# SCOTS at SCHOOL

# SCOTS at SCHOOL

## An Anthology

written and edited by
## David Northcroft

Edinburgh University Press

To Kathleen: a long-time Scot at School

Selection and editorial material David Northcroft, 2003

Edinburgh University Press Ltd
22 George Square, Edinburgh

Typeset in Bulmer by
Hewer Text Ltd, Edinburgh, and
printed and bound in Great Britain by
Antony Rowe Ltd, Chippenham

A CIP Record for this book is available from the British Library

ISBN 0 7486 1782 5 (paperback)

# CONTENTS

# Contents

Conclusion

# LIST OF ILLUSTRATIONS

# ACKNOWLEDGEMENTS

Copyright material has been reproduced unaltered except where cuts have been made for reasons of space. These are indicated by '. . .'. Since this is a work for the non-specialist reader, footnotes have not been used; it is hoped that sufficient explanation has been offered in the text itself.

I am grateful for the ready assistance provided by a number of schools, libraries, curators and archivists throughout Scotland. Among them I would like to mention those at: Abbotswell Primary School, Aberdeen; the University of Aberdeen; Balerno High School, Edinburgh; James Gillespie's High School, Edinburgh; Kirkcaldy High School; Montrose Academy; Northern College, Aberdeen; the Public Libraries at Aberdeen, Dundee, Inverness, Montrose; the Mitchell Library, Glasgow; Aberdeen Urban Studies Centre; the Education Museums at Edinburgh and Glasgow; the Scottish Life Archive; the Museum of Childhood, Edinburgh; and the Scottish Film Archive.

A number of individuals have generously helped me in specific matters: Karen Benson, Dunnottar Primary School; Mabel Brockle-hurst, Newtonhill; Winnie Brown ('Carnegie') of Torphins; Mrs Campbell, Dingwall; Ian Campbell, Edinburgh University; Lindy Cheyne, the *Leopard*; Gordon Craik, 'Glenesk Hotel', Edzell; Scott Duncan, Anstruther; Mike George, *Banffshire Journal*; John Leiper, Westhill; Lizzie MacGregor, Scottish Poetry Library; Peter Mitchell, 'Mitchell's Diary'; Peter Murphy, Carnoustie; Brian Osborne, Kirkintilloch; Lindsay Paterson, Edinburgh University; Jean Scotland, Aberdeen; Katie Turner, Glasgow; Carol Tyson, Aberdeen; and the late Archie Watt, Stonehaven.

I dearly wish to thank my close family for enthusiastic and participative support. The names of this incomparable – and Scottish-educated – group of human beings are Kathleen, Jonathan, Matt, Alice, Elaine and little Erin – a future Scot at school.

Grateful acknowledgement is made to the following sources to reproduce material. Every effort has been made to trace copyright holders but, if any have been inadvertently overlooked, the publisher will be pleased to make the necessary arrangements at the first opportunity.

Aberdeen City Libraries for the photograph of *Frederick Street School, 1907*.

Aberdeen Journals for the photographs of *Aberdeen College of Education Graduation, 1968*; *St Leonard's, Banchory, 1962*; *Aberdeen Grammar School Ablaze, 1986*.

University of Aberdeen for extracts from *Education in the North*; Alexander Murison, *Memoir of 88 Years*, Aberdeen University Press, 1935.

Aberdeenshire Education department for the extract from *Schemes of Work for the Primary School*, 1953.

Acair Ltd for the extract from Isobel Macdonald, *A Family in Skye 1908–1916*, 1980.

Balerno High School, Edinburgh, 2002 for a downloaded image of its website.

Winnie Brown for the extract from Winnie Carnegie, *Ugie Days*, Buchan Observer, 1996.

Mrs Campbell, Dingwall for the photograph of *Balloch Public School, 1907*.

Campbeltown Library, Argyll for the photograph *Campbeltown Grammar School, 1900*.

Centre for Educational Sociology, University of Edinburgh for extracts from *The Best Years?*, Joan Hughes (ed.), 1984; *Tell Them from Me*, Lesley Gow and Andrew McPherson (eds), 1980.

Centre for Scottish Studies, University of Aberdeen for extracts from Flora Youngson, *Dominie's Daughter*, 1991.

T. and T. Clark for the extract from Charles Warr, *Principal Caird*, T. and T. Clark, 1926.

James Clarke and Co. for the extract from George Seaver, *David Livingstone, Life and Letters*, Lutterworth, 1957.

Dr Linda Croxford, Centre for Educational Sociology, for the extract from 'Why Comprehensive Schools work for Scotland's youngsters', *Scottish Educational Journal*, 2002.

Dundee City Libraries for the photographs of *Dundee High School, Opening of New Library, 1958*; *Harris Academy, Infant Department, 1916*; *Harris Academy, 1916*.

Dunnottar Primary School, Stonehaven for examples of pupil work (Chapter 13).

City of Edinburgh, Education department for the extract from *Education Week, 1936*; *Flora Stevenson's School, 1914*; *North Canongate School, 1914*.

The Educational Institute of Scotland for the extracts from *The Centenary Handbook of the Educational Institute of Scotland*, A. J. Belford (ed.), 1946; *Towards 1970*, 1966.

Robert Gibson and Sons, Glasgow Ltd. for the extract from William Haddow, *My Seventy Years*, 1943.

Glasgow City archives for the photographs of *Primary Class, London Road, Glasgow, 1914*; *Garnetbank School, Glasgow, 1914*; *Glasgow Higher Grade School, 1914*; *Kelvinside Academy, 1916*.

Evelyn Glennie for the extract from *Good Vibrations*, Hutchinson, 1990.

HarperCollins Publishers for the extracts from John Boyd Orr, *As I Recall*, MacGibbon and Kee, 1965; Sheila Mackay, 'Community Activist' in *Scotland's Century*, Colin Bell (ed.), HarperCollins, 1999; Molly Weir, *Shoes Were for Sunday*, Hutchinson, 1970.

The *Herald* for the extracts from Elizabeth Buie, 'Too many targets, so little joy', 1999; Andy Drought, 'Govan's class act meets his heroine', 1999.

Highland Council Archive, Inverness for the photographs of *St Kilda Schoolroom, 1902*; *Central School, Inverness Prize-giving, 1900*.

Leslie Hills for the extract from 'The Senga Syndrome', *Girls in their Prime*, Scottish Academic Press, 1990.

A. C. Hunter for the extract from Helen Cruickshank, *Octobiography*, Montrose Standard Press, 1976.

Jeyes Group for the advertisement for *Jeyes' Special Fluid, 1909*.

Ethel Kilgour for the extract from *A Time of Our Lives*, Aberdeen City Libraries, 1992.

Kirkcaldy High School for the extract from *Kirkcaldy High School Souvenir*, 1958; the photograph *Homeward Bound*.

## Acknowledgements

The *Leopard* for the extract from Archie Baird, 'The Happiest days of our Lives . . .', 1999.

Tim Luckhurst for the extract from 'Scotched myths', *Guardian*, 2000.

Mrs Diana MacKenzie for the extract from R. F. MacKenzie, *The Unbowed Head*, 1976.

Alexander McRobbie and Richard Stenlake Publishing for the extract from *A Privileged Boyhood*, 1996.

Mainstream Publishing for the extracts from Hugh MacKenzie, *Craigroyston Days*, 1995; Leslie Duncan, ' Jock Tamson's Bairns. A Scottish Childhood' in *The Glasgow Herald Book of Scotland,* Arnold Kemp and Harry Reid (eds); Jack McLean, *Hopeless But Not Serious: The Autobiography of the Urban Voltaire*, 1966; Jack Webster, 'Bertie Charles Forbes: Magazine Magnate' in *A Legacy of Scots*, C. Walker (ed.), 1988.

Magnus Magnusson KBE for the extracts from *The Clacken and the Slate: The story of the Edinburgh Academy 1824-1974*, Collins, 1974.

Mercat Press for the extracts from Eddie Mathieson, *Voices from War: Personal Recollections of war in our century by Scottish Men and Women*, Ian MacDougall (ed.); Katherine Stewart, *A School in the Hills*, 1996.

James Murray for the extract from *Three Tears for Glasgow*, Murray Promotions, 1991.

Museum of Education, Edinburgh and Balony Primary School for the photograph of *Balony Primary School, 2001.*

Orkney Education department for the extract from A. H. Stephen 'Ending an Era' in *From Sang School to Comprehensive*, 1976.

Orkney Museum for the photograph *Kirbister School, 1955.*

Oxford University Press for the extract from Patricia Hollins, *Jennie Lee: A Life*, 1997.

Peters Fraser and Dunlop Group for the extract from *The Christian Watt Papers* edited by David Fraser (copyright David Fraser 1983) by permission of Caledonian Books and PFD on behalf of Sir David Fraser; Robert Anderson, *Education and Opportunity in Victorian Scotland*, Oxford University Press, 1983.

The *Press and Journal* for the extracts from Bill Howatson, 'Never too late to sow the seeds of knowledge', 1999; John Nickson, 'Countdown to maths muddle', 1981; 'Back to basics in schools', 1999; Norman Harper, 'Scotland spirals down to blissful ignorance', 1999.

Mrs Jean Scotland for the extracts from James Scotland, *A History of Scottish Education*, University of London Press, 1969; *History of Aberdeen College of Education*, 1983; Graduation speeches at Aberdeen College of Education, 1969 and 1983.

The *Scotsman* for the extracts from Susan Dean, 'St Margaret Mary's School', 1992; Andrew Denholme, 'Villagers fight to save their primary', 2001; Gillian Harris, 'James Gillespie's High School', 1992; Tom Little, 'Education for the millennium', 1999.

*Scottish Educational Journal* for the extracts from a speech by James Inglis, 1953; Alex Russell, 'From a Dominie's Notebook', 1950.

Scottish Executive Library and Information Service for the extracts from publications by Scottish Education Department; Scottish Office and Education Department and Scottish Executive.

Scottish Life Archive, Edinburgh for the photographs of *Balerno School, 1900*; *Cullerlie School*; *Edinburgh Ladies' College, 1920*; *Moray House Training Centre, 1880*.

Scottish Screen Archive for the quotation from *The Children's Story*, 1938.

Professor T. C. Smout for the extract from 'The Scottish Identity' in *The Future of Scotland*, Robert Underwood (ed.), 1977.

Alan Spence for the extract from 'Boom Baby' in *Jock Tamson's Bairns*, Trevor Royle (ed.), H. Hamilton, 1977.

Thomson Publishing Services, on behalf of Routledge, for the extract from F. G. Rea, *A School in South Uist*, Routledge, 1964.

Time Warner Books for the extract from Finlay J. Macdonald, *Crowdie and Cream*, Macdonald and Co., 1982.

*Times Educational Supplement Scotland* for the extracts 'An educational explosion', 1965; Muriel Macleod, 'A Democratic Intellect?', 2000.

Tuckwell Press for the extracts from Patrick McVeigh, *Look after the Bairns*, 1999; *Bondagers*, Ian Macdougall (ed.), 2000; Roderick Wilkinson, *Memories of Maryhill*, Canongate Academic, 1993.

Whitehill School, Glasgow for the extract from the *Whitehill School Magazine*, 1929.

Sydney Wood for the extracts from 'Education in Nineteenth-Century Rural Scotland', *Review of Scottish Culture*, 1991; 'School History and the Shaping of Scottish Identity', *History Scotland, 2002*.

# PREFACE

*Scots at School* tries to do three things: to bring together a selection of first-hand accounts of individual experience in Scotland's schools over the last two and a half centuries; to give an accompanying analytical commentary on developments and issues during that time; and, thus, to indicate something of the central role that 'education' has played, both in the life of the country and in its sense of itself as a distinct and distinctive nation, albeit within the British framework. The result should be a book which can be dipped into for its human interest or consulted as an intimate history of a significant Scottish topic.

The concentration has, therefore, been upon the individual witness, not the political or the socio-economic commentator. A wide range of extracts has been deployed, taken from biographies, from local histories, from contemporary journals and from interview transcripts. Some of the latter belong to the author's own continuing researches into an oral history of twentieth century Scottish schooling. Brief biographical notes have been appended to most of the witness accounts.

The great variety of materials uncovered has necessitated some cruel omissions; nor has it been possible to treat every part of the country and each one of its cultural groups equitably. I am, for instance, conscious that the Catholic sector has been under-represented and that the multi-cultural character of contemporary Scotland has not yet yielded the kind of retrospective testimony which would have done justice to its growing importance. Other aspects of focus should also be noted: 'at school' has been interpreted in terms of the publicly provided mainstream experience – pre-school, university, 'further' and private education are not central to its consideration.

This has meant that, regretfully, the self-help 'mutual improvement' and 'mechanics' institute' movements of the nineteenth century, which, along with the later trades union classes, did so much to compensate for the inadequacies and economic inaccessibility of the official system – despite all those democratic pretensions – have also had to be bypassed.

For similar reasons, some of the more contentious issues which have complicated Scotland's school history have, in the accompanying commentary, had to be briefly summarised or even omitted. Amongst these are the 'true' standard of literacy pre-1872, especially as compared to England's; school attendance rates; the claimed breadth of the curriculum; the place, permitted or not, of the native tongue(s) in the classroom; the various attempts to deal satisfactorily with technical subject matter. These are expertly treated in Robert Anderson's *Education and the Scottish People, 1750–1918.* A pair of recent compilations also cover the ground more thoroughly than *Scots at School* is able to do: *Scottish Education,* edited by T. Bryce and W. Humes, Edinburgh University Press (1999); *Scottish Life and Society. Education,* edited by Heather Holmes, Tuckwell Press (2000).

The intention has been to bring together a series of witness accounts which will act as the human characterisation of what has been a continuous, and continuing, narrative, one that has been charged with great abstracts – 'discipline', 'tradition', 'work', 'superiority' (over the English), 'identity' and- above all – 'excellence' and 'democracy'. A broad chronological structure has, accordingly, been adopted – '1750–1840', '1840–1918', '1918–2000'. Of these boundary points, the ending of the First World War makes '1918' an obvious choice; '1840' has been selected because that is the start of the decade which saw the introduction of significant government intervention, through the grants and inspections which would eventually transform the old parochial and burgh arrangements into a 'modern' centralised system.

It should further be explained that the selection has confined itself, on this occasion, to the non-literary, non-fiction account. Nearly every one of Scotland's noted writers has been the product of common public provision; a great number of them have used episodes of school life in their work. Some, indeed, such as James Kelman (*A Disaffection*), George Friel (*Mr Alfred MA*) and Christopher Rush (*Last Lesson of the Afternoon*) have done so pivotally. In addition, many – Thomas

Carlyle, Edwin Muir and Liz Lochhead, for example – have penned striking accounts of their own school experience. The local school has, in fact, played an illuminating, if underconsidered, role in the literary life of the nation – so much so that a proper treatment of it would demand its own volume, rather than suffer diffusion in one that is devoted to the more direct, day-to-day witness of the diverse collection of Scottish men and Scottish women whose memories make up this, the democratic history of the nation's many schoolings.

'Children of Scotland, it is a great thing to be a Scot and it is a great thing to be taught in our Scottish schools . . . You have inherited a great tradition. You must prove yourselves worthy of it. That, children of Scotland, is the part you have to play and if you play it well, you may rest assured that the fame of Scotland will continue to be great among the nations'

Sir William McKechnie, Secretary to the Scottish Education<br>Department 1929-36. Words used as conclusion to documentary<br>film The Children's Story 1938. Scottish Screen Archive.

# 1 THE TRADITION OF
# SCOTTISH EDUCATION

*Bertie Charles Forbes: Magazine Magnate*: Jack Webster, 1988
*Brigadoon High School*: Douglas Osler HMCI, 1999
*Scotched myths*: Tim Luckhurst, 2000
*A Democratic Intellect?*: Tom Devine, 2000
*Govan's class act meets his heroine*: Herald, 1999
*Never too early to sow the seeds of knowledge*: Bill Howatson, 1999
*The History of Scottish Education*: James Scotland, 1969
*Remarks on Parochial Education in Scotland*:
Aberdeen Magazine, 1832
*Education and Opportunity in Victorian Scotland*:
Robert Anderson, 1983

Figure 1. **Aberdeen Grammar School ablaze, 1986** The fire caused by a painter's careless
blow-torch threatens one of Britain's oldest schools. First mentioned in civic records in 1262,
the Grammar became one of Scotland's great burgh schools. Here the statue of its most
famous ex-pupil, Lord Byron (1795–98), stands firm against the blaze. However, the 'AGS'
where he 'threaded all the classes to the fourth' was not this splendid baronial edifice – the
product of local nineteenth-century investment in prestigious public building – but a squat
little pile enclosed within the city centre. The fire was contained, leaving the Grammar to live
on, but now as one of Aberdeen's ten comprehensive schools. *Aberdeen Journals*

**a)** Before he left Whitehill that day he visited the old school and, from its gateway, gazed out over the landscape of Buchan. Here is no scenic beauty of the Highlands but to him it was beautiful just the same, the rolling fields of fertility representing the soil from which his own heritage had sprung. He stood breathing in the fresh air, drooling over its invigorating properties, as if he were reluctant to leave it.

Malcolm Forbes had come home to *Cunnyknowe* and left the trappings of unimaginable wealth behind. Now he was just a vulnerable human being, in reverie perhaps with the spirit of the baggybreeked boy who trod those fields a century ago and dreamed dreams of life in a land that lay over the hill and far, far away.

Webster, Jack (1988). 'Bertie Charles Forbes: Magazine Magnate. (1880-1954)' in C. Walker (ed.), *A Legacy of Scots*. Edinburgh, Mainstream.

**b)** Speaking before a major conference in Edinburgh today, Douglas Osler condemned critics of current teaching standards and 'retreat into the Celtic mists in search of Brigadoon High School' . . .

He will expand on his comments in a speech to the Education in the Millennium conference, sponsored by *The Scotsman*. This sell-out event will be attended by politicians, parents and teachers and is being addressed by experts from around the world . . .

Mr Osler said yesterday that it was a myth that in the past the school system was so good that any 'lad o' pairts' could do well, as long as he arrived armed with a 'satchel of books and a monthly sack of meal'.

In his speech today he will say: 'Much is made of emulating the best of Scottish education's past as a cure-all for any perceived weaknesses. There is a nostalgic perception about Scotland's educational golden age when standards were high. [But] we must not retreat into the Celtic mists in search of Brigadoon High School . . . the hard evidence would lead us to question whether there has ever been a golden age in Scottish education'.

Mr Osler, a former history teacher, will back up his assertion by observing that fewer pupils obtained exam success in the 1950s than today, and even in the 1970s a much smaller proportion of youngsters stayed in education beyond the minimum school leaving age.

Osler, Douglas (1999), Senior Chief Inspector of Schools,
speech to the 'Education for the millennium' conference,
as reported by Little, Tom. *Scotsman*, September 3.

## A Personal Tradition

When – according to his biographer Jack Webster – Malcolm Forbes crossed the Atlantic in June 1987 to hold a picnic for the children of Whitehill, Aberdeenshire, he was doing more than simply revisiting the scenes of his father's own boyhood.

Malcolm was the third son of a man who had been born in 1880 and whose own father had been a poor country tailor. The family had had a hard time of it, patching together a meagre living among customers who worked the stony soil of the Buchan farmlands. When the time came, young Bertie, like all the other five-year-olds of the parish, started out at the little local school. The home he walked the daily two miles from was so poor that the clothes on his back hung there only by the repeated skill of the family trade. He was known as Patchy Forbes.

Whitehill Public School, however, proved to be a place of riches. 'Geographically remote' though it was, it formed a 'settled seat of learning which sent youngsters like Bertie Forbes into the world with an education as broad and as enlightened as you would now find at a much later age'. Part of the reason for this lay in the excellence of its headmaster. This was Gavin Greig, famous as a composer and collector of North-east folk songs, but also a noted teacher.

As Webster is concerned to point out, this advantage sprang from the educational system, of which Greig was an outstanding representative, and whose ethos, in turn, supported him in his own scholarly interests. His work among the oral traditions of his native region would grow to constitute 'the finest collection of its kind in the world'. But he was always the country schoolmaster, equally solicitous in his efforts to teach the Classics 'to those country bairns who came pleitering in from the farm-touns, crofts and cottar houses'. In this, Webster assures us, he was playing the part of the local 'dominie' of the time, one who was devoted to the service of 'his small country school at the turn of the century'.

*4*

It was Greig who sought out the contacts that gave the lad his first post, aged fourteen, at the *Peterhead Sentinel*. By twenty, Bertie was off to New York, in pursuit of what became an imaginatively expansive, endlessly striving career in journalism. If the parochial school at Whitehill had given him nothing in the way of formal qualification, it had instilled the values of hard work, of rock hard integrity and the nerve to succeed.

He immediately seized hold, as the twentieth century gathered pace, of the opportunities for new titles and new markets within the thrusting American magazine industry. By the time they found him slumped dead, the pen still warm in his hand, over his desk in the Forbes Building off Wall Street, he was the multi-millionaire chief of a vast media empire. Yet, as Webster insists, not once did Whitehill's great son forget his origins there: his 'whirlwind life in the United States did nothing to dim his memory of the little corner of Scotland which gave him his roots, nor blunt his gratitude to those who gave him a start in life'. Every two years, he would come back and host a vast picnic for his old friends and their families. Among them were the children of dominie Gavin Greig.

Bertie Forbes died in 1954. For the next thirty years, there were no summer reunions on the straw bales in the field down 'beside Whitehill School'. In 1987, however, Malcolm, the son who had done the most to build upon the Forbes business, decided to revive the custom. At the end of a great village day, full of sausage rolls, egg-and-spoon and sack races and the tug o' war, Webster pictures the man, who was now said to be worth more than £55 million, seeking a moment of reflective communion, as he gazes out over the plain, hard-worked Buchan landscape. And he does so while standing at the threshold of the common starting point of a thousand life journeys – the little parish school.

What begins as a simple biographical sketch has ended in an affirmation of root identity, even if, in the case of Malcolm Forbes, who was born and schooled in the USA, it can only be one that exists in the tribal memory.

'Bertie Forbes: Magazine Magnate' is one of a collection of similar portraits, brought together in 1988 under the title of *A Legacy of Scots*. As with the other nineteen subjects, his story is told in a way which invites us to look, once more, upon the wealth of men – and the occasional woman – which Scotland has continued to produce and, then, to move the eye backwards to alight on the abiding phenomenon of a humble Scots beginning. Each of the *Legacy* twenty – men like Patrick Manson, 'Oriental Dairy Farmer' and Thomas Lipton, 'From Message Boy to Millionaire' – has gone on to accomplish exceptional deeds but, like little Patchy Bertie, none of them set out from anywhere grander than some recognisably native place.

Jack Webster, himself, is the son of Buchan farming stock and also, a couple of generations later, attended the nearby Maud School. His family had run the Whitehill Farm; Gavin Greig was his great-grandfather. Webster, too, grew up to become a noted journalist and to tell his own story beneath the generic title of *A Grain of Truth* (1981). Both there, and in his sketch of an illustrious predecessor, he is concerned to stress the possibilities for cultural reproduction, for the continuity of achievement that rests upon the ethic of hard work, upon respect for the word and upon the sound academic grounding which, both of them, Bertie and Jack, had received as the offspring of a small Scottish country school. That is why the final paragraph depicts the worthy son of a famous father, drinking in the cleansing air of a devoutly remembered homeland, a century on from that first enrolment in the parochial school. It is a scene which brings to a flourishing close the story of one who did, indeed, scale the ladder of ethnic opportunity and whose example in so doing lives on into the present day.

A Living Tradition?

The title of this section comes with a question mark. The range of viewpoint, even within the small sample of texts used in it, will show why this is so. For Jack Webster, writer and local historian, the democratic character of the nation's education is a quality embedded in the unpretentiously fertile terrain of his own Aberdeenshire and made manifest by the stories of individual success that continue to be lodged in the annals of its rural parishes. Douglas Osler, a professional educationist, charged with the problems of his own, later times, would question whether any of this heroic stuff was ever a reality for the general run of Scottish boys and – especially – Scottish girls. To his contemporary eye, Webster's evocations would be a matter for myth, his Whitehill idyll a scenario for a piece of Hollywood tartanalia, a nostalgia land of little relevance to the challenges of the twenty-first century.

Chief Inspector Osler was addressing a conference in the early autumn of 1999. By the summer of the following year, his Scottish Education Department was caught up in a sequence of administrative calamities which led to their being branded as the 'biggest disaster' ever to be visited upon the nation's education system. This was the embarrassing run of errors and delays which had attended the first year of the administration's new-style Higher examination results. The catastrophe was widely reported, even in the London-based press, where the stories were motivated in part, no doubt, by the opening these mishaps gave its writers to throw new light upon a system which had, for the past several hundred years, been accustomed to claim superiority over anything on offer south of the border.

The *Guardian*'s Tim Luckhurst also employs the term 'myth' (**1A**). And, when he does so in order to deride the traditional claims of perpetual excellence, it is clear that he means us to interpret the word as denoting something that is dangerously misleading. 'Myth', here, is a gilded version of the 'true' – and ugly – state of affairs. He acknowledges, however, that the traditional account does at least have a grounding in history and that somewhere, lurking within the Scotch mist, is the noble 'vision' of a teacher within every single parish. This, as he points out, is a commitment which stretches back into a period that was lived out a century and a half before the union with England. Belief in education as a universal right is, therefore, strongly rooted within the Scots' consciousness of what has made them Scots. It has sufficient substance for Tom Devine, author of *The Scottish Nation* (1999), to describe the educational system as central to the country's ability to sustain a sense of itself as a distinct and distinctive society, even within the British state (**1B**).

In recounting this development, Devine is happy to bring into play the familiar mythology of 'lads o' pairts', of 'ladders of opportunity', and of the 'democratic intellect' as the supreme value. By recounting their role within the national progress, the historian is demonstrating that to shape events into a 'mythical' pattern is not the same as bearing false witness. Figures, such as the lads from humble circumstances who get on in life and the village dominies who selflessly drive them onwards, might well be the exceptions but, if that is so, they are to

7

be judged as the outstanding representations of an ideal for self-betterment, one whose influence is to be found in every Scottish home. A 'myth', in this sense, emerges as the story which a community tells itself in order to keep in view those principles which best define its highest aspirations.

The historical analysis is one way of investigating the myth's solidity. Another is to test its imaginative claims against our actual experience. That the spectacle of an ordinary Scots pupil of an unexceptional district school, who goes on to achieve international fame, continues to compel the nation's attention is illustrated by the media's treatment of the outstanding football manager, Sir Alex Ferguson. And the story of his sentimental return visit to the place where it all started is irresistible (**1C**).

'Fergie's' day in Govan to promote his best-selling autobiography is turned into a familiar Scottish parable. There is the modern superstore and the pile of books to be shifted; but there, too, is the old caring Primary Miss, busily devoted, capable still of inspiring awe. And so a grateful nostalgia lights up the demands of a commercially motivated present.

The 'class act' of Sir Alex makes for an eye-catching re-enactment of a timeless Scottish drama: successful ex-pupil meets grand old teacher. Bill Howatson's account of his adventures among his daughter's homework jotters in her little Kincardineshire primary school shows how, beyond the spotlights, the story of Scottish education continues to be lived out as a quietly persistent daily experience (**1D**). His newspaper piece develops into an extended family saga, in which a present day concern, that the value of diligent effort is grasped from the very outset, merges with recollections of his own boyhood wrestlings at the kitchen table over Latin declensions, and with classic mathematical posers that feature variously timed trains passing through tunnels of diverse lengths. And these, in turn, open out into the haunting memory of how, at the tail-end of each Sunday's visit by elderly relatives, young Bill would 'by custom' be told to look to his books for the serious business of the following week. In personal stories such as these, which are offered to his readers as the record of his and of their common Scots experience, 'myth' mingles with the actuality of the humdrum, domestic event, the one enriching and confirming the other.

## The Public Tradition

'. . . a strong instinct that goes back to the Protestant reformers and the desire to have a school in every parish'. Howatson's piece makes it clear that his present day experiences are part of a long, unfolding national story – and that it is the personal awareness of his country's distinctive history which presses down upon his insistence that his own children will also receive a good Scots education.

As its fountainhead, he cites the kirkmen of the sixteenth century and their mission to make of Scotland 'a godly commonwealth'. In such a kingdom, the moral and the social improvement of each one of its members would become the solemn charge of every parish community, as led by its minister and its lairds. This was the age of John Knox, whose *First Book of Discipline* proposed that all 900 of the nation's parishes should become the sites of a schoolmaster and a school.

If the full implementation of this scheme had to await the legislation of the Scottish parliament in 1646 and 1696, by the date of the Union of 1707, there was visible across the land a solid network of parochial schools, each managed by a properly lettered master, whose appointment had been approved by the local presbytery, working in a schoolhouse that had been underwritten by the district's leading landowners.

The values which such a system engendered were those which expressed the spirit of its foundation: individual responsibility, the ethic of work, a respect for academic achievement, and the importance of universal literacy, so that all may read the word of God.

Bill Howatson's ready ability, in 1998, to draw upon these historical sources is evidence that the story of the nation's education is sufficiently recognised to form part of the wider meaning which he invites his readers to give to his parental concern for a young daughter's homework. In this way, his little family anecdote is able to fill out the reasons noted by Professor Devine in his explanation of the role that the school has played in establishing the Scottish identity. Not only was it one of the 'civic' agencies left intact by the Union but it is also an inheritance, one which may be traced back to the spiritual reformers of more than 450 years ago. A system, in which so much of the people's cultural and religious experience has been invested, has itself become a defining tradition.

This is why historians have customarily pointed to the 'Scottish

Tradition in Education' as the essential reference point in their accounts of the development of the country's schooling. When, for example, James Scotland came to the final chapter of his two-volume *History of Scottish Education* (1969), he devoted the whole of his summing up to that theme, thus treating 'the Tradition' as a body of implicit commandments that had guided the direction of the preceding five hundred years. What his account has demonstrated, he concludes, is the working out of a set of socio-historical forces. These may be set out as a number of key characteristics: 'Pride'; 'Pietism'; 'Poverty'; 'Devotion'; 'Militant Democracy'; 'Academic Bias'; 'Conservatism'; 'Authoritarianism'. Indeed, so strong has been the power of precept that even this brief listing may be simplified into a one-paragraph group of binding 'dicta' (**1E**).

As the then Principal of Aberdeen College of Education, James Scotland would have been familiar with the declaration with which, 140 years previously, *The Aberdeen Magazine* had swept the reader into its 'Remarks on Parochial Education in Scotland' (**1F**). Its style is that of a patriotic rallying call, one in which 'education' has been recruited to serve as a verse within the national anthem of Northern Britain. Yet, empurpled though it may be, the paragraph deploys the same essential features which are carefully laid out in the academic's twentieth-century account – a small and poor country whose true riches are to be found in the cultivation of its human stock and in the moral stature of its meanest citizens. By setting James Scotland's properties in a landscape of hard terrain and unyielding climate, but also of pure and elemental qualities, the earlier writer has demonstrated another abiding feature of the national treatment of its educational capital – the desire to seek out, in the archetypal Highland landscape of rock and cloud and running water, a vivid poetic equivalent to all those aims whose emotive power can only be partly conveyed through the historian's factual summations. Here, in 1832, as on many occasions since, the national geography is made to join forces with the national history in order to bind the Scottish people to their educational system and to make of it a sacred, common possession.

The *Magazine*'s argument was that the Scottish system owed its strength to its 'simplicity'. In her Oxford and her Cambridge and in her celebrated endowed colleges, England might have the more elaborate superstructures but, in terms of the underlying fabric, she could not compare to the universal strength attained by the one-parish-one-school provision of her northern partner.

The dominant note, which emerges from accounts such as these, is that of 'democracy'. However limited in resources their schools might be, however partial they were in their fostering of an academic elite, there is little doubt that Scots were being brought up to think of their school as a common and inherited possession – and to acquire the rhetoric by which to claim it imaginatively and emotionally as their own.

Since the work of James Scotland, the historian who has done most to establish a definitive account of Scotland's educational history has been Robert Anderson. His *Education and the Scottish People, 1750–1918* (1995) and the earlier *Education and Opportunity in Victorian Scotland* (1983) are characterized by a clear ordering of evidence and a sharply rational analysis. Yet, he, too, accepts that the nation's progress has been empowered by a set of emotive beliefs, which demonstrate the force of myth, as well as socio-economics, in its shaping. Central to its progress is the belief that Scottish education was peculiarly 'democratic', not in any encouragement of a sense of an ethnic, as opposed to a competitively British, identity but, rather, as an expression of classless, social values. At the very outset of his investigations, Anderson sets out a clear statement of the importance he has come to attach to this 'Tradition' (**1G**).

In adopting this as his leading hypothesis, Anderson, the modern historian, is recognising that 'democracy' is the standard against which its actual progress must be judged. It is the belief that, in Scotland, above all other nations (and especially the one that lies to its south), the school belongs to the people.

James Scotland's roll call of Educational Traditions was, however, summed up in 1969. Since that time, we have become less inclined to rest easy upon the notion that there exists a reliable way of describing Scottish education through a set of well-established 'dicta'. As the comments of Osler and Luckhurst have indicated, a spirit of questioning, of debunking even, has sprung up. Although this pair are more interested in making a topical point, the serious historian has also reacted against any straightforward acceptance of the old wisdoms of 'democratic' superiority. Over the last thirty years, researchers have been busy probing the national myths of lads o' pairts, of dominies and of the little village school. Their aim has been to set such representations in a wider, more questioning sociological context than that of handed down folk tradition or the patriotically vainglorious chronicle.

This revisionism has raised a series of uncomfortable counter-claims. Scottish Education has recently come to be indicted as: sexist (where is the lass o' pairts?); as Anglo-centric (Scottish history, Scottish culture and, most culpably, the Scots tongue all banished from the classroom); as grimly anti-children (too much soulless, repetitive work, not enough arts, not enough play and definitely too much tawse); obsessively academic (a few got on but what happened to the silenced majority?).

Worst of all, perhaps, is the implication that an over-flattering reputation has allowed the Scottish system to act as an instrument of political control. According to this version, the favourite old stories of democratic classrooms, of getting on and of efficiently high standards have been deployed to mask the realities of hidebound methods, of general underachievement and of comfortably entrenched officials who have used the standard myths to convince both themselves and the world at large that all continued to be well. The conclusion has been that, far from belonging to the people, Scottish education has been in the possession of a small circle of establishment figures with a vested interest in maintaining the illusion of a well-run, equitable regime.

Undoubtedly, the work of researchers, such as Walter Humes in Glasgow, of the Centre for Educational Sociology at Edinburgh University and of feminist critics everywhere has offered a series of bracing re-evaluations, which must lead to a sharpened understanding of exactly how democratic the national system has been – and continues to be. This is an issue which will re-emerge in later chapters, when the myths and the counter-myths may be tested against the day-to-day actualities that form our subject matter.

In their search for evidence, the critics – like the historians before them – have tended to focus on the motives and the pronouncements of the policy makers and the professionals. Robert Anderson has, however, recommended that what we should now do is to look at the experiences of the countless thousands who, down the generations, have been 'on the receiving end' – the pupils, their parents and, perhaps, the rank-and-file teacher. This volume is an attempt to do just that.

*Scots at School* is built up from a range of first-hand accounts:

biographies, local histories, interviews, the journal and newspaper pieces of the day. This has been done in the belief that it is the experiences of the Scottish people, as much as the public statements, the bureaucratic memoranda and the official documentation, which has made the national education truly Scottish.


1A                                                    London, 2000.


Certain truths about Scotland are held to be absolute. King among them is that Scottish education is excellent. The nation that first saw the vision of a teacher in every community in 1561 still leads the world in matters pedagogical. Or so the myth runs – and heaven help any curmudgeon who dares challenge it. So the crisis that has enveloped Scottish education since the revelation that this year's Highers results are unreliable has dealt a blow to national pride. The SNP's education spokeswoman, Nicola Sturgeon, calls it 'the biggest disaster ever to hit Scottish education'.

Luckhurst, Tim (2000). 'Scotched myths', Guardian, 16 August.


1B                                                    Glasgow, 2000.


A few years before David Stow opened his 'Normal seminary' in Glasgow in 1837 . . . Sir Walter Scott offered a pessimistic analysis. He saw Scotland's sense of itself crumbling as a result of fundamental economic change and the new political and cultural relationships which were growing with England after a century of union. As Scott put it, 'what makes Scotland is fast disappearing'. Before long it would simply become 'North Britain', a mere provincial extension of the Union state.

We know that this did not come to pass. On the contrary, a striking feature of the development of the Union in the Victorian era was not only the robust survival of 'Scottishness' but its adaptation and reinvention within a changing world. Pride in Scotland proved to be entirely compatible with loyalty to Great Britain.

One reason for this was the strength and endurance of Scottish civil society and particularly the powerful influence of those three institutions, the church, the legal system and education, which had survived the Union. Education in Scotland during the nineteenth century became not simply a matter of schooling and learning but a badge of identity.

Together with Presbyterianism, education became a way of marking out Scotland's distinctiveness from its powerful neighbour to the south. The belief developed, and has been accepted uncritically until recently, that Scottish education was excellent compared to that of England and most other countries; that even before compulsory schooling after 1872, literacy was well-nigh universal; that the Scottish system was both meritocratic and democratic, resting on a ladder of opportunity which ascended from the famous parish schools through to the universities and enabled the 'lad o' pairts' (never girls) to climb towards academic and material success. The Scots came to see themselves as a nation with egalitarian values, the home of the 'democratic intellect'.

Not all of this can be dismissed as mere myth. Before 1872 education was neither free nor compulsory. But marriage signatures for that date indicate that 94 per cent of bridegrooms and 89 per cent of brides were literate and that there had been a conspicuous increase in female literacy over the previous quarter of a century. Only in the Western Isles and in Glasgow – with its Irish immigrants – were poorer averages recorded.

Remarkably, by the 1860s, the proportion of children on the school roll was close to the levels achieved in Prussia, where elementary education was already compulsory and unmatched elsewhere in Europe.

Devine, Tom (2000). 'A Democratic Intellect? The Scottish tradition in historical perspective'. The annual Stow Lecture at Strathclyde University. As reported by Macleod, Muriel, in the *Times Educational Supplement,* 24 March.

For 'David Stow', see Chapter 6.

1C                                                          Glasgow, 1999.

Manchester United manager Sir Alex Ferguson was reunited with an old flame yesterday when he met his former teacher Elizabeth Thomson for the first time since revealing that he had a schoolboy crush on her.

The Govan-born legend has stayed in close contact with Mrs Thomson since she taught him in his final year at the local Broomloan Road Primary School and also refereed some of his playground football matches.

But it was only when Sir Alex's autobiography was published recently that she learned of his amorous prepubescent yearnings. Yesterday, as he signed copies of his book for hundreds of fans at the Asda superstore in Govan, Sir Alex credited her with inspiring his trademark steely determination, and added: 'She shoved me over the line educationally that year'.

When asked whether his feelings had remained constant over the years, he smiled; 'She's still a cracker'.

Drought, Andy (1999). 'Govan's class act meets his heroine', Herald,<br>7 September.

1941– : multiple trophy-winning manager Aberdeen FC and Manchester United.

1D                                    Kincardineshire, 1999.

Long before the first born came into this world, a small resolution was passed within the confines of our household. It rested solely on a desire to ensure that, whether male or female, the new arrival would get every encouragement in his or her education. In the event, the first born was a female and the process was repeated four years later when the second child came on the scene.

The desire to make the most of what education is available is a strong Scottish instinct which probably goes back to sixteenth-century Protestant reformers and the aim to have a school in every parish. It has a place in Scotland which is rightly valued and prized. The idea that a thorough grounding in the basics of education would stand a child in good stead and help counter some of the myths and misconceptions that society throws up has long appealed to me . . .

I was certainly keen that the girls got a good start and, while huge swathes of the elder daughter's years have been shaped by her mother, I have taken an interest in what goes on at school. This week was one of those parents' nights when the truth is revealed. In practice, however, apart from trying to interest her in the nation's story through occasional visits to places which I deem of interest, my part has been largely confined to homework supervision. Homework, I kept telling the first born, is good for a number of reasons, not least because it affords some degree of discipline and application. It is, in my Calvinistic view, better for the mind than kicking a bus shelter to pieces.

At any rate, I have of late been casting an eye over the work that requires sentence formation, spelling and readings. I particularly enjoy the section that calls for a sentence to be formed by using a specified and predetermined word. The trick in this, however, is to act in a supervisory manner and to be on hand to offer some guidance. The danger is to rush in and do the work. I was reminded the other day of a teacher who, on reading the homework of one of her pupils, asked the child to inform her father that, if he desired homework, it could easily be set for him – a revealing little anecdote which speaks volumes about over-eager parents . . . But perhaps the most vivid memory of homework springs from the tail-end of a Sunday visit by relatives when I would, by custom, be told to 'look to my books' for the following day. Relatives, who meant well, had an unfortunate knack of wanting to participate in this academic exercise and to 'help'.

This would have been tolerable had they observed the basic principles I set out earlier. But faced with mind-numbing problems about how long it took a train of certain length to go through a tunnel of another length, or perplexed by some bizarre geometric puzzle, they could not resist chipping in with varied and varying answers, all of which were characterised by a total lack of consistency, rationale or anything approaching the correct answer.

Howatson, Bill (1999). 'Never too early to
sow the seeds of knowledge', *Press and Journal*, 12 November.

1E                                                              Aberdeen, 1969.

The vaunted Scottish devotion to education may often have been superstitious, illogical – often, but not always. For centuries education was respectable, but it was more than that. There were in each generation men who cared sufficiently about it to spend their money and their energy and their time freely on its development – men like Andrew Melville and Bishop Kennedy, Robert Owen and David Stow,

Robert Gordon and Allan Glen and Andrew Carnegie, the founders of the Gaelic Societies, the Education Societies, the Infant School Societies, the S.S.P.C.K. [Society in Scotland for Propagating Christian Knowledge], the Free Church Committee. The sentimental image of Scottish educational democracy, personified in the lad of parts who was to become a colonial governor or a university principal or a law lord, may be idealised through an intellectual soft-focus lens. But there were many lads of parts, and they did attain eminence, and it was easier for a Scottish boy to reach a university than for his brothers in most countries of the western world. The Scottish educational tradition then may be found in a few positive dicta:

that education is, and always has been, of paramount importance in any community;

that every child should have the right to all the education of which he is capable;

that such education should be provided as economically and systematically as possible;

that the training of the intellect should take priority over all other facets of the pupil's personality;

that experiment is to be attempted only with the greatest of caution;

that the most important person in the school, no matter what the theorists say, is not the pupil but the (inadequately rewarded) teacher.

Scotland, James (1969). *The History of Scottish Education.* University of London Press.

1F                                                            Aberdeen, 1832.

It is a system of which Scotland has just reason to be proud . . . Of silver and gold, she has ever but possessed a trifling share; nor has nature bestowed upon her the warmth of unclouded sun and the rich products of a luxuriant soil. But although physically speaking she may be frequently regarded as a land of mists and storms, yet has her moral atmosphere for a succession of ages been generally serene and unclouded. While the benefits of knowledge in other countries have been, comparatively speaking, locked up from all those whose fortunes have not raised them above the lower or even the middling ranks of life, the son of the most humble peasant in our native land has it in his power to approach the fountain of learning and to drink unmolested from its pure and invigorating and ennobling stream.

'Remarks on Parochial Education in Scotland' (1832). *Aberdeen Magazine*, 5.

1G                                                                  Edinburgh, 1983.

This democratic myth became, and has remained, a central part of the Scottish sense of nationhood and of the image which others have formed of the Scots. In the history of European nationalism, education often had a vital role in transmitting, or helping to revive, national languages and cultures. In Scotland this has not been the case – indeed, the schools became notorious for their neglect of Scottish literature and history. Instead it was the institutional forms of the educational system, and their articulation with each other, which were seen as the distinctive heritage to be preserved against alien influences and unsympathetic reforms. From this point of view, four distinct aspects of the 'myth' may be identified. First there was the ideal of 'universality', of a school system which would put religious education and the elements of literacy within reach of the whole population through the provision of a school in every parish. Second, there was the role of the school in affording opportunities to the 'lad of parts'; poverty should be no barrier to talent, and individuals from whatever background should be able to climb the educational ladder. Third, the school was seen as a place where all the social classes rubbed shoulders . . . The fourth aspect of the tradition was that the three parts of the educational system – parish schools in the countryside, burgh schools in the towns, and the universities – should be seen as forming a national system, with no social barriers between them, and that since this system served the community as a whole it should be established by law, supported from public funds, and supervised by the authorities of Church and state. Parish schoolmasters, teachers in burgh schools and university professors were all in a sense public officials, paid a fixed salary which they supplemented by charging fees for their services. In this, of course, there was a marked contrast between Scotland and England, where the idea of a national system hardly existed . . .'

Anderson, Robert (1983). *Education and Opportunity in Victorian Scotland: Schools and Universities.* Oxford University Press.

1750–1840

# 2 SCHOOL AND SOCIETY: A PEOPLE'S SYSTEM?

❧

*Some Account of my Life and Writings*: Sir Archibald Alison, 1883
*Independent Spirit of the Lower Classes of the Scotch*:
*New Monthly Magazine*, 1817
*Scottish Parochial Schools*: Lord Henry Cockburn. 1827
*Abstract of Education Returns (Scotland):* 1837
*The Autobiography of a Working Man*: Alex Somerville, 1848
*The Christian Watt Papers*: Christian Watt, 1988
*A Letter to the People of Laurencekirk*: Lord Gardenstone, 1780
*The Parish School*: George Menzies, 1840
*The Mem, or Schoolmistress*: John Galt, 1834

Figure 2. **Balloch Public School, Upper Strathdon, 1907** All nineteen pupils of this remote Aberdeenshire school have presented themselves for the photographer, along with their one teacher, Miss H. Singer. Depopulation led to its closure after the war. The school building has long since become overgrown by foliage.
*Mrs Campbell, Dingwall (granddaughter of Miss Singer)*

Figure 3. **Flora Stevenson's School, Edinburgh: fire drill, 1914** A scene which demonstrates not only the onset of world war, but the daunting décor common to the large urban School Board institution of the period – many of which, like this one, were built to direct over a thousand pupils throughout their whole, elementary, school career.
*Edinburgh Education Department*

Even at the cost of £1,500 a year and a grieving congregation, the Reverend Archibald Alison's decision to uproot his family from their comfortable Shropshire living and have his boys receive a proper 'Scotch' education seemed a sound one (**2A**). By 1800, his native land could point to more than a hundred years of educational achievement. During the preceding century, the old Scottish Parliament's legislation had been translated into a system that now reached out into every community. In each parish, the leading land owners – 'heritors' – had, as required by law, provided a school-house and funds for the salary of a properly equipped master. They had done this in partnership with the Kirk, whose local presbyteries were responsible for monitoring the content and the standards of the curriculum. Every attempt was made to appoint a learned man who was capable of teaching Latin and the Scriptures, as well as the three Rs. His presence would ensure that no village lad of outstanding ability would be without the opportunity to rise up to a university career and thus to get on life.

In those towns which had been granted burgh status (by 1800, there were 80 of them), provision was on a somewhat different footing: there, the magistrates or Council held the responsibility for maintaining the school. If, in the larger settlements, it often developed into a prestigious academic establishment that carried several staff and concentrated on the secondary ages, the principle of a properly administered public school in every legally defined centre of population held good.

Land-Kirk-School; Burgh-Magistrates-School: at the start of the new century, the Alisons were returning to a country which had succeeded in establishing a secure and public educational presence in every parish in the land. The assumption on both sides of the border was that, however poor and disfavoured the northern partner within the British union was, in academic terms she was certainly the superior.

**2B** and **2C** are typical of the kind of pieces which were appearing in the journals at that time. As, in the early decades of the nineteenth century, England began to inch its way towards a properly organised system by which to replace its haphazard series of charitable and

Church-run institutions, Scotland was usually cited as the model to emulate. In **2B**, the anonymous English journalist is remarking upon the moral power of its parish schooling. **2C** shows a leading social commentator of the day, Lord Cockburn, writing to similar effect in the *Edinburgh Review*, a periodical which had a wide circulation throughout the United Kingdom.

Yet, although each writer rests his case upon the virtues of a universal system, their articles are as much about keeping the 'lower orders' in check as they are about high educational aspirations. The hope is that, by being schooled into an 'independent spirit', the 'labouring classes' will come to practise a self-reliance which will enable their social superiors to rest easy they will not become a burden on their prosperity or a threat to the peace. Both extracts are designed to appeal to their readers' need for reassurance: by conjuring up a warmly domestic picture of old folk, humbly bringing out the pennies which testify to the national thrift; and by reiterating the myth of a poor little country which, by giving itself up to education, became miraculously reborn out of savagery.

How 'democratic' was this vaunted system? To what extent could it be said to belong to, and to serve, the interests of all the people? There were, certainly, solid grounds beneath the rhetoric. In the 1790s, the *Statistical Account of Scotland* had completed a parish-by-parish account, detailing the chief human and material features of the whole country. Its sections on 'Education' convey an overall impression that illiteracy was a rare exception and that, everywhere, school attendance was engrained in the culture of daily life.

Later, as the government began to debate the issue of public education, it commissioned a number of surveys. These yielded a mass of information, not only as to the extent of Scotland's provision but how its parochial scheme actually functioned. As an example of this, take the sample entries from the inquiry initiated by order of Parliament in 1834 (**2D**). Summing up a pair of representative rural parishes in Aberdeenshire, the lists of syllabus subjects, of attendance patterns and the confident pronouncements on their inhabitants' literacy, all suggest a national system that had, indeed, entered effectively into people's lives.

But the Inquiry also exposes a fast growing problem. As a contrast to the stable rural places, **2E** sets out two of the entries from Aberdeen City. These reveal a system under strain. It is clear that, by the 1830s and now well into the great industrial upheaval that would turn Scotland into a predominantly urbanised society, the old parochial scheme was struggling to cope with the needs of the rapidly expanding towns.

Indeed, if we read further into even the rural data, it becomes clear that, although the principle of a public school to every parish holds, it usually had to be supplemented by a myriad of private, 'venture' establishments. The summary figures that were attached to the Aberdeenshire section tell the story here: in the county as a whole, there are 440 schools listed – but 347 of them are 'non-parochial'; 9,926 pupils go to these and only 5,410 to the 'public' remainder. Attendance figures, moreover, reveal that 'going to school' tends to be a seasonal matter for many families, whose young members had to take the summer months out to act as cheap agricultural labour; the all-important Latin – gateway to the professions – is confined to the parochial schools, which the majority were not attending; the lists of subjects seem imposing, but they have to be delivered by one master to all-age classes of up to 80 – and no uptake figures for them are given. Fees, even for the basic subjects, are universal.

Complexities such as these remind us that this is a society unused to any notion of a central government's intervention in the local community's management of daily affairs. The mixed economy of its education reflects this: the official parish or burgh school provides the model but for a whole range of private and sectional establishments which may be attended, singly or in serial combination, according to the individual family's varying circumstances. Clearly, the claim that, by the early 1800s, the people of Scotland were enjoying an open, democratic system has to be set against the standards of the time. Economic constraint was one important determinant and social ethos was another. In this connection, Alex Somerville's *Autobiography of a Working Man* offers us a first-hand account of a life whose early struggles show the problems that getting an education could create for the ordinary family. The parents took the matter seriously but, despite their scrimping, could only give their gifted young son an irregular, hand-to-mouth schooling – and his sister not even that.

What is almost as great an obstacle as money are the class-bound attitudes of the schoolmaster. The young of the district might be held together within the one schoolroom but the dominie's best endeavours are preserved for the sons of the well-to-do, whom he insists that the common lot addresses as 'Master'. It is a strict decorum, which is maintained by the lash of the belt and a summary form of socially prejudiced justice (**2F**).

The young Alex refused to be cowed: although forced into a series of degradingly hard, itinerant posts on the land, followed by a brutal enlistment in the Army, he continued to read improving literature wherever he could get it. This was sometimes through local sub-scription libraries but often it was by borrowing precious, tattered copies that belonged to his fellow workmen. In his twenties, he starts to send in pieces to the Edinburgh press. And so, from the humblest of beginnings, a noteworthy journalistic career takes shape. It is, in its way, an inspiring story, a tribute to the energies and will to learn of an ordinary 'working man' Scot. It is also one which shows that the ladder of opportunity could be as much of the individual's own making as due to any carpentry provided by the official system.

The struggles of Alex Somerville remind us of the importance of context when we attempt to judge the actual effectiveness of Scottish education as a democratic force. The dependency of the poor on the power of the farm owners, the sharp sense of class distinctions, which were frequently reproduced in the treatment of pupils, both tell us that the national system established its reputation in a society which was essentially rural and organised on fixed, hierarchical lines. Although there was always the chance left open for the really able and industrious boy to rise from his background, the greater expectation was that he and his kind would pass through the school and back out into the farm-labouring occupations of their fathers.

For half the population, there was not even that. The experience of Christian Watt shows how impossible it was for a working-class woman, gifted and independently minded though she might be, to escape from the expected role of part-time labour and full-time domestic duty. A woman of intelligence and fierce pride, avid for learning, she first had to endure social discrimination at her school and then a life as drudge, fishwife and prolific mother (**2G**). Ulti-mately, the frustration and the strain were too much: she lived out the last half of her life as inmate in an Aberdeen mental hospital.

The late eighteenth century had, however, witnessed a remarkable period of economic growth. This was generated not only by the burgeoning textile mills of the Central Belt but also by the advances being made in lowland agriculture. This was the age of the 'Improvers', when landowners were busy driving into their estates efficiently modern methods of draining, dyking and tilling the soil and for the breeding of cattle.

The Kincardineshire settlement of Laurencekirk is a typical product of this movement. In the mid-eighteenth century, it grew from insignificance into a thriving community, its marshes drained, its endemic ague cleansed away, its fields able to produce sufficient for a population which had expanded tenfold in fifty years. A publicly spirited landlord, Lord Gardenstone, had bought heavily into the area, engineered a straight new road and, alongside its six furlongs, laid out a model village.

When the place came to be rewarded with its charter as a burgh, his Lordship demonstrates a paternalistic regard for his people's welfare and this includes their education (**2H**). But sound schooling is only part of the grand mission by which he will civilise the local peasantry into the adoption of rational domestic habits and of 'INDUSTRY'. And that, he adds, will require 'no genteel or costly education'.

It was a provision sufficient to encourage the next generation to contribute to the national stock of patriotic nostalgia, as grateful sons looked back with softened reminiscence and a poetic desire to reclaim a native identity. One of them was George Menzies. He was the poor son of a farm servant but died a successful journalist in Ontario. In truth, it was Canada rather than the Mearns which had made him. But it was abroad, as chief of the *Niagara Mail*, that he composed 'The Parish School', 'the home', he assures us, 'of all/ The best and brightest of my days' (**2I**).

The local collections of the libraries of Scotland are full of gilded material, similar to the Menzies effusion. This is what makes John Galt so valuable. His best known work, *Annals of the Parish* (1821), gives us a nicely poised characterisation of small community Ayrshire life and its social development over some fifty years, as recorded in the journals of its Reverend Micah Balwhidder. The parochial school might represent the national system but its conduct is just as much subject to the humdrum pretensions of village life as the arrival of tea-drinking or Miss Hookie's embroidery classes for its young ladies.

It is a later and less well-known work, which fully demonstrates Galt's ability to place 'education' within the changing values of Scottish society in his lifetime. This is *Mem*, the story of a small burgh private school mistress, again set in Ayrshire, again observed through the musings of Balwhidder. With poignant force, he records the fate of Miss Peerie, the only child of the local grammar school headmaster. Fifty years before, she had been esteemed the most accomplished young lady in the whole district, as beautiful as she was intellectually able: Greek, Latin and Hebrew were as familiar to her as the ABC.

His story shows the cruel decline (2J). She has opened up a garret school, hoping soon to move on to bigger things. But she discovers no market for all her learning; she has to settle for imparting the arts of plain-work embroidery and table-laying to the daughters of the more socially ambitious parents. In a passage of delicate artistry, Galt shows something of how, in a typical Scottish small-town community at the end of the eighteenth century, learning could be valued. He ends with a question that neither he nor its inhabitants can properly answer.

Our opening episode of autobiography (2A) is further evidence of how, beneath the standard claims made for it, the essential character of Scottish education can only be located by entering into the experiences of the people as they lived it. Whatever Sir Archibald Alison's father meant by the 'Scotch system of education', he evidently did not include the local school in its fundamental definition. Once returned to Edinburgh, he hired a succession of private tutors by which to give young Archy Greek and Latin enough to enter the city's university.

It was a response which reflected the wider situation. The Scottish educational tradition rested upon simple historical principles but it was also of its own time. As such, the ideal of the 'common' school and the 'public' system was capable of yielding a range of individual interpretations. As the nineteenth century advanced, the relationship between the inherited mythology and the increasingly complex practicalities would become ever more intricate, ever more a matter of first-hand experience.


2A                                                    Shropshire, 1800.


My father, though bred up, after he left Glasgow at Balliol College, Oxford, where he spent eleven years in close study, was strongly impressed by the superiority for *general* students and practical life of the Scotch system of education . . . Influenced by these views, he embraced an offer made in the spring of 1800 by the Directors of the

Episcopal Chapel, Cowgate, Edinburgh, of the situation of the senior minister of that congregation, a charge which permitted him to retain his English livings. In doing so, he was not ignorant that he ran the risk of losing the chance of further preferment from Sir William Poultney, who had destined for him the rectory of Wern in Shropshire, worth £1,500 a-year. But that sacrifice appeared to him trifling in comparison with the advantages likely to accrue to his sons from the proposed change; and certainly neither my brother nor I have had reason to regret his resolution. We set out accordingly, on the 8th May 1800, for Shrewsbury on our way to Scotland, followed for several miles by the whole parish, most of whom were in tears, and finally left the home of infancy . . .

> Alison, Sir Archibald (1883). *Some Account of my Life and Writings: an Autobiography.* Edinburgh, William Blackwood.

1792–1867: Edinburgh historian, lawyer, literary critic and leading Scots Tory.

## 2B                                                  London, 1817.

Mr Editor, I fervently hope that the benevolent institution of cheap schools for our labouring population in England, may produce the salutary effects of parochial seminaries in Scotland. A taste for mental pleasures, in preference to sensual gratifications, has proceeded from an acquaintance with letters; and several communities have followed the example of the miners at Leadhills and Wanloch Head, in collecting libraries for the common good. A noble sentiment prevails, that it is disgraceful to depend upon charity, and infamous to have a parent an incumbrance upon the public; while on the other hand, all persons of any character make a point of providing for old age, that they may not become very burdensome to their descendents. This fact was remarkably apparent when the new coinage came into circulation: Crowds of poor old men and women brought out their little hoards, to exchange for new silver – shillings and sixpences, quite discoloured, by lying many years in their humble repositories. Baron Voght has recommended to discourage early marriage, as a preventative of poverty among the lower classes; but in Scotland, without legal exactions, or large voluntary donations from the opulent, the offspring of a sanctified union in the prime of life, are able to help the authors of their existence before old age and decrepitude wholly unfit them to help themselves – and so sweetly potent are local attachments and filial affections, that the undaunted soldier, discharged from service, returns with delight to his 'heath-covered mountains', which excite in his bosom admiration never awakened by the glowing scenery of southern continental provinces.

'Independent Spirit of the Lower Classes of the
Scotch' (1817). *New Monthly Magazine,* 8, November.


2C                                                        Edinburgh, 1827.

There probably never was a nation where a taste for education was less to have been expected than in Scotland at the time of the Revolution [Reformation]. Utter poverty, long persecution, and every species of internal disorder, seemed to make the country the natural abode of general and continued ignorance. Its disturbances, however, were no sooner settled, than the seed, which had been scattered abroad, began to spring, even on that stony soil. A process was set at work in every parish, which prepared all ranks for the coming harvest. There being few other objects of literary ambition at home, successive races of persons, distinguished by virtue and learning, were attracted to the profession of teaching, not so much by its emoluments, as by the honour in which it was held. Under the intellectual and moral tuition of those excellent men, the district in which each of them laboured was gradually reclaimed. Amidst the various outlets which opened to a poor but enterprising people, it was soon made evident that education was its own reward; and the success of every individual, who either raised up a name for himself in his own country, or returned to it enriched with foreign wealth or honour, increased that appetite of knowledge, which was not merely indulged in as a luxury, but valued as one of the most certain and cheapest means of worldly advancement. As the public establishment had never been complete, private schools arose to supply its deficiencies; but the excellence of the parochial seminaries – secured chiefly by the respectability of the men who found it their interest to devote themselves to their duties – enabled them in general to triumph over all competition. The example of a right school was thus kept up in every parish; and, each rival copying that visible model, the whole system of education throughout the country was maintained steadily and quietly.

Cockburn, Henry (Lord) (1827). 'Scottish

Parochial Schools', *Edinburgh Review*, 46, June.

2D                                                    Aberdeenshire, 1830s.

COULL Parish is entirely landward.

The instruction given at the Parochial School consists of English reading, writing, arithmetic and Latin; no other branches seem called for. The salary of the master (who is aged, and for the greater part of the year keeps an assistant), is 26*l* per annum, with 7*l* 14*s* 1*d* school fees, and 2*l* 2*s* 9*d* annually other emoluments, exclusive of the Dick bequest, which in 1832 amounted to 29*l* 3*s*. The School *not* parochial is kept by an aged female and her daughter, who only teach reading and writing.

Only one person is known in the parish, above fifteen years of age, who is unable to read, and he is not a native of Coull. A Sunday School is kept, during the summer months of every alternate year, by the clergyman of the parish, which is attended by about 35 of both sexes. A parochial library was established, under the superintendence of the clergyman, in 1831, containing chiefly standard works of practical divinity, with a select number of books of history, voyages and travels. It has succeeded well; and it is thought that similar libraries, if established in every place in the kingdom, would prove a great blessing. At all the above Schools the scholars are carefully instructed in the principles of the Christian religion.

(signed) *William Campbell*, Minister.

CRIMOND Parish is entirely landward.

The instruction given at the Parochial School consists of Latin, reading, writing, arithmetic, theoretical and practical mathematics, book-keeping and geography, frequently Greek, and French occasionally; no other branch could be taught conveniently. The salary of the master is 35*l* per annum, with 11*l* 12*s* 11*d* school fees, and other emoluments, arising from the interest of mortification, and perquisites from the office of session clerk, amounting together to 19*l* 8*s* 11*d* for the year previous to the harvest of 1834. The salary was only 28*l* per annum, until last year, when it was raised, by the liberality of the heritors, to meet the views of 'Dick's trustees'. At one of the Schools *not* parochial, reading, writing and sewing and arithmetic are taught; at another, the same, with sewing in addition; at another, reading, writing, and sewing; and at the other two, reading and knitting only.

The Schools returned in this parish contain 23 children from other parishes, and 7 children belonging to this parish (not included) attend Schools in other parishes. There is no child capable of attending School but what is sent.

(signed) *W. Boyd*, Minister.


2E                                          Aberdeen City, 1830s.

GREY FRIARS Parish

By the census of 1831, the population of Grey Friars was 4,706; but by a late *quoad sacra* division, it now contains about 5,500 souls. The population throughout is very much of the same class, and is the poorest in Aberdeen, so that the following may serve as a specimen of the whole, in answer to the first set of queries. It is found that, in a district containing about 660 souls, there are 25 children under five years of age, and 165 between five and fifteen, able to read, and 89 between five and fifteen able to write. There are about six adventure Schools within the parish, attended by about 200 children in all, some of which are *migratory*, and inefficiently taught. The only thing at all of the nature of a Parochial School is one established by the Minister, attended throughout the day and evenings of the week by about 240 children; in addition to which, there are seven Sabbath Evening Schools, attended by about 400 or 500 children, where, however, religious instruction only is communicated. These Schools (Week and Sabbath) are supported chiefly by the contributions of the congregation. The branches generally taught, both in the *Adventure* and other Schools, are reading, writing, arithmetic, grammar and geography, &c. In short, the means of education for the poorer classes in this parish are deplorably inefficient and defective, and the result has been, is, and will continue every day more strongly to show itself in the ignorance, irreligion and immorality of the inhabitants; in which respects it is not singular, but only the same with the other parishes of large towns in Scotland.

(signed) Abercromby L. Gordon, Minister.

## WOODSIDE Parish

Woodside is a parish *quoad spiritualia*, and has been disjoined from the parish of Old Machar, in consequence of the Act of the last General Assembly respecting Chapels of Ease. It consists of five villages, three of them contiguous to each other, and a considerable landward district. Woodside is no Burgh, neither is it part of one; it is distant one mile and a quarter from the Burgh of Old Aberdeen, and two miles from the Burgh of New Aberdeen.

There is no Parochial School at Woodside; the one belonging to Old Machar is situate [sic] in Old Aberdeen, and from its distance and other causes, can be of no use whatever to this parish. At the Schools *not* parochial (which include Evening Schools), reading, writing, arithmetic, sewing and knitting are taught.

The Schools are very inefficient; the teachers are in general totally unqualified. There is no encouragement for good teachers, the emoluments being trifling; the fees are almost universally paid weekly, and the income of the master, for that period varies from 5s to 12s. Very little good is done at the Eveninschools [sic], the attendance consisting principally of such as have been at work in the mills during the day, and are consequently too fatigued to make much progress in education; besides, the frequent changes in the mill hours prevent regularity of attendance.

There is no endowment of any kind for the instruction of youth; the state of education is most deplorable, there being many who cannot read.

(signed) Andrew Gray, Minister.

*Abstract of Education Returns (Scotland)*
(1837). London, H. M. Government.

2F                                                   East Lothian, 1810s.

One of the oldest and most infirm of the thatched houses was the school-room. The schoolmaster was a lame man, and was a teacher

*33*

only because he was lame. It was not a parish school; but he had a local fame as a good teacher, and though, as will be seen, I have no reason to remember him with much respect, I must say that, excepting the inordinate and cruel use of the *taws* for punishment, his system of teaching was better than that of any of the parish schools near us at that time.

My mother saw the schoolmaster in the house of George Dickison, the weaver, and some of the pupils, pleased to see 'new scholars' come, took us into the school, and so my education, having got a twopenny spelling book, began. The first six weeks were consumed in learning to forget to name the letters as my father and mother had named them; that once accomplished, I got on pretty well; for though the spelling books were made up of lessons with no meaning in them, or a meaning of sheer nonsense, I had a desire to know what the nonsense was. In short, I read as well as I could, and tried to read better, and ran before the lesson I was at, to see what the next one said. In this way I was getting on, and had not got much punishment, not so much as several other children reading with me, when one day I came in rather late in the morning. I was instantly called up and questioned as to why I was too late. The schoolmaster was a very polite man in his way, but he had never taught us the polite designation of vulgar things. After some hesitation, I, in my innocence, gave him an answer which offended him; upon which he took up his great leathern belt, thirty inches long, two and a half inches broad, which was split half way up into six thongs, the end of each having been burned in the fire to make it hard; the other end of the belt, having a slit in it, into which he put his hand and wound it round his wrist. With this instrument, called the *taws*, he thrashed me on the hands, head, face, neck, shoulders, back, legs, everywhere, until I was blistered. He wanted me to cry, but I would not, and never did for punishment or pain then or since, though my flesh is nervous and extremely sensitive. I have cried when excessive kindness has been used to me, not when cruelty was used. I sat sullen and in torture all the day, my poor sister Mary glancing at me from her book, she was not crying, but her heart was beating as if it would burst for me. When we got out of the school to go home, and were away from all the other scholars, on our lonely road to Thriepland Hill, she soothed me with kind words, and we cried then, both of us. We could not tell at home what had happened; our mother would have deeply grieved, and our father, we supposed, would think it all right what the schoolmaster had done, for he believed in his infallibility as a teacher.

My sister went to school no more than that quarter, having to go to the fields to help to work for the family bread. When the summer of 1819 came, I left school also, to herd the farmer's cows. In the winter of 1819 I again went to school, and got into severe trouble with the teacher on one occasion . . .

The term 'ragged radicals' was a common one in newspapers of that time, and the boys who heard their fathers read the newspapers or talk of the news, brought this name of reproach to the school. It was suggested one day by some of them, that an excellent play might be got up in the Eel Yards, a meadow with some large trees in it, if the scholars divided themselves into soldiers and radicals. As the soldiers were the most respectable in the eyes of the better dressed sons of farmers and tradesmen, and as they took the lead in everything, they made themselves soldiers; in addition to that, took upon themselves to pick out those who were to be the radicals. This was done according to the quality of the clothes worn, and I, consequently, found myself declared to be a radical . . .

As soon as I made my appearance, the cry of 'ragged radical' was raised; the soldiers charged on me, and knocked my infirm hat over my eyes with my head through the crown of it. Some laid hold of me by the feet to carry me off to be hanged and beheaded, *as the real law upon the real radicals had taught them to imitate in play.* I made a violent effort to free myself, and the rents of yesterday, which my mother had so carefully sewed, broke open afresh. The hat I raised from where it had sunk over my face, and saw part of the brim in the hands of a lad who was a kind of king of the school, or cock of the walk, with some of my poor mother's threads hanging from it. He was older than I, and was a fighter. I had never fought, nor had heard of two human creatures going together to fight, until I came to that school. Yet neither had I heard of the divine principle of forbearance and forgiveness, as regards blows upon the body, and the laceration of feelings worse than blows upon the body . . . I was a strong boy for my age, and I had received very bad treatment. My honour and the remembrance of my affectionate mother's toils made me feel like a giant. I amazed the king of the school by giving him a blow in the face that laid him flat on his back, and amazed the onlookers by giving several of them as much with the same results. Not that I escaped without blows myself. I got many, but they were returned with principle and interest. Some one ran to the schoolmaster and told that I was thrashing 'Master' Somebody, for he being a gentleman's son was called 'Master', while I had to submit to a nickname, derived from the state of my clothes. The school was summoned in at once, it being near the schoolhour in the morning. Some of those whose noses were bleeding ran to school with them in that state to let their disasters be seen. Another one and myself tried to get water to wash our faces, for mine was in as bad a condition as the worst of theirs; but the frost was so hard, that we could not break the ice to get water, and at last were compelled to obey the repeated summons to school in the dreadful guise we were in; my clothes being torn half off me in addition to the hideousness of the blood streaming from my face.

The schoolmaster stood with the *taws* ready to flagellate the moment I entered the school. He inquired who began the fight, and everyone named me. He at once ordered me to hold up my right hand, which I did, and received a violent cut on the edge of it, given with his whole strength. He ordered my left hand up, and up it went and received a cut of the same kind; then my right, which got what it got before; next my left, which also got what it got before; and so he went on until I had got six cuts (skults we called them) on each hand. He had a way of raising himself upon his toes when he swung the heavy *taws* round his head, and came down upon his feet with a spring, giving the cuts slantingly on the hand. He saw me resolved to take all he could give me without a tear, whereupon he began to cut at the back of my hands. I drew them behind me to save them, which seeing, he cut at the open place of my torn clothes, where my skin was visible; and always as I wriggled to one side to save those bare places, I exposed other bare places on the other side, which he aimed at with terrible certainty. After a time he pushed me before him, still thrashing me on the bare places, and the head, until he got me to the farther end of the school, where the coals lay in a corner. He thrashed me until I got on the top of the coals. Here he ordered me to sit down and remain until he gave me liberty to leave that place, which he did not do until evening. The day was piercingly cold. The house was an old place, with no furniture nor partition in it. I sat at the end farthest from the fireplace, and near to the door, which was an old door that did not fit its place, and which allowed the wind to blow freely through. It blew through and about me as if it had been another schoolmaster, and was as partial to the farmers' sons, and as cruel to the ragged boys of farm labourers, as he was.

> Somerville, Alex [1848] (1951). *The Autobiography of a Working Man*. London, Turnstile Press.

1811–85: after variety of jobs, including Army enlistment and 200 lashes for insubordination, developed journalist career, achieving national attention as independently minded commentator on radical issues.

2G                    Fraserburgh, Aberdeenshire, 1830s.

With my two young brothers, my cousin Annie and I went to Broadsea School to start our education . . . We had to take a bawbee, a lump of coal or peat each day, bairns who could not produce these things were not put out of school, only Mrs. Cox, the mistress would go on about it to scare them. She took a keen interest in those willing to learn, and in my first three years I could read, write and spell according to the standard. I left Broadsea school to help mother with the fish. My little brother and I in the dead of winter attended Mr Woodman's school on the Aberdeen road, it cost a penny a day. We were both good at the English and we learned the stops and interrogations in writing, every odd moment, I could never get enough to read, I read everything I could get my hands on. The school was largely attended by children of would be gentry from the Broch, Mr Woodman fauned on them and they looked down on us because we came from Broadsea which was by far older than Fraserburgh, our houses were ancient compared to any building in the Broch yet they regarded them as hovels. My father spent a lot of time with me and my little brother. He was a smart man who believed in learning. We had to work when we were 8 years old, but our schooling went on in the winter when fishing was slack.

> Watt, Christian (1988). *The Christian Watt Papers*. David Fraser (ed.). Collieston, Caledonian Books.

1833–1923: of North-east fishing stock; lost four brothers and husband at sea; subsisted by door-to-door fish selling; removed to Cornhill mental hospital, Aberdeen, at 47, where she received enlightened treatment and was encouraged to write her recollections.

Laurencekirk, Kincardineshire, 1780.

A due care and wise management in the EDUCATION OF YOUR CHILDREN is of equal moment to the prosperity of your private families, and the good of the community: – 'train up a child', says the Wise Man, 'in the way that he should go, and when he is old he will not depart from it'. – Unreasonable indulgence is a prevailing error in the education of children among our people: – 'He that spareth the rod, hateth the child'. – When he is perverse and peevish, you very commonly caress him, and give him something he likes to put him in good humour; – that is, you reward and encourage the ill temper, and obstinacy which you ought to correct. – Bad men grow up from bad children; – and if you would form your son to be a temperate, good-natured, honest, and industrious man, (perhaps the best character of the human race), you must take some pains on his education; – you must make use of rational arts, of little rewards and punishments to fall on him in that character from his earliest infancy . . .

There is another unhappy error in the common practice of our country-education, and that is, that you do not begin early enough to give your children lessons and habits of INDUSTRY. – Your boys and girls, till they are at least seven or eight years old, are for the most part in a mere state of idleness, and do nothing but play and ramble about, or begin to waste time at the grammar-school in the rudiments of Latin, whether they discover a genius for literature (which is early and easily discernable) or not. – You should exercise your invention and ingenuity to find early employments for them. – There is nothing more material to their welfare and success through the stages of life. – In all countries distinguished for industry, particularly in Holland and England, the children are very early set to some easy work or other: – In Aberdeenshire (where I think the people in general have the best habits of temperance and industry of any in Scotland) I have seen children, taught to weave the stocking very alertly at five years old. – The first thing you commonly set your children to, is what I must call an idle occupation; – the herding of cattle; – often but a single cow. – The child has little else to do but to saunter and look about him. – He grows excessively weary, and discovers it by the most natural symptoms. – I seldom pass one of them at any advanced time of the day, but he crawls to me and asks. – 'What o'clock is it?' – A plain and significant expression of their impatience and weariness; – In

Aberdeenshire, where they are employed at the stocking while they attend the cattle, they discover no such impatience . . .'

Lord Gardenstone (1780). *A Letter to the People of Laurencekirk, on the Occasion of presenting the King's Charter by which the Village is created into a Free and Independent Burgh or Barony.*


2I                                             Laurencekirk/Ontario, 1840.

> Close by our Parish Church there stands,
> Albeit a fane [flag] of lowlier kind
> Than those which rise in sunnier lands,
> The nursery of a nation's mind.
>
> That mind hath travelled far and wide
> O'er every land and every sea
> But still its proudest cause of pride,
> Our Parish School, is all of thee!
>
> Oh, glory to the Parish School
> And honour to it everywhere,
> For it hath been the vestibule
> To many, many a home of prayer!

Menzies, George (1840). 'The Parish School'. Woodstock, Canada.

1797–1847: forced to leave school early through family poverty; variety of jobs, including venture teaching, before penury led to emigration to Ontario, where he prospered in journalism.


2J                                                    Ayrshire, 1780s.

At last the rheumatics in her legs put an end to her solitary walks, and her narrow course was in consequence confined to her room; where, when the winter raged without, she had a small fire – just a pinch of chips and coals that, to folks used to galravaging [merry-making], would have made the cold sensible. But she was content with the spunk, and sat alone all night beside it, sometimes with spread hands

*39*

cowering over the flames, reading a book by the light of her cruise [lamp], and heaping up knowledge that it was plain to all that saw her could never be put to use in this world – in the next, all worldly wisdom is foolishness, as is well known.

One Sunday afternoon, when it was rather rainy, there came on a shower just as I passed her close mouth; and remembering her, I took the benefit of the wet to shelter there. Being constrained to wait longer than I expected, it came into my head to go up stairs and inquire for her. No doubt it was a fool thought of me to do so, for I was but slenderly acquainted with the ailing woman: we knew, however, each other well enough for need to give me the privilege. So I went up the wooden stair. I mind the place; it was very dark, and had a ravel of rope, useful to the lame and the aged in going up and down.

When I had reached her door, instead of rapping with my knuckle before entering, as maybe I should have done, in I went at once, and there was the clean, respectable-looking old woman taking her tea, beside her spark of fire. She had for her table a big stool, with a finger hole in the middle of it; and for her teapot, notwithstanding the grand row on her dresser, she had a coarse, stumpy, brick-coloured commodity, that held well enough, no doubt, for one. But when I told her what had driven me in, she invited me to take a cup with her, and the track pot was in consequence obliged that night to serve two; but her tea was very thin, and she had her small condiment of sugar in a tea cup, that shewed nothing was allowed for waste.

After I had solaced myself with her frugal beverage, the rain continuing to blatter on the windows, she made an endeavour to converse with me concerning many things, such as the Trojan war, and Numa Pompilius, a king of Rome, wherein she gave me a sample of the lore she had learned from her father. But she was not like an earthly creature, for her mind ran on old things, such as the building of the pyramids of Egypt, and Queen Cleopatra, and Isaac and Abraham, the fathers and founders of the Israelitish people.

Saving that accidental visit, which was most interesting, I never had a specimen of the great learning that she inherited from her father. She was, however, a dungeon of wit, and made no brag of what she knew.

Soon after that visit she was constrained to give up her school, and to prepare herself for another and better world, which made me very woeful to hear; for though it could not be said that her life was barren of utility, as she taught the daughters of many mothers thrift and good conduct, it was sad to think that all her days were just a struggle to flee from the fangs of famine.

The only good fortune that befel this innocent creature was that death did not make her latter end a kittle [troublesome] case, but stopped her breath in a sudden cough, when she had no complaint but the pains in her knees and ancles [sic]; and fortunately this happened when the misses were coming in the morning to school, so that she did not die unseen, as many feared she would do.

Dreadful was the cry made by her scholars when they saw that she was dead. Some ran home, others to the doctor's shop; but it was all in vain – the unblemished soul of Miss Peerie had taken the wings of the morning and flown away into Abraham's bosom. Great was the lamentation that ensued. Mothers wondered what they would do with their daughters, and really were in as great an affliction as if they had all been marriageable. However, their grief was not of a durable nature, and was soon forgotten when Miss Peerie was laid in the churchyard. But still she has been a mystery to me. For what use was knowledge and instruction given to her?: I ponder when I think of it, but have no answer to the question.

Galt, John (1834). 'The Mem, or Schoolmistress. From the Papers of the Late Rev. Micah Balwhidder, of Dalmailing', *Fraser's Magazine*, 9, August.

1779–1839: Ayrshire man; author of 60 books, many offering incisive commentary on provincial Scottish life.

# 3 THE LADS WHO GOT ON

*The Life of Dr Alexander Duff*: George Smith, 1879
*The Life and Letters of John Cairns*: Alexander McEwan, 1895
*Rhymes and Recollections of a Hand-loom Weaver*:
William Thom, 1847
*Phases of Girlhood*: Janet Hamilton, 1870
*My Schools and Schoolmasters*: Hugh Miller, 1854
*David Livingstone, His Life and Letters*: George Seaver, 1957
*Reminiscences of a Long and Busy Life*: William Chambers, 1882
*Biographic Sketches, Dr Adam*: *Chambers's Journal*, 1832

Figure 4. **Campbeltown Grammar School, Argyll, c. 1900** A 'master-and-boys' shot which evokes both the regimentation and masculine ethos which many have seen as characteristic of Scottish education. *Campbeltown Library*

Figure 5. **A Glasgow Higher Grade School, 1914** At this date, girls were being given a thorough domestic science training in solidly equipped, purpose-built rooms.
*Glasgow City Archive*

By the end of the nineteenth century, the public libraries of the land would hold a shelf or two on which were lined up biographies of favourite Scottish sons. Their intention is to lay before the world a record of the exemplary life, one that is capable of giving dramatic shape to the native virtues of perseverance, piety, self-discipline and the common, homely touch.

Origins are vitally important to this larger aim. Early chapters carefully depict the warmth of a humble parental cottage, long days of youthful toil to assist the meagre family budget, the ingesting of scriptures along with the daily porridge, and, crucially, the enlightenment that is assuredly available at the little local school.

As the subject moves his way upwards, it is possible to discern one of a pair of complementary model careers taking wing. There is the Scot who goes forth to bestow his native powers upon the whole wide world; there is the brother who stays behind, there to renew the national wellsprings in the continued service of his own people.

An example of the former is Alexander Duff, the farmer's boy who was born in 1806 in the remoteness of the Perthshire hills and who spent forty years waging missionary war against, as the *Dictionary of National Biography* put it, 'the absurdities of the Hindoo' in British India, at the same time founding the University of Calcutta in order to cast the light of the European mind on that obscure subcontinent. In doing this, Duff was simply applying the principles of his own education, a mixture of devoted tuition and personal piety (**3A**).

One who stayed at home was John Cairns. Although he became a national church leader, for thirty years he was content to minister in his native Berwickshire. There he had acted out the cycle of heroic family sacrifice, of trial by dominie ordeal, of early morning conjugations and snatched moments of study at the sheep, which constitute the classic Scottish drama of the lad of parts (**3B**).

The experiences of Alexander Duff and John Cairns were, however, more dramatic than typical. For others, 'getting on' could be a much more hazardous affair. That this applied to individuals every bit as talented is shown by the case of William Thom. At ten, he was working a cotton loom in Aberdeen's Schoolhill Factory. The lad was, however, gifted in both words and music. He began to compose, initially for the delight of his fellow workers, the songs and the ballads which led to his being taken up by metropolitan literary circles. The moment of fashionable acclamation passed; he died in penury at fifty.

Significantly, the country's celebrated education system had done nothing for his native talent. Taking a neat swipe at Lord Chancellor Brougham's famed boast concerning the irresistible march of education in his native land – 'the Schoolmaster is abroad' – Thom sets down the haphazard reality of the curriculum that was available to him and his kind at their local backstreet dame's establishment (**3C**).

The 'wifie's skweel' shows that, if by 1800 there was female participation in the national education, it constituted little more than an extension of the strictly domestic part assumed in adult life. While the Dame's School had now become common, its age range was limited to the infant years appropriate to the maternal role. Mixed education had always been the parochial norm but the daughter's schooling tended to be shorter and her syllabus a narrow concentration on the basics – and, even here, the 'coontin' and, indeed, writing were often dispensed with, although 'sewing' and, significantly, 'sewing schools', were a common feature. The parliamentary survey of 1834–37 indicated girls' school attendance to be only 70 per cent of the boys' and, up to the 1872 Act, their literacy figures ran significantly lower – in the 1850s, for example, 77 per cent against the male 89.

Girls did not 'get on'. The social assumptions of the period, strengthened by a strong male-centred Presbyterian ethic and the basic facts of working-class domestic economy, suppressed any aspiration for higher study, even in the most independent of feminine spirits. One of these was Janet Hamilton, the 'Lanarkshire Poetess', daughter of a shoemaker and, despite her own lack of formal education, able to pick up sufficient inspiration at the village subscription library to become an accomplished writer on the changing social scene. But, although her volume is dedicated to 'Her Brothers and Sisters of the Working Classes', she is also aware that, essentially, she is 'the daughter, wife and mother of working-men'. In all her urgings for self-improvement, she never departs from counselling her own sex in the lessons of home-making or warning against over-'radical' thinking. Her wishes for her own Maggie anticipate, not question, the destiny of domestic servitude (**3D**).

The literary achievements of Thom and Hamilton show that there were other sources of education at work in the Scotland of the time, beyond the famed parochial provision. Despite the privations, as a weaver, Thom grew up within a supportive and, in its own way, intellectually alert community. He and his fellow workers inhabited a lively subculture of dance, rhyme and theological and political debate – one which drew upon the oral traditions of their rural backgrounds, as well as the opportunities for book and pamphlet circulation now made possible by their being part of a mass urban work force.

One of Thom's favourites was the Paisley poet Robert Tannahill, a cotton worker who had, despite a schooling which was so threadbare that it forced him, in later life, to turn to a private tutor for proper 'grammar', also achieved a transitory national fame. He had started out as a boy composer of workplace riddles, or 'speer guesses', before graduating to the ballads which were memorised and recited among the clattering machines. There were others – John Duncan, the Drumlithie weaver boy, who became a noted botanist, and Alexander Wilson, also of Paisley and, later, America's first great ornithologist.

But these were workers for whom the traditional route of parish school, followed by classical honours at university, had been, not so much bypassed, as simply shut off. Taken together, their example showed nineteenth-century Scotland both the deficiencies within its national system and the necessary alternative to it. In Hugh Miller's autobiography, the model of self-education within a supportive community found its most powerful advocate. It is the intensely personal story of how its author used his own readings in theology and literature, alongside highly idiosyncratic field research among the rocks and on the beaches of his native Cromarty, to pull himself up from the position of stonemason apprentice to become essayist, banking accountant, poet, collector of folklore, journalist, theologian, pre-eminent geologist and nineteenth-century polymath.

He called his story *My Schools and Schoolmasters*. As his own introduction (3E 1) affirms, the title is more declaration than description. Running through all that follows, whether it be a rapt account of summer evenings spent pouring over the gneiss and rock pools of the great slabbed sands of the Cromarty Firth or pained recall of days cramped behind the hard-edged desks of the local school, there is this message: that, in Scotland, as elsewhere, for the working man, a true education is to be experienced as an encounter between the inner spark and the open world that lies about him. Against all this, the official school can appear to be no more than an oppressive incarceration (**3E 2**).

As the nineteenth century moved on and as its biographical portraits were harvested, the two pathways of local school or self-education began to be merged into the one celebration of the capacity of the 'ordinary' Scot to conquer all life's adversities, through the power of studious application. This is demonstrated in the homage accorded to that greatest of all cotton-mill icons, David Livingstone. As his lovingly remembered anecdote shows us, what entered the national memory was the evidence of an heroically homespun ability to use 'education', whether gained at the parochial school or as an act of individual will, as the means to better one's own material and spiritual self (**3F**).

Ultimately, it is all a matter of moral steadfastness rather than the actions of any one particular social agency. As the rapid expansion in the publication and circulation of mass reading material, led by such Edinburgh-based titles as the *Edinburgh Review* and *Blackwoods*, drew in an ever wider circle of readership, the stories that Scotland told itself – and readers elsewhere in Great Britain – confirmed this self-image. In 1832, the brothers Robert and William launched their successful *Chambers's Journal*. Fifty years later, William used its columns to give an account of his 'Long and Busy Life' (**3G**). He is dismissive of his own parochial schooling. But the brothers shared an ethnic hunger for knowledge, which drove them to fashion their own garret room 'college' out of the books and periodicals that came their way.

The result was their determination to use their *Journal* to give the 'poorest labourer' the 'power to purchase . . . a meal of healthful, useful and agreeable instruction'. The same first edition, which sets out this promise, also launched a series of 'biographical sketches'. Both the opening subject and its preamble are indicative of the mixture of edification and national pride which were to run through the ensuing portraits, whenever, as was frequently the case, they alighted upon a Scottish subject. The tale of Alexander Adam, the peasant boy, who slogged his way through hypothermia and starvation to become rector of the country's leading school, made up a pattern of self-advancement which was archetypal in its content and its shaping (**3H**).

Other moral fables followed: there was Robert Watt, the carter's boy who grew up to compile the *Bibliotheca Britannica*; there was John Ferguson, the unlettered Banffshire day-labourer who became a renowned astronomer; there was James Watt and the power of steam.

By the middle of the nineteenth century, the reader into Scottish life had available a range of biographical experiences in which 'education' was shown to play a dynamic role. They drew upon two traditions: the model of the self-educated man who, in many cases, owed his emergence in large part to his early membership of a supportive working community; or the star product of the ancient parochial system who, thanks to the skilled devotion of the master and his own dogged ability, studied his way ever upwards.

In reality, even in the second category, the collaborative efforts of neighbours could be as influential as any dominie. Most accounts cite the extent to which the local practice of raising a library through a subscription scheme, or of individual households banding together to purchase a journal for shared reading, had a precious impact upon their subject's intellectual awakening. And in artisan workshops, such as the earlier, more intimate weavers' sheds, it was common practice to nominate one of the employees to read to the rest as they spun.

Yet, in each of these instances, 'Scottish education' would emerge as being vindicated. This was because underlying all these success stories was the inspiring figure of the lone individual who was possessed of the native character, as well as the wit, to overcome all obstacles, including the very real inequalities in economic and social circumstances. And because, as in the century before it, the early Victorian age continued to throw up examples of men who turned family misfortune and disfavoured backgrounds into triumphant demonstrations of a generic devotion to self-betterment, their stories could still be used to confirm the reputation of the national education as a truly democratic possession.

But, if that were so, it was a particular kind of democracy. Recently, social analysts have come to term the prized Scottish notion of 'getting on' as an example of 'contest mobility' – that is, an institutionalised arrangement by which a toughened and able minority, from whatever background, is given the chance to fight its way towards educational honours. Consequently, in the biographies and commentaries of the day, the commonly vicious hardships of the sort registered by William Thom and Alex Somerville could be viewed as affirmation, not indictment, of the Scottish way. Indeed, privation, lack of funding, inequalities of class, sickness, climatic rigour were all there to be positively celebrated, not softened by some Westminster government intervention in the shape of welfare provision or public finance. The people's system? There was nothing egalitarian in this shaping of the democratic intellect: rather Scotland is to be shown to be the testing ground for educational heroes.

3A                                                        Perthshire, 1810s.

Mr. Mcdougall was master of Kirkmichael school. In his family and under his teaching Alexander Duff laid the foundation of a well-disciplined culture, for which, so long as his teacher lived, he did not cease to express to him the warmest affection . . . Such was the teacher's ability, and such his well deserved popularity, that the thinly peopled parish at one time sent eleven students to St. Andrews. 'I have not forgotten the days I passed under your roof,' wrote Duff when he had become famous, to his old master, 'nor the manifold advantages derived from your tuition, and, I trust, I never will. And when the time comes that in the good providence of God I shall visit Kirkmichael, I know that to me at least it will be matter of heartfelt gratification'. 'What would I have been this day', he wrote again, 'had not an overruling Providence directed me to Kirkmichael school?' Of every book and pamphlet which he wrote he sent a copy to his first benefactor.

Before he left Kirkmichael to pass through the then famous grammar school of Perth to St. Andrews University, he was to carry with him from his home another experience never to be forgotten.

The winter at the end of 1819 was severe, and the snow lay deep in the Grampians. The Saturday had come round for young Duff's weekly visit to his parents. Taking the shorter track for ten miles across the low hill by Glen Briarchan and Strathire, from Kirkmichael to Moulin, he and a companion waded for hours through the snowy heather. The sun set as they got out of the glen, no stars came out, all landmarks were obliterated, and they knew only that they had to pass between deep morasses and a considerable tarn. To return was as impossible as it was dangerous to advance, for already they felt the ice of the moss-covered pools and then of the lake cracking under their feet in the thick darkness. Still going forward, they came to what they took to be a precipice hidden by the snow-drift down which they slid. Then they heard the purling of the burn which, they well knew, would bring them down the valley of Athole if they had only light to follow it.

The night went on, and the words with which they tried to cheer themselves and each other grew fainter, when exhaustion compelled them to sit down. Then they cried to God for deliverance. With their heads resting on a snow-wreath they were vainly trying to keep their eyes open, when a bright light flashed upon them and then disappeared. Roused as if by an electric shock, they ran forward and stumbled against a garden wall. The light, which proved to be the flare of a torch used by salmon poachers in the Tummel, was too distant to guide them to safety, but it had been the means of leading them to a cottage three miles from their home. The occupants, roused from bed in the early morning, warmed and fed the wanderers. To Alexander Duff's parents the deliverance looked almost miraculous. Often in after years, when he was in peril or difficulty, did the memory of that sudden flash call forth new thankfulness and cheerful hope. Trust in the overruling providence of a gracious God so filled his heart that the deliverance never failed to stimulate him to a fresh effort in a righteous cause when all seemed lost.

> Smith, George (1879). *The Life of Dr.
> Alexander Duff*. London, Hodder and Stoughton.

1806–78: pioneering Church of Scotland missionary to India; established number of educational centres there, culminating in University of Calcutta.

3B                                             Berwickshire, 1830s.

'Before my brother came to Cockburnspath', writes Mr. William Cairns, 'he had been thoroughly trained in ordinary English branches and in arithmetic, and well-exercised in repetition of the Bible, the Shorter Catechism, the Psalms and Paraphrases. Even then he had the reputation of a "grand learner", who read everything that came in his way. During his three or four years of constant attendance at Mr. M'Gregor's day-school, he made considerable progress in Latin, some progress also in Greek, had worked his way pretty well through Euclid, as well as practical geometry, and was well advanced in Algebra. When he was about ten, Mr. M'Gregor expressed a wish that he should join a Latin class that was then being formed. The propriety of this step was eagerly discussed. Father, with his anxious turn of mind and severe conscientiousness, was doubtful as to the wisdom of setting one of the family before the others, and obviously all could not be put through such a course. The usual fees of 3s. or 4s. per quarter were raised to 7s. 6d. when Latin was taken. I think that the schoolmaster offered that in this case there should be no addition. Our mother was all for "John going on"; and, while grateful to Mr. M'Gregor, she was sure that the fees could be furnished by some economy. Small as was our father's wage, it was generally paid in kind – so much grain annually, with house, firing and the keep of cow and pig, so that the actual value of the wages could be enlarged by the housekeeper's carefulness. Our mother's fine management, without being painful or sordid in its thrift, I have never seen surpassed. The minister, too, who was taken into counsel, was clear for the classics, and so a beginning was made. The Latin class met an hour before the rest of the school, and having now joined the school contingent with my twin sister, I remember the great terror which fell on me when I was left outside, amid what seemed to be an innumerable throng of curious savages, and the relief that came when John appeared to lead us into the awful presence. Day by day for the next few years he watched over us younger ones while drinking his deeper draughts of the sacred stream . . .

When Greek was added to his other school lessons, the evening stir and bustle of the small though lightsome house hindered his preparation; and he used to stipulate with our mother that she would call him in the morning when she rose to prepare breakfast for those who had to go out at six o'clock. He would be heard conjugating his verbs by the solitary oil lamp, or in the dim twilight of the early morning, while we were still snug in bed. In this way he saw more or thought more of the devoted mother's constant toiling and moiling, and was ever eager to find ways in which he could lighten her burdens, by cutting firewood, carrying water and such services; and he was sometimes quoted against those of us who were not quite so helpful.

He was twelve years of age when the day-school days ended. Although my father was nominally shepherd, his duties were very multifarious, and the charge of the sheep had principally fallen upon our oldest brother Thomas. But the time came when Thomas could earn a larger wage than was allowed for the shepherd's boy and so it was John's turn and time to take his place. When father spoke to Mr. M'Gregor about this, the old man was moved with regret at the prospect of losing his favourite pupil, and proposed that if John would find time to carry on his studies during the day, he should come to him two or three nights a week that they might read together. Such a proposal from such a quarter was thought a marvellous testimony, for the old teacher had got into habits of isolation. Yet his pupils stood in such awe of him, that few would have looked forward with pleasure to hours of private intercourse. But to John it seemed a great opportunity, and the closer he came into contact with the grim old man, the more he liked and respected him.

It was in 1831 that he began his course as "herd laddie". Hitherto he had done nothing at field-work, save occasional days at harvest time. But he had the hereditary instinct for sheep; so that the responsible care of them came easily to him. This was something like his daily course for the next three years. There were two parts of his office, "looking" and "herding". Starting by 6 a.m. at the latest, he made a circuit of three or four miles, counting the sheep to see that all were afoot. If there were cattle in some of the parks they also had to be "looked". When the last field was reached, the sheep that were to be taken out for the day had herded in the unfenced lawns would be generally be found lying near the gate, waiting to go forth to the better pasture. This flock at the time of John's herding generally consisted of about fifty or sixty well-bred Leicester ewes, solid responsible sheep, which knew exactly the road to take down the brae to their feeding-grounds, and the shepherd might leave them, while he hurried home for his own breakfast of porridge and milk, for which his two hours' round had fully prepared him. The books for the forenoon's reading were slung into the plaid-neuk with a hunch of bannock, and he rejoined the flock . . . A place therefore would be chosen – some sunny knoll with a clear outlook on the salient points, and if there was no hurry-scurrying of dogs or other disturbing force, the sheep would feed very quietly, and a long spell of reading might be indulged in, or even a process of abstract thinking, with open eye, however, all the while. Or if the danger of too near proximity to forbidden fruits threatened, a quiet stroll, book in hand, to the point of attack would turn back the sheep, and sheep once turned when feeding will lead a whole flock to change their line of grazing . . .

Of course it was very different in stormy and wet weather. At all hazards the sheep had to be "looked" and those in the foldfield, where the grass was pretty bare, must be taken out for their full food. Then haps and wraps were needed, and reading out of doors was well-nigh impossible. But even in this emergency there was a resource, for the ruins of the old church stood in the herding-ground, with the roof intact in portions and quite waterproof, and through the doors and window, all woodless and glassless, there were good views of the lawn, so that shelter was provided both for book and boy, and on the sandy floor Euclid could be demonstrated.

The old people still tell how surprised Sir John Hall was to discover the sort of books the herd-boy was reading, and how Professor Hope of Edinburgh, Lady Hall's uncle, came upon him buried in Greek in the old church ruins, and was "rale taen-up wi' him" ' . . .

The above graphic narrative is fully borne out by reminiscences which survive in the locality. Aged people who were pupils with John at the village school, preserve memories of his incessant study, and describe him as wandering over the fields book in hand, with a pease bannock sticking out of his pocket. One old woman tells how the grim Mr. M'Gregor was actually seen to laugh as he left school one day, and explained the laugh by saying that he had given John Cairns an exercise 'that would gar him los' his sleep the nicht'.

McEwan, Alexander (1895). *The Life and Letters of John Cairns.* London, Hodder and Stoughton.

1818–92: became noted as spell-binding preacher; after 30 years of quiet Borders ministry became leader of United Presbyterian Church and Principal of New Hall, Edinburgh.

3C                                        Aberdeen, 1800s.

Ere yet the schoolmaster was so much abroad, the schoolmistress was very much at home. In Aberdeen, about thirty years ago, at any of fifty lowly firesides, could be found one of those simple academies yclept a 'Wifie's Squeel'. In one of these was imparted to me all the tuition I ever received in the way of letters – gatherings in after-life being only 'crumbs from the rich man's table'. *Our* Wifie had always twenty scholars, one cat, one *taurds,* and one opinion. The scholars exercised her patience, the cat her affections, and the opinion, simply that the *taurds* (a cordovan improvement on the feebler birch) was, as an exercise, the best panacea on earth for rheumatism in the right shoulder. When Elspet Gillespie wanted a bit of exercise in this way, there was no long waiting for a defaulter to give a duty-like interest to her emotions. The evolutions of the *taurds* then awakened some excitement throughout the establishment, accompanied by strong marks of disapproval in the party honoured by her immediate regard, and stirred curious sympathies even in those who sat by in safety – if, indeed, safety could be coupled with such an hour. When the pangs of rheumatism were lulled by a sense of weariness about the shoulder blade, Elspet resumed her proud elevation above the trembling assembly, who felt there was one great woman in the world, and there she sat. Boys five years old and upwards brought the fee of three 'bawbees' and a peat weekly. Our junior class was composed of little ones, who were too young to talk, but who, of course, made most noise. These were charged sixpence. I cannot say what portion of the sum was entered to 'din'. She had, indeed, much trouble with these, and longer time of it, having to tend them during the whole day, until their poor mothers returned from the spinning-mill or the field. The outfit for grown-up *students* was a Bible, a Westminster Catechism, and a stool, all of which were removed on Saturday, and fetched again on Monday. Oh, that I could tell, and tell it rightly, the 'skailing of the squeel!' or paint yon joyous little mob, gushing forth from the *laigh* [low] door of Elspet Gillespie!

Thom, William (1847). *Rhymes and Recollections of a Hand-loom Weaver*. London, Smith and Elder.

1798–1848: 'the Inverurie Poet'; weaver and self-taught man of letters; fêted briefly as 'Second Burns'; died in penury.

3D                                Coatbridge, Lanarkshire, 1830s.

> Now my girl must go to school,
> Be subject to her teacher's rule;
> At home were trained the budding beauties
> Of her mind – her moral duties.
> Well she knows her gentle heart
> Is tender, true, and void of art:
> On that mind, so pure and good,
> May never evil thoughts intrude;
> In that loving little heart

May never shame or grief have part;
In that motley congregation –
A common school – contamination
From falsehood, evil words and strife,
Sully the streams of youthful life –
From every ill that would infect
Her mind, may God my child protect;
And much may she, my darling daughter,
Profit by the knowledge taught her.
When school she leaves, be still my pearl,
An innocent and happy girl.

My girl is but a workman's child,
And so not Miss but Maggie styled.
At school four years has been at most,
And now she leaves – not for the cost,
For that is small – at home she's wanted;
A little colony is planted
Upon the hearth and round the table.
There's more to do than mother's able
To perform, and Maggie's clever
And now is set to washing, scrubbing,
Baking, cooking, wringing, rubbing;
Nursing little sis or brother
To relieve poor, weary mother.
Time goes on, now Maggie's tall,
Very pretty, too, withal;
Getting forward with her teens,
All too soon shall Maggie know
The hopes, the doubts, the bliss, the woe
Of love. Oh! may good angels guard,
And virtue have its full reward.
Thank God, from sin, from shame, and peril,
He still preserves my virtuous girl.

Hamilton, Janet (1870). 'Phases of Girlhood',
*Poems, Essays and Sketches*. Glasgow, Aird and Cornhill.

1795–1873: recorded life in Coatbridge during its rapid industrialisation;
champion of working-class consciousness; self-taught poet and essayist.

**1)** It has occurred to me, that, by simply laying before the working men of the country the 'Story of my Education', I may succeed in first exciting their curiosity, and next, occasionally at least, in gratifying it also. They will find that by far the best schools I ever attended are schools open to them all – that the best teachers I ever had are (though severe in their discipline) always easy of access – and that the special *form* at which I was, if I may say so, most successful as a pupil, was a form to which I was drawn by a strong inclination, but at which I had less assistance from my brother men, or even from books, than at any of the others. There are few of the natural sciences which do not lie quite as open to the working men of Britain and America as Geology did to me.

**2)** It so chanced, however, that in what proved the closing scene in my term of school attendance, I was rather unfortunate than guilty. The class to which I now belonged read an English lesson every afternoon, and had its rounds of spelling; and in these last I acquitted myself but ill; partly from the circumstance that I spelt only indifferently, but still more from the further circumstance, that, retaining strongly fixed in my memory the broad Scotch pronunciation acquired at the dame's school, I had to carry on in my mind the double process of at once spelling the required word, and of translating the old sounds of the letters of which it was composed into the modern ones. Nor had I been taught to break the words into syllables; and so, when required one evening to spell the word "*awful*", with much deliberation – for I had to translate, as I went on, the letters *a-w* and *u* – I spelt it word for word, without break or pause as a-w-f-u-l. 'No', said the master, 'a-w *aw*, f-u-l, *awful*; spell again!'. This seemed preposterous spelling. It was sticking in an *a*, as I thought, into the middle of the word, where, I was sure, no *a* had a right to be; and so I spelt it as at first. The master recompensed my supposed contumacy with a sharp cut athwart the ears with his tawse; and again demanding the spelling of the word, I yet again spelt it as at first. But on receiving a second cut, I refused to spell it any more; and, determined on overcoming my obstinacy, he laid hold of me and attempted throwing me down. As wrestling, however, had been one of our favourite Marcus's Cave exercises, and as few lads of my inches wrestled better than I, the master, though a tall and tolerably robust fellow, found the feat considerably more difficult than he could have supposed. We swayed from side to side of the school-room, now backwards, now forward, and for a full minute it seemed to be rather a moot point on which side the victory was to incline. At length, however, I was tripped over a form; and as the master had to deal with me, not as a master usually deals with a pupil, but as one combatant deals with another, whom he has to beat into submission, I was mauled in a way that filled me with aches and bruises for a full month thereafter. I greatly fear that, had I met the fellow on a lonely road five years subsequent to our encounter, when I had become strong enough to raise breast-high the 'great lifting stone of the Dropping Cave', he would have caught as sound a thrashing as he ever gave to little boy or girl in his life; but all I could do at this time was to take down my cap from off the pin, when the affair had ended, and march straight out of school. And thus terminated my school education.

Miller, Hugh [1854] (1993). *My Schools and Schoolmasters*. Edinburgh, B & W Publishing.

1802–56: self-taught geologist and theologian; pioneer of popular science books, attempting to reconcile Darwinian evolutionary theory with fundamental religious belief; leading light in Free Church after 1843 Disruption.

3F                                    Blantyre, Lanarkshire, 1820s.

At the age of ten he was put into the cotton-factory as a piecer. His task was to walk back and forth between the reels of the whirring spinning-jenny and tie the broken threads. Having purchased a Latin Grammar with part of his first week's wages he placed the book on a portion of the frame, and memorized sentence by sentence as he passed to and fro. 'I thus kept up a pretty constant study undisturbed by the roar of the machinery. To this part of my education I owe my present power of completely abstracting the mind from surrounding noises, so as to read and write with perfect comfort amidst the play of children or near the dancing and songs of savages'. His hours were from 6 a.m. to 8 p.m., with intervals for breakfast and dinner. But with the close of the day's work his real work was just beginning – at least from the age of thirteen when the local schoolmaster, Mr. McSkimming, opened an evening class for Latin. 'I pursued the study of that language for many years afterwards, with unabated ardour, at an evening school, which met between the hours of eight and ten'. One wonders how he managed to get any supper, for it is certain that he was as punctual as he could be. Perhaps he took a 'piece' with him in his pocket. But even then his ardour was unsatisfied. 'The dictionary part of my labours was followed up till twelve o'clock, or later, if my mother did not interfere by jumping up and snatching the book out of my hands'. And he had to be up – and at work – at 6 a.m.! There has been many a poor Scottish student who has shown a similar grit (such as by reading under a street lamp for lack of light at home), but a display of such will-power in a lad's early teens is surely something phenomenal.

Seaver, George (1957). *David Livingstone,*
*His Life and Letters.* London, Lutterworth.

1813–73: at 24 succeeded in escaping cotton factory work to study medicine; achieved national fame in southern Africa as missionary, explorer and general Victorian hero.


3G                                    Peebles/Edinburgh, 1820/30s.

I was not fated to receive more than a plain education in the place of my birth, a small country town in the south of Scotland. Matters there were still somewhat primitive. In the schools I passed through, there was not a map, nor a book on geography, or history or science. The only instruction consisted of the three Rs, finishing off with a dose of Latin. It was a simple and cheap arrangement, diversified with boisterous outdoor exercises, and a certain amount of fighting, in which I was forced to take part. My instruction in Latin came abruptly to a conclusion. Lieutenant Waters, in one of the old novels, says, with more energy than elegance, that he still bore the marks of 'Homo' on his person. I likewise have the honour of bearing similar evidences of my acquaintance with Homo. One day, not being quite prompt in answering a question in Latin grammar, my teacher, in one of his irascible moods (which were always distinguishable by his wearing a bottle-green coat), lifted a ruler and inflicted a sharp blow on the top of my head, which almost deprived me of consciousness, and which, while leaving a small protuberance, is on occasions, after an interval of seventy years, still felt to be awkwardly painful. So much for my acquaintance with Homo. With every respect for his agency in mental culture, I shortly afterwards bade the academy good-bye; and so ended my classical education, or school education of any kind.

It was a miserable business; but after all, I have reason to think it was the best thing that could have happened. An over-cramming of classical learning might have sent me in a wrong direction. I had secured the means of self-instruction through books, and that was deemed sufficient. All depended on making a proper use of the means. My brother Robert, two years younger, more docile and meditative, took kindly to Homo, and continued to prosecute his studies in that direction some time longer. Both, however, were alike anxious to make up for deficiencies by self-reliance. A little room we occupied was our college. Every spare hour, morning, noon and night, was devoted to books. We went right through a circulating library, which the small town had the happiness to possess, besides devouring every book within the domestic circle. Light and heavy literature were equally accepted. The object was to fill the mind with anything that was harmlessly amusing and instructive. At from ten to twelve years of age we had in a way digested much of the 'Encyclopedia Britannica' and by this means alone we acquired a knowledge of the physical sciences, not a quarter of which could have been learned at school.

Chambers, William (1882). 'Reminiscences of a
Long and Busy life', *Chambers's Journal*, 28 January.

1800–83: with brother Robert, founded Edinburgh publishers which produced numerous popular educational works, including the eponymous *Journal*.

3H                                      Morayshire/Edinburgh, 1740/50s.

Perhaps no country in the world, in proportion to its size, has produced so many eminent men, who have risen from the humble ranks of life, as Scotland; and no species of reading with which we are acquainted can yield such striking instances of the value of honest perseverance, under the most adverse circumstances, as the biography of the individuals who have so distinguished themselves. A most instructive lesson of this nature is afforded us in the life of the late Dr Adam, at one time rector of the High School of Edinburgh, and the author of a number of meritorious classic works, well known to every young man who attends our schools and colleges.

Alexander Adam L.L.D., was born at the hamlet of Coates of Burgie, in the parish of Rafford, and county of Moray, about the month of June 1741. His father, John Adam, rented one of those small farms which were formerly so common in the north of Scotland. In his earlier years, like many children of his own class, and even of a class higher removed above poverty, he occasionally tended his father's cattle. Being destined by his parents, poor as they were, for a learned profession, he was kept at the parish school till he was thought fit to come forward as an exhibitioner, or, as it is called in Scotland, a bursar, at the University of Aberdeen. He made this attempt but failed, from the alleged inferiority of his acquirements, and was requested by the judges to go back and study for another year at the school. This incident did not mortify the young student, but only stimulated him to fresh exertions. He was prevented, however, from renewing his attempts at Aberdeen, by the representations of the Rev. Mr Watson, a minister at Edinburgh, and a relation of his mother, who induced him to try his fortune in the metropolis. He removed thither early in the year 1758 but, it appears, without any assured means of supporting himself during the progress of his studies. For a considerable time while attending the classes at the college the only means of subsistence he enjoyed consisted of the small sum of one guinea per quarter, which he derived from Mr Allan Macconochie (afterwards Lord Meadowbank), for assisting him in his capacity of a tutor. The details of his system of life at this period, as given by his biographer Mr Henderson, are painfully interesting. 'He lodged in a small room at Restalrig, in the north-eastern suburbs; and for this accommodation he paid fourpence a week'. All his meals, except dinner, uniformly consisted of oatmeal made into porridge together with small beer, bought at the nearest baker's shop; and if the day was fair, he would dispatch his meal in a walk to the Meadows or Hope Park, which is adjoining to the southern part of the city; but if the weather was foul, he had recourse to some long and lonely stair, which he would climb, eating his dinner at every step. By this means all expense for cookery was avoided and he wasted neither coal nor candles; for when he was chill, he used to run till his blood began to glow, and his evening studies were always prosecuted under the roof of some one or other of his companions. There are many instances, we believe, among

Scottish students of the most rigid self-denial, crowned at length by splendid success; but there is certainly no case known in which the self-denial was so chastened, and the triumph so grand, as that of Dr Adam.

'Biographic Sketches, Dr Adam', *Chambers's Journal*, 1, 1832.

1741–1809: noted teacher and classicist; appointed Rector Edinburgh High School at 27.

# 4 AND THE DOMINIES WHO HELPED THEM

*Memorial drawn up for the Parochial Schoolmasters
in Scotland*: 1782
*Autobiography of Thomas Guthrie and Memoir*:
David and Charles Guthrie, 1874
*Hawkie – the Autobiography of a Gangrel*: 1888
*In School in the Forties*: Centenary Handbook,
*Educational Institute of Scotland*, 1946
*The Country Schoolmaster's Vacation*: Scots Magazine, 1823
*Memorials of his Time*: Lord Henry Cockburn, 1856
*Principal Caird*: Charles Warr, 1926

Figure 6. **Central School, Inverness: prize-giving, 1900** Most of the school's 750 pupils appear to be jostling for attention. Despite the row of prizes and the visiting dignitaries, none of them would have risen to anything higher than an 'Elementary' level award.
*Highland Council Archive, Inverness*

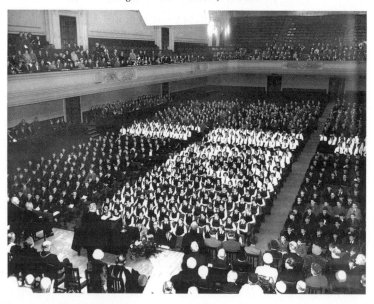

Figure 7. **Dundee High School: opening of new library, 1958** An independent school run not by any local authority, but its own board of governors. The emphasis on ordered ceremony speaks of a different ethos, as well as history, to that of the Inverness Central.
*Dundee City Libraries*

In 1782, the parochial schoolmasters of Scotland presented their 'Memorial' to the British Government (**4A**). In it, they unfurled an epic depiction of 'North Britain' as an inhospitable wilderness, whose darkness was lit up only by its educational heritage and the missionary devotion of its teachers to that cause. They were, of course, putting in for a pay rise. And, in so doing, they were highlighting a disparity between the nobility of their calling and its meagre recompense which, along with the curses of inflation, has never since quite departed the Scottish scene.

Yet, historically, the position of the Scottish parish teacher was far from pitiful. One of only 900 in total, he stood as the sole guardian in his own community of the proud national system, a professional man in a society composed mostly of labourers, mechanics and farm servants. At his back, there was the legal authority of an Act of Parliament, which entitled him to a house, a garden, a guaranteed income and the right to levy fees for his services. Above all, he had security of tenure – only a reckless fornication or some outrageous blasphemy could imperil his reign.

To acquire his post, he had to prove his academic and moral credentials before the local church and the heritors or, in the burghs, the magistrates. Indeed, about half of the nation's 'old parochials' would have been full university graduates and most of the rest would have had sufficient learning to enable them to grapple with the Odes of Horace or to proffer smart answers on the Westminster Confession. In the town, their standing was likely to be even higher, since its Grammar or its High could charge bigger fees and, thus, attract a better standard of academic. There, they often proved to be men of sufficient cultivation to become influential contributors to the learned societies and the improving associations which were developing into such a bustling feature of burgh life at that time.

In both town and country, the master filled a position of moral authority, licensed by the Presbytery or the burgh authorities and ranked alongside the minister as the guardian of the minds and souls of the parish flock. If, in a poor land, his material benefits were scanty, then that served to establish a contrast between the elevation of his vocation and the frugality of his living which could only augment the sense of selfless nobility which hung around his drab, time-worn clothing. And, in many cases, he had himself fought to arrive at his honoured position in ways that would inspire the next generation of able lads and, thus, add a further round to the nation's annals of educational heroism.

Thomas Guthrie's two teachers belong to a life in which the author – later to be a famous educational missionary among the slums of Edinburgh – was able to look back on the academic opportunities that were available in his native Brechin, in the first two decades of the century (**4B 1, 2**). His first 'pedagogue', James Stewart, was, essentially, a weaver who, although not able to escape the loom long enough to become a fully qualified dominie, is still impressive enough to show that the private teacher, too, could offer solid schooling and a commanding classroom presence. Robert Simpson, with whom he rounded off his studies, was the parish master at neighbouring Dun – and, Guthrie points out, he could have got his 'Euclid, French, Latin and Greek, and all for five shillings the quarter', at any one of three other local establishments.

At the age of thirteen, and more than prepared for it, the lad from Brechin took a seat on a carrier's cart and trundled off to a glittering career at Edinburgh University. Such an event, and such reportage, have the stuff of myth about them. It is little wonder that, given his own marvellous progress, Thomas Guthrie's memory should people his youthful Scotland with giant-sized dominie figures. His account also reminds us of the part played by the private 'venture' teacher in the educational provision of the day. That not all of them, however, could match his own Brechin mentor is to be seen in a survey carried out by the *Aberdeen Censor* of 1825 into that city's academic establishments. It includes, among other choice specimens, the school of one, Janet P. Hendrick. Situated at the foot of Jack's Brae, it bears this sign: 'Reading and spelling and the Single carritch and Scholing are Teached hear for 2d. weekly'.

The place that, in practice, teaching could assume in the hierarchy of vocations is illustrated by the story of *Hawkie* (**4C**). The son of a distillery worker in Stirling, in the 1810s, the young Hawkie managed to pick up the basics at his parish school and, over the next few years, to spare a little money for the purchase of some further arithmetic and a course in elocution. But, by the age of twelve, he had quit any regular education to become apprenticed to a tailor. Always restless and devoid of prospects at home, he took to the road and, thus, became 'a gangrel' – one who lived off his wits and picked up whatever odd jobs he could find. As the extract shows, one of these was 'teaching'.

Although it would appear that this gangrel had a talent for it, he shows that, below the level of the parish school, the calling of 'teacher' was to be treated like any other casual trade – a matter of sporadic openings and energetic self-promotion. Nor, even for the parochial opposition, was it always possible to attain the ideal of the mature university man; in many cases, the village had to settle for a bright youth, one who was forced to put in a few broken years of school-mastering while he worked up the qualifications to become that substantially better remunerated being, a parish minister. In other instances, the reverse was the case and the schoolroom was grudgingly occupied by one who had failed in that quest or who, hanging on for the pulpit that never came, earned the sour title of 'stickit minister'. In too many cases, the incumbent was not even that: sometimes, physical disability, and a consequent incapacity for manual work, appeared to be the major qualification.

The conditions under which the men of learning and cultivation laboured out their days were likewise grim. Even when, as the nineteenth century wore on and most schoolrooms rose to the heights of the functionally austere, there were still sixty or so assorted village progeny to be kept under, with only tattered books, a grimy wall map of the British Empire and the faithful tawse for helpmates. When the Educational Institute offered the public its *Centenary Handbook* in 1946 and attempted to reconstruct a schoolroom of a century before, it did so in graphically oppressive terms. **4D** is a composite picture, partly drawn in order to measure the progress accomplished in the intervening hundred years. But it contains what was, for the survivors of that – and later – regimes, their abiding image of the Scottish dominie: one who was sentenced to be recalled with that blend of half-forgotten childish fear and adult disdain, which is popularly caught by the dismissive tag, 'A man among boys; a boy among men'.

Indeed, for the early nineteenth century journal, dominie deflation could provide a popular theme. A common slant is to present the old Scottish master as too unworldly and precious a figure to survive outside the puerile confines of his schoolroom. The *Scots Magazine*'s 'country school-master' on holiday is an example of what was then fast becoming a minor genre (**4E**). In the decade of its publication, the same journal added the episodes of 'Mr MacDominie', of 'Ill Tam', and 'The Feelings and Fortunes of a Scotch Tutor' as further examples of hapless, highly schooled innocents, who attempt to use their classical learning to fumble their way into the 'fashionable' world that lies beyond the 'cramping and chilling influence of a country school'.

A major problem was that, in his attempts to hold the line before the advances of an increasingly complex world, the traditional dominie had only a rudimentary, time-honoured pedagogy, to guide him. His teaching was based on a model that envisaged him to be a solitary operator, with little but rote, drill and the tawse with which to communicate his learning to the parochial hordes. While there is truth in Robert Anderson's claim that, 'in the first decades of the nineteenth century, Scotland was a lively centre of educational thought and experiment', the examples he refers to – the callisthenics of New Lanark and David Stow's experiments with a more child-centred 'infant' education – were largely confined to the drive to penetrate the unruly cohorts within the new city slums. They had little impact upon the practices to be found within the traditional parish and burgh establishments.

This was certainly the case in the institution which was commonly reckoned to be the nation's leading public school, the Royal High School of Edinburgh. The young Henry Cockburn, who was to grow up to be a leading legal and Whig party figure of the day, has left a record of his own vicissitudes there (**4F**). It is one that testifies to the pedagogical cluelessness, and consequent resort to corporal tyranny, which could undermine the scholarship of even so distinguished an eminence as Dr Alexander Christison, the man who was later to become Professor of Humanity at the University and author of the nationally self-flattering tract, *The General Diffusion of Knowledge, One Great Cause of the Prosperity of North Britain* (1802).

Cockburn goes on to praise his next teacher – Dr Adam – as warmly as he denounces the brute efforts of his colleague. The contrast makes the larger point: the old dispensation could, indeed, produce examples of academic saintliness but Adam was the Rector of an establishment in which there was no tradition of team work, no practice of collaboration that could have made a wider use of his personal gifts.

Even in the large burgh school, the old dominie model was left to rest on the assumption that individual academic prowess, stiffened by repetitive drill and sharpened by the lash, was sufficient to rear the next generation of scholastic heroes.

Significantly, Cockburn is writing as an elderly citizen, who, in his same *Memorials* journals, forty years on, laments the decline of the very Latin he used to regard as gratuitous juvenile torture. It is, he worries, being forced to give way to the 'overeasy' appeal of such seductively 'practical' subjects as modern languages and chemistry. In the end – and in his old man's memory – it is Dr Adam which comes to dominate his assessment of the old place, a scurrying, dark-suited figure, who gathers about his blinking personage the anecdotes which will immortalise him as an example of 'true' dominie eccentricity and memorable devotion.

Ultimately, when attached to the drama of a personal success story and set in a more purely Scottish land than the inevitable corruptions of a later age can ever permit, it is the Dr Adams and the Mr Simpsons who come to stand for Scotland. The professional poverty, which the parochials of 1782 had so deplored, was fated to join the dominie to the lad of parts as icons which perpetuated the worship of Scottish education, as founded upon the national verities of stern landscape, self-denial and a scholar's devotion to the higher cause.

It is in this sprit that **4G** must be read. Although its subject, the future theologian John Caird, grew up in the rapidly industrialising port of Greenock in the 1820s, this description of the all-important schooling given him by his own Dominie Brown was published a whole century later. By that time, the story of the masters of the earlier age had become fashioned into the making of the nation's spirit.


4A                                                  North Britain, 1782.


Scotland, or North Britain, struggles with many natural disadvantages; the climate is cold, the sky seldom serene, the weather variable, the soil unfruitful, the mountains bleak, barren, rocky, often covered by snows, and the appearance of the country in many places very forbidding to strangers; yet, by an early attention to the education of youth, to form good men and good citizens, she has uniformly maintained a high character among the nations, has always been deemed an excellent nurse of the human species, and has furnished not soldiers only, but divines, generals, statesmen, and philosophers to almost every nation of Europe.

Our ancestors towards the end of the last century, turning their attention to this subject, beheld with pleasure the progress already made in useful knowledge and arts. They saw that the laws of nature and religion required of parents the virtuous education of their offspring; but they saw also that the increasing cares and avocations of civil life, together with the ignorance of many parents, rendered it necessary to call to their assistance a body of men appointed by the state to attend upon this one thing.

The schoolmasters, thus legally established, were supposed to be men who had turned their attention to the improvement of their minds, to the dignity, virtue, and happiness of human nature, to the distinctions between right and wrong in human conduct; and who were, besides, 'apt to teach', patient, diligent, and faithful.

The encouragement appointed by the state for this respectable and useful body of men, though not great, was yet well suited to the times, the funds, and distinction of rank at the period. The emoluments of their office placed them above day-labourers, and the poorer class of mechanics and farmers; nay, raised them to an equality with the more opulent farmers, respectable tradesmen and citizens; among whom their employment, their manners, and prospects in life, procured them a degree of respect very advantageous to their profession.

Ninety years have produced such a change, and so great improvements, in the agriculture, navigation, commerce, arts, and riches of this country, that 15 l. sterling per annum, at the end of the last century, may be considered as a better income than 45 l. sterling per annum at this present time.

Suppose, then, that in Scotland there are 900 parochial schoolmasters, which is very near the truth; 800 of these will be found struggling with indigence, inferior in point of income to 800 day-labourers in the best cultivated parts of this island, and receiving hardly half the emoluments of the menial servants of country gentlemen and wealthy citizens.

*Memorial drawn up for the Parochial Schoolmasters in Scotland, anno 1782.*

1) James Stewart, our pedagogue, was by trade a weaver; a very little man, dressed in the old fashion, his broad, blue bonnet covering a head of great size, and full of brains . . . The single room of this good old man, where he lived with his wife and daughter – the loom standing in one corner and their box-beds in another – was our school. There were some half dozen of us who sat on stools, conning our lessons to the click of his shuttle, while he sat weaving, gently reminding us from time to time of our tasks, by the use of a leather thong at the end of a long stick, with which he reached us without having to leave his throne.

Having learned our letters, and some small syllables printed on a fly-sheet of the Shorter Catechism, we were at once passed into the Book of Proverbs. In the olden time this was the universal custom in all the common schools in Scotland, a custom that should never have been abandoned. That book is without a rival for beginners, contain-ing quite a repertory of monosyllables and pure Saxon – 'English undefiled'. Take this passage, for example, where, with one exception, every word is formed of a single syllable, and belongs to the Saxon tongue – 'Train up a child in the way he should go; and when he is old, he will not depart from it'. What a contrast to the silly trash of modern schoolbooks for beginners, with such sentences as, 'Tom has a dog'; 'The cat is good'; 'The cow has a calf!'.

2) His father, an elder of the Church, and a man of excellent character, was by trade a weaver. But, though possessed of some little means – what the Scotch call a *'bein' body'* – he could not well afford to educate a son at college out of his own resources. So my friend began life at the loom. But, a youth of superior talents and early piety, he was fired with a holy ambition to be a minister of the gospel. *Tenax propositi* [firm of purpose] – the characteristic of our countrymen – he commenced the Latin grammar, and, placing the book before him on his loom, as he plied the shuttle, he studied and finally mastered it.

Such a case was that of my excellent tutor Mr. Simpson. He had only a year or two at school; but, by dint of determined application, made such advances in study as to venture on competing for a bursary at the University of Aberdeen. He came out first on the list. His foot was now on the ladder, and round after round he manfully climbed, till he found himself Professor of Hebrew in the university of that city, a position he left to become minister of the parish of Kintore: where, after 'going out' at the Disruption, receiving the honour of Doctor in Divinity, living and labouring for many years, he died last summer – few in life so much esteemed, few in death so much regretted.

The accommodation provided by law for teachers in those days was very inadequate. Mr. Simpson's house at Dun contained only two rooms besides the school-room. The heritors of Scotland, in most instances, grudged the schoolmaster (though, it might be, more highly cultivated than themselves) anything beyond this, the provision required by law. To them, with honourable exceptions, the country owed little gratitude. They grew rich by the spoils of the Church; starved the teachers and opposed with dogged determination every reform in Church and State, reminding one of what Dr. Chalmers related as the speech of a professor at St. Andrews to his students: 'Gentlemen,' he said, 'there are just two things in nature that never change. These are the fixed stars and the Scotch lairds!'

Guthrie, David and Charles (1874). Autobiography of Thomas Guthrie and Memoir. London, Daldy, Isbister and Co.

1803–73: evangelical ministry in east-end Edinburgh; founded 'Ragged School' movement – designed to offer accommodation, welfare and education to homeless young of the city.

4C                                                      Stirlingshire, 1800s.

I was now at the parish school of St Ninian's, where I began Latin; I attended this school through the day, and at night went to one Robert M'Callum for arithmetic, who was a great arithmetician in his way. His system was one hundred years back, and was not mercantile, being all of a puzzling nature. I also went through a system of book-keeping, mensuration, and trigonometry, and considered myself far enough advanced.

During the time I had a number of breaks at the tailor trade, not for love of it, but whenever my father and I had words I went for it. It is bad for a youth to have a *backdoor*, and I knew that the tailor trade rendered me independent of my father . . . I made off for Glasgow, having left my teachers without the knowledge of my parents. I joined a journeyman tailors' house of call, then in the Pipe Close, High

Street. It was in the heat of the summer's trade. I got a call to a tailor at the Cross, whose name was M'Luckey, I wrought with him some weeks. Another journeyman and I, one Sabbath morning, were taking a walk in Glasgow Green, where we came across a field preacher holding forth to a large audience, while the lining of his hat spoke more for the feelings of his hearers than himself. The sound of the pence, dashing against each other, to a person of feeling, formed a concert of the most harmonious music, although the preacher was but a 'lame brother'. We stood for some time and listened, when I happened to say that, 'I could beat him myself'. The next day at our work, merely for pastime, one of the men said, addressing me, 'You think you could beat the preacher'. I said that 'I could', not thinking that it would go any further, but on Saturday night, after our work was over, we fell in with some tailors, when the preaching was brought up. I still said that, 'I could beat him', when it was agreed that it should be tried the next day. I had no black clothes; the other journeymen went to the 'cork' ( master) and asked him for the loan of his black suit, pretending that it was for the purpose of attending a funeral.

The next day about 40 of the principal journeymen tailors assembled in the house of call, when I was dressed in the blacks in order to try my 'say' in the new profession. I insisted against going to the Green, lest any person from Stirling coming forward might know me. We arranged to go to Westmuir, on the road leading to Airdrie.

At about twelve o'clock we set out, about 40 or 50 strong, and by the time we got to Westmuir we had a good congregation. A precentor was selected, 'Donald Bell', a journeyman of Mr Lockhart's, a tailor above the 'King's Arms' in the Trongate. My father and mother were Burghers, and possessed the works of Ralph Erskine of Dunfermline, whose sermons my mother took great pleasure in reading and hearing read. I had often read them aloud to her, which although to her a pleasure, was to me a punishment; and, having a good memory, which was much improved at school, I preached one of Ralph Erskine's sermons. I took for my text St John xiii. 7. 'What I do thou knowest not now, but thou shalt know hereafter'. I pleased the congregation well, and no thanks to me, for Erskine has handled the subject well.

I had got a number of lessons in elocution, for which I had a peculiar liking, and, my voice at that time not being broken, I made a favourable impression on the people. We had an elder chosen to go round with the 'hat', but the 'dust' (money) came in so quick that there was no need for that.

At the conclusion I thanked them for their kindness, letting them know I was sent by the Haldane Society on an itinerating mission to the West of Scotland, with little more to depend on than the generosity of the Christian public, when a lash of more 'blunt' (money) was pitched into the hat.

We then came to Camlachie, where we counted the collection: it amounted to 13s. and some odds; that night we spent every 'ring'.

Next Sabbath there was another sermon planned, but I preferred to go to Stewartown, in Ayrshire, where I wrought till the end of the harvest. I was engaged by three farmers at a place called Bloack to keep a school all winter; none were to be admitted but the children of the three farmers and their cottars. I was boarded in one of the houses at 10s. a-week; I behaved exemplarily, and carefully studying the nature of my scholars, they made rapid advance.

I returned to Glasgow, and began the tailor trade again, and remained at it for nearly two years, but doing no good. Always when I was in trouble I went home, and when I left home, they got no further word from me till I turned up again. At one of my retreats about five miles from home, I engaged to keep a school at a coal work, at a place called Planemure. They had stoned a number of teachers out of the place before I went; my chance was dull, but I undertook it, and found it the hardest task I had ever met. There were only three persons in the whole place who knew their letters; however, with a mixture of patience and diligence, I succeeded beyond expectation; in six months I had a class of 30 reading the Testament, and during that time I never needed to lift a hand. Their former teachers used physical power over their scholars, and it was not likely that the collier, come to the length of manhood, would take one stroke without giving another. However, I worked on other principles, and for English and arithmetic I would put them on a par with any school in Scotland.

*Hawkie – the Autobiography of a Gangrel* (1888).
Strathesk, John (ed.). Glasgow, Robertson.

Attributed to John Tod, well-known Glasgow street character in mid-nineteenth-century Glasgow.

Next the door, on rude, low forms, sat the younger scholars, confined for four hours a day, and perhaps supervised for five or six minutes at a time by some of the older pupils. Near these a helper superintended a class in the Old Testament. In another quarter, at tables, sat the arithmeticians, or 'counters' as they were called, some mumbling over the multiplication table, and wondering why all the lines were not as easy as the tenth; most, however, engaged in the game of 'nine-ticks'. Beyond, sat, in more dignified position and seclusion, the Latin scholars. Not far off, at a broader table, sat a few mathematicians, who were regarded by the other pupils with an eye of reverence, indeed, as magicians, when they wielded their scales and compasses. Beside them, unmindful of their occasional frays, would sit some thoughtful lad, who, in consequence of an 'in-come' in his leg, had been advised to turn his mind to learning, and who was now engaged in balancing a set of book-keeping by double entry.

All these advanced pupils prepared their lessons during the day, while the master attended to the classes which, one by one, were drawn up successively to the middle of the floor, where, forming a ring, they rehearsed their lessons. The general hum, or rather continuous roar, of the whole school rendered it necessary that every boy in the ring should, in order to be audible to the master, stretch his lungs to the utmost extent, the vehemence of the recital dilating each eye and contracting each forehead. Around them incessantly flitted the dominie, whose attention was distracted by hosts of enquiries on all asides from the various regions of learning. One of the young fraternity whines for leave to go out; an arithmetician hovers round with a slate, complaining that he cannot get his count 'to come out'; an emissary from the classical department reports that such and such a word is not to be found in the dictionary. The distraction increases; complaints of injustice by the helper, announcements of bad words in one quarter, of nicknames in another, and of unprovoked blows, pour in. With a sudden resolution the master brushes the whole host of enquirers and complainers from him, banishes the class *en masse* to its bench, and tears out the utterer of bad words to the bar of the school. Immediately all business ceases; everyone rises, witnesses are summoned, admonition follows, and then punishment. A dead silence marks the reign of terror. But short was the respite. With the business of the various classes, the hum again prevailed and the sound of the school rose to fever pitch.

'In School in the Forties', *Centenary Handbook of the Educational Institute of Scotland*, (1946). Belford, A. J. (ed.). Edinburgh, EIS.

4E                                                              'The Country', 1820s

I confess I have sometimes, after dismissing the noisy tenants of my little mansion, sat at my desk, leaning my cheek on my hand, and mentally exclaiming, 'Oh! the fatigues – the vexations – and the privations of a schoolmaster!' Had Thomson ever been doomed to the drudgery of being a country schoolmaster, his conscience would never have allowed him to have written the often-quoted apostrophe, so pleasing to the ear, and soothing to the heart of every poetical reader, except to him who has long practised the wearisome trade:

> Delightful task! to rear the tender thought,
> To teach the young idea how to shoot,
> And pour the fresh instruction o'er the mind!

All this is very fine in theory, but come to the practice: it is not then pouring the *fresh,* but the *stale* instruction, which has been fifty times poured before, and will probably require to be as often reiterated before it can be made efficient. To encourage the timid, check the forward, goad the sluggard, stimulate the careless, overcome the obstinate, inform the dull, and vainly attempt to put brains in a blockhead; these are the daily and *delightful tasks* of a schoolmaster. To be teased by the pride of one parent, the ignorance of another, and the boorish rudeness of a third, are specimens of his vexations. Then, for his privations, for eleven months of the year he must plod on in the same monotonous track. The tailor who sits cross-legged on a board is comparatively his own master; he can make a holiday to town and country as suits his inclinations.

Such have been my melancholy musings; and I doubt not many of my brethren have indulged similar feelings. It will not, therefore, be wondered at, if the heart of the teacher, like those of his pupils, bounds with anticipated pleasure as he contemplates the approaching autumnal vacation, which is hailed as the annual jubilee of both master and scholar . . . I would, like the mountain bee, rove from flower to flower, my purpose being, in imitation of my betters, to see a little of the world, and study men, their manners and their ways; enjoying, also, the sweets of Nature in her rural beauty. For these purposes, the clustered village, the lonely glen, and heath-clad hill, were to be the objects of my attention. My projected plan was to cross the Forth, see the folks of Fife, the bodies of Angus, and, if time permitted, the men of the Mearns . . .

As mine was to be a pedestrian tour, it will not be supposed that I encumbered myself with superfluous baggage; a couple of shirts, and some other necessaries, tied in a silk-handkerchief, constituted my wardrobe; in my pockets, I stowed a small paper book, pencil and inkhorn, for making memoranda; a Lilliputian edition of Horace, when I might lack company; and a sufficient stock of fine-flavoured Macabau, as the snuff-box generally serves as a pass-key to open the door of conversation with a stranger. Dressed in black, with new velveteen small-clothes, a silk umbrella in my right hand, and the bundle containing my wardrobe under my left arm. I started early, on a fine morning, for Leith, to which I had a walk of several hours, and arrived just in time for the passage-boat. I seated myself beside a young lady in a rich satin pelisse. We had many passengers, and a fine stiff breeze. Then about mid-water, I took out my snuff-box to have a pinch, when a sudden motion of the boat made both the lady and me change our positions, in consequence of which, she received the contents of the box right in her face, while, by a twitch of her elbow, she jerked the snuff-box full into the water. The pain in her eyes, I have no doubt, was excruciating, as, in spite of herself, she writhed, and cried, and soon began to sneeze sans intermission; the tears streaming from her eyes on her cheeks, blended with the titillating dust with which her face had been so liberally bestowed. Some other of her own sex coming to her assistance, I hastily arose to give them place, when the handle of my umbrella, being entangled in the satin pelisse, made a rent of at least half a yard in length. The lady, who had hitherto borne her distress with a surprising meekness, now exclaimed, 'Was there ever such an awkward—!' The sentence was left unfinished; perhaps it was intended to be filled up by the word 'accident', although it is more probable the suppressed substantive was some appellation mentally applied to me, although not uttered. I staggered to another quarter of the boat, turning my back on the distress I had occasioned. By the time we reached Kirkcaldy, the lady was tolerably recovered. On emerging from the boat, the pier was somewhat slippery, and wishing to display my agility, I stumbled and fell, rising with a most unfortunate and capacious hiatus in my new velveteens. My fellow passengers set up a universal laugh, and I heard the lady say, much vauntingly, 'so much for my wrongs!'

'The Country Schoolmaster's Vacation' (1823). *The Scots Magazine,* March.


4F                                                    Edinburgh, 1790s.


In October 1787 I was sent to the High School. Having never been at a public school before, and this one being notorious for its severity and riotousness, I approached its walls with trembling, and felt dizzy when I sat down amidst 100 new faces. We had been living at Leith, for sea-bathing, for some weeks before; and I was taken to school by our tutor. The only thing that relieved my alarm as he hauled me along was the diversion of crossing the arches of the South Bridge, which were then unfinished, on planks. The person to whose uncontrolled discipline I was now subjected, though a good man, an intense student, and filled, but rather in the memory than the head, with knowledge, was as bad a schoolmaster as it is possible to fancy. Unacquainted with the nature of youth, ignorant even of the characters of his own boys, and with not a conception of the art or the duty of alluring them, he had nothing for it but to drive them; and this he did by constant and indiscriminate harshness.

The effects of this were very hurtful to all his pupils. Out of the whole four years of my attendance there were probably not ten days in which I was not flogged, at least once. Yet I never entered the class, nor left it, without feeling perfectly qualified, both in ability and preparation, for its whole business; which, being confined to Latin alone, and in necessarily short tasks, since every one of the boys had to rhyme over the very same words, in the very same way, was no great feat. But I was driven stupid. Oh! the bodily and mental wearisomeness of sitting six hours a day, staring idly at a page, without motion and without thought, and trembling at the approach of the merciless giant. I never got a single prize, and once sat *boobie* at the annual public examination. The beauty of no Roman word, or thought, or action, ever occurred to me! nor did I ever fancy that Latin was of any use except to torture boys.

After four years of this class, I passed on to that of the rector, Dr

Alexander Adam, the author of the work on Roman Antiquities, then in the zenith of his reputation. He had raised himself from the very dust to that high position. Never was a man more fortunate in the choice of a vocation. He was born to teach Latin, some Greek, and all virtue. In doing so he was generally patient, though not, when intolerably provoked, without due fits of gentle wrath; inspiring to his boys, especially the timid and backward; enthusiastically delighted with every appearance of talent or goodness; a warm encourager by praise, play, and kindness; and constantly under the strongest sense of duty. The art of teaching has been so immeasurably improved in good Scotch schools since his time, that we can scarcely estimate his merits now. He had most of the usual peculiarities of a schoolmaster; but was so amiable and so artless, that no sensible friend would have wished one of them to be even softened. His private industry was appalling. If one moment late at school, he would hurry in, and explain that he had been detained 'verifying a quotation'; and many a one did he verify at four in the morning. He told me at the close of one of his autumn vacations of six weeks, that, before it had begun, he had taken a house in the country, and had sent his family there, in order that he himself might have a bit of rustic leisure, but that having got upon the scent of some curious passages (his favourite sport) he had remained with his books in town, and had never seen the country house.

Cockburn, (Lord) Henry (1856). *Memorials of his Time.*
Edinburgh, Adam and Charles Black.

1779–1854: leading political (Whig) and legal figure in Edinburgh life.

4G                                                     Greenock, 1820s.

The child John Caird, who was destined to be perhaps the greatest preacher the Scottish pulpit has produced, was born on the 15th December 1820. He was the eldest of six surviving sons. His education he received at the Grammar School of Greenock, an institution established about the middle of the eighteenth century, and served from its foundation by a succession of those ill-paid but cultured dominies who created the great tradition of Scottish parochial education. The atmosphere in which they laboured for their miserable pittance must have been depressing in the extreme, for

Greenock in the eighteenth and early nineteenth centuries was intellectually barbarian. Its traders, carpenters, seamen, and ship-masters composed a rough, unlettered population concentrated on their commercial interests and crassly indifferent to the appeal of science or of literature . .

It behoves us therefore to look at James Lockhart Brown, master of the Grammar School of Greenock and preceptor of the future Principal of Glasgow University. He was an eccentric and extraordinary creature. A mighty protagonist for the classics, he was serenely at home wandering with the poets of antiquity among the Sabine hills or on the shores of Hellas as among the Ayrshire fields with Robert Burns. Of the width, extent and accuracy of his massive scholarship there can be no question, and his presence as the teacher of a hundred and fifty grubby brats in an uninviting Clyde port is testimony to the standard of the old Scottish dominie of the late eighteenth and nineteenth centuries. There we can see him, this man of splendid gifts which Glasgow University recognized with a Doctorate of Laws, struggling with the ineptitude of sulky children in his shabby, congested school, which had neither lamp nor candle nor gas-jet to alleviate its gloom. There he is, enthusiastic in his evening classes for young men in advanced Latin and Greek, opening up for them wide horizons, revealing to them their kinship with the ages. Or on a winter day we find him crouching blue in the face over the inadequate fire in his little classroom, declaiming the *Iliad* to half a dozen boys, by its fitful, smoky light. No country but Scotland was able in those days to commit its bourgeois youth to the care of men like that.

And Brown taught them well. He grounded them in the classics, knocked into them the elements of mathematics, led or herded them into the fields of English literature, taught them to write with a penship that is now a forgotten art. His methods were his own. He addressed his urchins always as 'Gentlemen', but he flogged them with unwearied zeal, beating his own gawky son more than anyone else, doubtless in order that there might be no suspicion left in the minds of his victims as to his strict impartiality. He shared Dr Johnson's almost superstitious reverence for corporal punishment, and John Caird's success in after life he quite sincerely attributed to the fact that as a boy he had thrashed him well.

Warr, Charles (1926). *Principal Caird.* Edinburgh, T. and T. Clark.

1820–98: leading theologian; Principal Glasgow University.

# 5 AN EDUCATED PEOPLE: IMAGES OF SCOTLAND

*Caledonian Sketches*: The Gentleman's Magazine, 1809
*Proceedings in the late Session of Parliament*:
*The Gentleman's Magazine*, 1807
*A Tour of Scotland in the Year 1749*:
*European Magazine*, 1806
*Female Schools of Cleanliness, Morals and Decorum*:
*Scots Magazine*, 1804
*Reminiscences of Auld Langsyne*: Scots Magazine, 1822

Figure 8. **North Canongate School, Edinburgh: dinner time, 1914** The 1908 Act allowed schools to provide subsidised hot meals – a much-needed step, given the widespread poverty evident in this picture. *Edinburgh Education Department*

Figure 9. **Kelvinside Academy, Glasgow: art class, 1916** While the inner-city elementaries were preoccupied with the basics, their secondary counterparts in the suburbs were pursuing the graces – albeit through the formality of the 'still-life' study.
*Glasgow City Archive*

By the middle of the nineteenth century, 'Scottish education' was as much a matter of history as of current actions. And 'history' meant heritage. For those who took it upon themselves to speak about the nation's schools, the events of the past had become collected together to form a storehouse of exemplars, ones which had been placed in the memory in order to express a living ideal by which to guide the present. Indeed, the Scottish school, in such reconstructions, had come to stand for the nation itself and its defining, non-English values.

What these might be – and how such a process of representation worked in the familiar literature of the day – is to found in *The Gentleman's Magazine* of 1809 (**5A**). Sir John Carr's 'Tour' shows how, as communications improved and advances in agriculture and industry stimulated a curiosity as to how such matters were proceeding in other parts of the island, the travelogue became increasingly popular. The individual expedition into the stranger regions of the kingdom could also become a vehicle for the projection of a particular image of North Britain, which would then act as confirmation to the natives of their self-image and as edification to the rest. Habitually, Scotland's renowned education system was given centre stage.

Sir John's account follows the common script. There is the usual exotic backcloth of 'Scotland' in terms of its wildest and most rugged – if sparsely populated – Highland aspects; the dramatically austere living conditions and domestic simplicity of its characters are deftly evoked. But then, in the foreground, comes the contrastingly vivid appearance of the educated peasant and, with him, the rhetoric of elevated moral values.

The authorship of 'Caledonian Sketches' is evidence that the homespun idealisation was by now becoming the widely accepted version, even – and gratifyingly – among English audiences. Its members included those who were responsible for considering how best to develop England's more rudimentary system. Mr Whitbread MP's citation is but one of a whole series of Parliamentary compliments paid to the neighbouring example during this period (**5B**).

The MP's preamble also demonstrates one of the leading attractions the assumed achievement of Scottish education held for those who were concerned to maintain social control, whether in the civil or the religious domain. As the golden references to a Latin-speaking proletariat and its knowledgeable piety demonstrate, the 'democratic' spread of schooling was to be embraced for the moral benefits it promised to secure. At a time when parliament and churchmen were beginning to look nervously at the fast expanding labouring popula-tion of the industrialising valleys and the slum-filled towns, an assurance that education could mean a training in the more orderly virtues of ecclesiastical deference and rational conduct was a most timely one.

This is why many of the accounts of the 'Scottish Tour' take on the shape of a Biblical narrative. The incident recounted in *The European Magazine* of 1806 is the parable of the Guid Samaritan (**5C**). It begins with the customary fascinated distaste for the primitive lifestyle, which immediately becomes visible north of Carlisle, as the southern visitor gamely struggles past bedraggled fields, encounters women who go barefoot along rutted roads and risks pestilence in grimy, fly-blown inns. But the carefully assembled Anglocentric disdain is there to act as the background that will permit the translucent literacy and moral probity of the humbly learned native to shine forth all the more brightly.

By the 1830s, the scenario had become axiomatic to both sides of the border: the 'Scotch' led the harsher lives but sustained the richer values. Ruggedness of environment, it would appear, bred indepen-dence, good sense and sturdy, reliable morals; the ubiquitous parish school fashioned these qualities into a system; the ever-ready contrast with a cosseted England turned the system into an expression of national identity.

But as the century advanced, the picture was becoming more blurred. The Scottish economy was now advancing rapidly; there was a consciousness of catching up, of 'poverty' ceasing to be a distin-guishing feature. By 1832, *Chambers's Journal* was reprinting the '1749 Tour' but now as a historical curiosity, 'a specimen of the amusing mixture of truth and falsehood that was written regarding Scotland and its inhabitants 80 years ago'. The essay in nostalgia concludes on a comfortable note:

The Scotch of the present day have reason to thank more than blame writers like this. With much that is objectionable and scandalous, they told some plain disagreeable truths, and were partly responsible for schooling the people into better habits. We can now afford to laugh, as well as our neighbours, at the condition of *old* Scotland.

The juxtaposition of 'schooling' and 'better habits' is, however, significant. Despite this breezy display of parity, the journals of the day had, for some time now, been evincing an uneasiness as to whether in some respects the average Scot, better schooled though he might be, was not backward compared to the cotton hands of Bolton or the smocked yokels of Kent. As both his landed and his newly middle-class compatriots began to seek the refinements of carriage and dress and table, which would enable them to hold a place in any English drawing-room, they were becoming embarrassedly aware of the filthy taverns, the tubs of excremental deposit scattered on to the streets of the capital, and of the dub and the dung in which the countryside beyond its limits wallowed.

The remedy proposed by *The Scots Magazine* is a symptom of an increasing discomfort over such domestic matters (**5D**). By pointing to a fresh type of 'school ' as a source of cleansing, the article also sums up the extent to which an educational system, which had hitherto maintained a rigorous concentration on matters intellectual and of the spirit, was now beginning to be viewed as deficient in certain respects. The English might, after all, have something to teach them.

Towards the end of our period, then, observers within Scotland were beginning to reappraise its own traditions in ways that were guided by a growing sensitivity towards its standing within the United Kingdom. Frequently, the plea for a measure of modernisation was accompanied by some uncomfortable stocktaking in which debit, as well as gain, was to be registered. In the good old *Scots Magazine* of 1822, the reader was given an early example of what, over the next 150 years, was to gather into a persistent minor genre, the exercise in educational nostalgia (**5E**). Its 'reminiscence', significantly, is not of any one specific place, but of 'Auld Langsyne'.

5A                                                    Caledonia, 1807.

By the wise and salutary diffusion of education, particularly in parts which appear to be impenetrable to civilization, upon the sides of frightful mountains, or in dismal glens, seldom visited by the rays of Heaven, the astonished and admiring traveller beholds a spectacle at once gratifying and affecting. In a hut of branches and sods, when the hour of labour is over, the young, enlightened by those institutions which do honour to human nature, are seen, instructing those who are younger, or consoling the last hours of venerable and sightless Age by reading aloud the Scriptures, or some pious book, printed in their own language; yet in this sorry dwelling the benighted traveller may rest in safety amid the howling storm . . . It is equally singular and true that one can scarcely meet with a poor man in any part of Scotland who is not possessed of the knowledge particularized in the commencement of this chapter; and to this he frequently adds a little Latin. The results of this system of education are of the most beneficent nature. If the poor remain at home, their deportment is sedate, upright and orderly; if they attempt their fortunes in other countries, they bear with them a superior understanding, and a knowledge sharpened by poverty, which enables them to do honour in any situation, and frequently to improve those arts, studies and pursuits, by which the power, prosperity, and character of a country are at once extended and secured.

'Caledonian sketches or A tour through Scotland in 1807, by Sir John Carr'
(1809). Review in *The Gentleman's Magazine*, 79, February.

5B                                                    Westminster, 1807.

Mr Whitbread moved the farther consideration of the Report of the Parochial Schools Bill . . . The preamble stood thus, – 'Whereas the instruction of youth tends most materially to the promotion of morality and virtue, and to the formation of good members of society, whereof we have the most convincing proof, by long experience, in that part of the United kingdom called Scotland; and it is expedient that provision should be made for the instruction of the children of the Poor of England and Wales'.

'Proceedings in the Late Session of Parliament' (1807).
*The Gentleman's Magazine*, 77, October.

5C                                        Galloway, 1749.

I take the liberty to send you the account (I promised) of my journey into Scotland, the idea that my memory retains of the country in general, the particular places I saw there, and the people I conversed with. I am afraid you will find no entertainment to make it worth the trouble of reading; but that you may not complain of *me*, if you *do* read and dislike it, I warn you before hand, it is nothing but a description of a barren land . . .

Soon after this, I was taken ill at a place called Sanchor, was well when I left my chamber, but fainted in attempting to mount my horse; the inn was so execrably bad and nasty, that I resolved to leave it as soon as possible. I bore riding pretty well for three miles, but then found myself scorched with a fever, and so violent a thirst, that I could not resist my impatience to drive immediately at every spring and stream I came to; was forced several times to alight, and rest myself upon the ground, and at last lay down without the least hope of riding any more; my servant and guide were gone different ways to seek for a wheeled carriage. In the meantime, a country fellow came up to me, and seemed sensibly touched with my distress, and would fain have carried me on his back to his own house, or an inn; at last, by his assistance, I was seated, and supported on horseback till he brought me where I got some new milk, that gave me so much refreshment as enabled me to ride on to the inn he told me of, which had not a chimney belonging to it. The wall of my bed chamber was of mud and stone, with a hole, instead of a window, to let in light and air. The first seven hours that I lay there, it could hardly be discerned whether I was alive or dead . . . Luckily, a young fellow (student of one of the universities) was making a visit to the neighbourhood, who came to me, and at length, by his extraordinary skill and incessant attendance for three days and nights, recovered me. I must not forget to tell you, that when I offered a reward to the poor man whose kindness, I believe, saved my life, the generous creature refused it absolutely, saying, it gave him joy enough to have done such an act of charity, for which he neither wanted nor would take money . . .

I was astonished at the discernment and knowledge of the young fellow (of about two-and-twenty) who first came to me, till he gave me this account of his education . . . The Scotch are in general very polite, of free and easy address, and it is rare to find a man of that nation, of any rank but the very lowest of all, without some tincture of learning; for the pride and delight of every father is to give a liberal education to his son . . . No wonder, then, that the Scotch are accounted so wise a people; for, if amongst us, every man's capacity was improved to the utmost with care and judgement, what an immense decrease there would be of our present multitude of fools!

'A Tour of Scotland in the Year 1749' (1806).
*The European Magazine,* 49, April.

5D                                                        Edinburgh, 1804.

Among the many imperfections in our present political economy, it has often occurred to me, that a want of sufficient attention to moral order, decency, and cleanliness, among the lower ranks of society in Scotland, deserves just reprehension, and reflects no small portion of disgrace on those who not only possess the power, but have long had the means to rectify the evil. Among the various causes which tend to improve, civilize, and refine national character, I consider CLEANLI-NESS as not the least powerful. Without those pleasurable sensations, arising from conscious purity and a consequent disgust at what is offensively filthy, I maintain that a proper *purity of mind* cannot possibly exist . . .

Of all the tribes of uncivilized society, the most disgustingly filthy in their habits, and at the same time, the most deplorably indolent, stupid and defective in intellectual powers, is the *Hottentot*; of all the civilized nations, with whose manners and dispositions we are acquainted, the *English,* taken collectively, are perhaps the most cleanly . . . Scotch poverty, and Scotch nastiness, have long been subjects of national reproach from our cleanly southern neighbours. The first cause has ceased; the other remains . . .

Sluggish and slow as the Scotch are in most of their operations, they certainly are not naturally stupid; much as they resemble their Dutch neighbours in their torpidity, it proceeds more from habits of *indolent indifference* than from any radical defect of mental energy, or constitutional laziness; rouse them from their habitual slumbers by touching their passions, few or none are more ardent; excite their attentions by what is interesting and beneficial, few are more active, persevering, and acute. The great object, therefore, is to overcome habit, and produce impressions, to awaken *perception,* and excite *action;* and as I am clearly of opinion that nothing can promote these more effectually than habits of cleanliness, I am laying the axe to the root of the tree at once, by instituting proper *schools* for the instruction of our *females,* to produce a new class of beings with such perceptions, ideas, and predilections, as will produce a new conduct.

'Female Schools for Cleanliness, Morals and Decorum' (1804).

*The Scots Magazine,* 66, March.


5E                                                 Auld Scotland, 1822.


Next day was Saturday, and it rained so heavily that there was no stirring out; we were therefore confined to the parlour, talking, to beguile the 'joyless day', with all the younger branches of the family present. Of these, the eldest was Sophia, a fine blooming girl of about eighteen; Peter, the eldest boy, appeared to be about fifteen. I inquired whether the boys were at school, the object of their studies, the economy of the school, and character of their teacher? 'Our school-master', said my cousin, 'is a fine dashing young fellow, lately licensed to preach, very clever, and most excellent company. I hope he will be home from his vacation jaunt before you leave us. You shall see him. Respecting the methods followed in the school, Peter will inform you'. 'Well, Peter, what does he teach?', said I. 'We have, Sir, a Latin, French and a Geography class, besides all the lower branches of education'. 'Ah! these are improvements upon my school-boy days; we had Latin, to be sure; but French and Geography were unknown. You have got a new school-house too, I presume?' 'Oh, yes, Sir; would you wish to see it?' 'I should have liked better to have visited the old one; although it would have grieved me to see another in the place of that venerable man, whom fancy still places before me, in the act of morning or evening prayers'. Here Peter stared at me, repeating the word, 'Prayers!'. 'Yes, prayers', said I; 'sure your teacher prays for a blessing upon his labours?' 'Perhaps, he does, but it is not in our hearing – your master had been a Seceder!' 'No, he was not; but I believe he was a pious man, who had the welfare of all under his charge seriously at heart'. 'And how often did your dominie pray in the school?' 'Twice every day – morning and evening'. 'And were you all very devout?' 'His manner commanded outward attention; but I hope many joined him in their hearts. His style and supplicating attitude made an impression on the minds of his pupils. He stood as if surrounded by his children, and the expressions of tender regard which we heard him utter made him be esteemed as a father. But how often do you repeat your Catechism?' 'Sir?' said Peter, not because he did not hear, but from not understanding the question. 'How often do you answer questions?' said I. 'Every geography lesson, Sir? – we are fashed with them. I have worn out a set of maps, and cannot yet answer half of them. Tam, there is the boy for questions; he can tell you all the Kings of England, and all the battles from William the Conqueror, at the battle of Hastings, down to Bunker's-hill'. 'And all the Assembly's Shorter Catechism, with the Scripture Proofs, of course?', said I. 'We have no such book, Sir'. 'What! Do you not learn the Single Catechism?' 'No; I never saw it, since the time I was learning the A,B,C at Marion Lindsay'.

'Reminiscences of Auld Langsyne' (1822). *The Scots Magazine,* 89, April.

1840–1918

# 6 CRISIS IN THE CITY

*Scotland: A Half Educated Nation*: George Lewis, 1835
*On the System of Parochial Schools in Scotland*:
Thomas Chalmers, 1819
*Memoirs of Thomas Chalmers*: William Hanna, 1852
*The Schoolmaster in the Wynds*: Robert Buchanan, 1850
*Among the Masses*: Dugald MacColl, 1867
*The State of Scottish Towns*: *North British Review*, 1847
*Granny and Leezy – a Scottish Dialogue*: David Stow, 1860
*Elementary Education*: (Sheriff)William Watson, 1863
*Autobiographies of Industrial School Children*: 'A.H.', 1864
*Some Notes: Personal and Public*: William Lindsay, 1898

Figure 10. **Jeyes' Special Fluid, 1909** A famous brand's contribution to the war on germs which became such a priority following the increased responsibilities for child welfare imposed on schools by the 1908 Education Act. *Jeyes Group*

Figure 11. **Cullerlie School, Aberdeenshire, late nineteenth century** Bairns and teacher at play outside what was a typical country schoolhouse of the period. The teaching was done on the ground floor, while the teacher inhabited the upstairs. Cullerlie was closed in the 1930s. Its renovated building has now become a fine private residence. *Scottish Life Archive*

In 1835, the Reverend George Lewis issued his pamphlet with the shocking title. In it, he sets out the 'plain-spoken statistics' which will justify the claim that Scotland was now no better than a *Half Educated Nation*. While a school attendance rate of one in six of the overall population was considered to represent universality, Glasgow could only muster one in fifteen- in its inner city districts half that – and Aberdeen one in twenty-five. Cotton-rich Paisley contained 3,000 illiterate adults.

Such data pointed to a system which was becoming overwhelmed by the surging of the population, especially in the manufacturing areas, and by the resulting social dislocation. But, as **6A** shows, Lewis did not allow figures to do all the preaching. Although he makes great play with his attendance ratios, they are enveloped in a rhetoric which is sufficiently heated to beat out visions of spiritual dereliction and collective guilt.

The language may be on fire, but the pamphlet's argument is actually a conservative one. Despite the depth of a crisis which, in other quarters, is beginning to stir thoughts of a radically new system that would be run by central government, Lewis demands that public money be furnished – in order to subsidise the Church in its ancient responsibilities. A regular injection of grants would enable her to erect new schools, appoint new masters and, thus, shore up the trusted old regime.

With its brew of Biblical invocation, of modern statistics, pleas for the restoration of inherited values and menacing glimpses of civic collapse, the spectre of a 'Half Educated Nation' sets the emotional as well as the material agenda, which will infuse Scottish opinion through the forty years of national soul-searching, towards its final adoption of a secular, government administered regime in 1872.

At its centre, was East-end Glasgow. There, Lewis depicts a Scotland in despair. Although the city could count 200 schools by which to civilise its 202,000 souls, only eight of them were being provided through the original parish framework. In the main, families had come to rely upon an inchoate network of private establishments and charitable institutions. Lewis's conclusion was that 'the opulent city of Glasgow has done nothing for education'. He can point, however, to one exemption from the shameful neglect – the Church. While the city magistrates were looking the other way, its pastors and its congregations were striving to provide for the educational needs of their flocks.

The outstanding example was the work of Thomas Chalmers in his inner-city parish of St John's. There, he had succeeded in organising his parishioners into building new schools and mounting a pro-gramme of vigilant home visits to bring in the pupil recruits. The overall aim was local self-sufficiency within a framework of communal discipline and support. Finance must come from parent fees as well as by congregational support.

What Chalmers was attempting was to carry the traditional rural model into the very depths of the city – and, with it, the continued rule of the Church (**6B**). In his campaigning, he frequently evoked his own days as a pupil in the fishing village of Anstruther when he had shared his desk with 'children of all ranks and degrees'. In practical terms, these messages could only have limited impact on a situation where the sheer scale of need continually outran resources. Their import was, moreover, dependant upon the ability of their preachers to deliver them through sustained personal involvement. That Chalmers had this missionary gift is undoubted (**6C**); that his own endeavours had to be constantly repeated by bands of ever newer and fresher crusaders is shown by what happened next.

By 1823, Chalmers was gone, off to accept a Chair at St Andrews, exhausted by the intensity of the effort. Others would follow to repeat the pattern. In the 1830s, Robert Buchanan swept into St John's with a similar combination of hard-headed organisation and committed evangelism (**6D**); Dugald MacColl carried the Word into the next decade – but when he arrived he found that Buchanan's 'Candle school' had fallen into disarray: the children were staying away, their parents irredeemable – 'like rotten wood, they winna haud the nail'. Ten years on, George Troup was to take up the cause and write about it in his *The Question of the Day! How are the Masses to be Educated and Evangelised?* (1857). It was one that would not go away.

In an environment which held a shifting, expanding population, whose members were assailed by poverty, fluctuations in trade, disease and the necessity for child labour, the raw circumstances of survival always seemed to outrun the schemes of the evangelists.

MacColl's words reveal a further limitation (**6E**): examples of child conversions are intended to inspire but they also indicate that the focus of their crusading was not on the relief of poverty but rescue from its spiritual consequences. In a situation that cried out for concerted social action, they were intent on the individual soul.

Yet, while Chalmers and his followers had been striving to adapt their pastoral eighteenth-century thinking to the actualities of the modern industrial city, the government was beginning to stir. From the 1830s onwards, it had been commissioning a series of inquiries into a range of environmental issues. As these were commonly set within a British context, their findings made for some sharp comparisons. When the committees on the 'Health of Towns' and the 'Sanitary Condition of the Labouring Population' delivered their reports, their common verdict was that 'the condition of the population of Glasgow was the worst of any we had seen in any part of Britain'.

That this environmentalist approach was beginning to intrude itself into evangelical circles may be seen in how the *North British Review* reported their work (**6F**). Significantly, the hygiene issue is set in the context of the Scottish education system. The familiar references to the parochial school are there, the usual flattering contrast to the intellectual naivety of the English peasant is made – but, now, these appear in order to raise an urgent concern over comparative standards of living and the importance of an educated cleanliness. The native domestic habits are now being viewed as a matter of wider social concern, not simply a question of individual refinement. The writer has recognized that the new urban conditions have changed everything: no parish system would be able to counteract the effect of the city's daily horrors upon the young mind. To imagine differently would, the article continues later, be to oppose a raging torrent with nothing but a 'few twigs'.

That is why, the periodical argues, the era of voluntary, localised action must yield to concerted national action. It is its source which makes this conclusion particularly significant. By now, the Church of Scotland had split. In the Disruption of 1843, the evangelist wing, led by Chalmers, at odds over the issue of congregational autonomy and tiring of the quietist policies of the 'Moderate' majority, had broken away to found the Free Church of Scotland. The *North British* was established to represent its viewpoint. At its time of writing, its new

Church was busy establishing a rival national network of parochial schools.

This was a development which struck at the very concept of an integrated and historically validated system, through which all Scots could receive their education in the one community school. Yet, if it was to take a further thirty years before a unified – and secular – system was finally reinstituted, it could at least be said that, in the interim, the evangelical movement generated a great wave of energetic concern, one which attracted forceful lay, as well as ecclesiastic, adherents. Among them none achieved more than David Stow. The son of a well-to-do Paisley mercantile family, he came to Glasgow in 1811, at the age of 18, ready to embark upon his own commercial career. Distressed at the spectacle of deprivation which he was daily forced to observe on its streets, Stow set up a series of Sunday, then day, schools, by which to rescue the young, before their corruption set in.

In 1828, he founded the Glasgow Infant Society. Its aim was to spread child-centred methods, with a particular emphasis upon creative play. Concerned with educating teachers in the appropriate methodologies, he began to open up his schools as model or 'Normal Seminaries'. From them, emerged the organised system which led to the establishment of Jordanhill, as Britain's first teacher training centre He also attempted to change the attitudes of parents. **6G** is taken from his exemplary dialogues: Leezy represents the decent working-class parent, anxious to do the best for her children; Granny is the old generation, doubtful whether any 'real' school can so happily eschew the grinding pedagogy of her own brief experience.

Stow's interest in the school as a protective, rather than coercive, environment was taken up by other reformers. In 1841, Britain's first 'Industrial School' was opened in Aberdeen by Sheriff William Watson. The new institution was an ambitious attempt to deal with the scourge of vagrant juvenile delinquency, which was now threateningly visible on the city's streets.

A distinctive feature of the Industrial School was that it gave the pupil welfare as well as letters. It acted as a domestic environment where, in addition to literacy and the Bible, the homeless young would find soup and a heated stove. Watson's argument was that to offer the starving child no more than the bare school place was 'like offering a stone instead of bread'. Personal responsibility was certainly woven into the daily round and there were sessions where they would be making salmon nets and unpicking hair for mattresses, but there would also be times to eat, study and wash.

Watson was a resourceful publicist for what developed into a nation-wide movement, with offshoots soon appearing in Glasgow, Falkirk, Ayr and even Liverpool. They were guided by his pamphlets; one of these displayed the child biographies he used to demonstrate the depths from which his pupils had emerged and the literate extent they had travelled (**6I**). He also became anxious to spread the cause of child-friendliness to the old parochial system. His forays into it convinced him that what the standard 'Elementary' school offered was punitively austere (**6H**).

He was not alone. In Edinburgh, Thomas Guthrie instituted the Ragged School concept, through which he set up establishments that would furnish bodily care, useful training, a Christian ethos and residential accommodation. By the middle of the century, Watson and Guthrie had emerged as the latest heroes of a movement which by then had pervaded Scottish middle-class life, the voluntarist principle of individual good works. In her *Philanthropy in Victorian Scotland* (1980), Olive Checkland has tracked the successive attempts to translate this principle into effective social action. The aim was to mobilise the force of charitable giving into an attack upon the sin, intemperance, disease, ignorance and general squalor, which had become rampant within the city's lower quarters. By 1850, there had sprung up a whole spread of welfare schemes, which ranged from the orphanage, to the House of Refuge, to training ships. Each aimed at removal of the vulnerable young from domestic corruption.

It was a logical culmination. The originally inclusive, and pre-dominately academic, vision of Chalmers and Buchanan had now evolved into schemes which combined schooling with welfare and concentrated on the most pressing of the daily casualties which the modern city incurred. This targeting was, given the urgency of the matter, an inevitable scaling down of the initial priorities. But it, too, was accompanied by rhetoric which broadcast a dramatic emphasis upon the wasteland within which the East-end poor were seen to scramble and wallow. It was one that was to leave its mark when the schools of the state-run system came to be planted down among them.

Caught up in the immediacy of their urban horrors, the mid-century reformers' message was bound to be a highly charged one. Historical distance has led to a more balanced assessment. The data they brandished has been shown to be as much propagandist as analytical. The more dispassionate scrutiny of such contemporary analysts as Donald Withrington and Robert Anderson has indicated that, all through the period, literacy rates were, in fact, steadily rising; the 1871 census reveals that fewer than fifteen per cent, even in the darkest slum, escaped some significant schooling. While the explosive conditions of the mid-century – Irish immigration, the full arrival of the factory system, the sheer rate of urban expansion – had created its crises, by the 1860s the system had regrouped itself and a sufficiency of school places was being regained.

But their utilisation followed its own particular shapes. Within the city, the older patterns of provision and attendance, which had characterised the rural areas, had evolved into their urban equivalents. It is illuminating to track the career of William Lindsay who, the son of an Aberdeen shoemaker, eventually succeeded in becoming a noted journalist. Having first been taught his letters at home, he worked his way through a range of local schools – Dame, Venture, Lancastrian. Spells of full attendance were interspersed with part-days and full employment. As important as any institutionalised experience was the influence of his adult colleagues in the workshop, especially that of John Duncan, the artisan poet and theologian, who emerges as a formidable example of the self-taught working man. As he looks back on it all, at the end of the century, Lindsay shows his city to be a lively, expansive place, one that housed a pluralistic range of opportunities from which the willing individual could piece together his own continuing education. It was also – he held – one that could produce results as sound as any accomplished 'under our modern system, with all its magnificent and expensive appliances'.


6A                                                              Scotland, 1830s.


We have been accustomed to compassionate our Highland country-men; but it is not in the Highlands, but in the streets and lanes of Glasgow, Edinburgh, Dundee, Paisley, and Aberdeen, that ignorance and profligacy have now their strongholds. It is not where ignorance dwells alone, but where it is surrounded by intelligence and opulence – where the extremes of society meet in dismal contrast – that the destitution is most lamentable. Though the corrupting influences of a town life are incomparably greater than those of rural society – though a large city be a common sewer and receptacle of all iniquity – though vice is there found on a magnificent scale, and her facilities and allurements are there multiplied a thousandfold – yet no means of instruction have been devised, expanding with the population, to elevate, purify, and strengthen, virtuous habits and holy principles. 'Is it not amazing?', you will hear good people exclaim, 'that with all our churches, and schools, and benevolent societies, ignorance, and vice, and irreligion, should be continually increasing among the poor!' Not the least strange, we reply: neither our churches nor schools are for the *poor*; they help only those who can help themselves. Our churches and schools are open; but only to those who can pay for them. Here and there are to be seen a few labourers at work; but what can they do to reclaim a wilderness! We magnify the little that is doing under our eye; we observe not all that is left undone. All that has been yet done for the education of the poor in Glasgow, serves only to evince the entire impotency of the voluntary system to educate either an entire nation, or an entire city. A few plain-spoken statistics are all that is necessary to expose the vanity of trusting to the broken reed of a spontaneous demand for education, or even to the spontaneous benevolence of the good: and unless the Legislature go forward in good earnest to meet the wants of the ignorant and irreligious population of our towns, as our cities increase, ignorance and irreligion will increase also; discontent, and turbulence, and pauperism, will increase: and if the nation will not pay for the schoolmaster, to prevent crime, it must pay tenfold for the repression of social disorder, and for coercing an unhappy, dissolute, and reckless population.

Lewis, George (1835). *Scotland: A Half Educated Nation, both in the Quantity and Quality of her Educational Institutions.* Glasgow, pamphlet.

6B                                                              Glasgow, 1819.

And yet we will not despair of this cause, when we think of its many recommendations; and that, with all its cost, it would still form the best and cheapest defence of our nation, against the misrule of the fiercer and more untoward passions of our nature; and that the true secret for managing a people, is not so much to curb, as to enlighten them; and that a moral is a far mightier operation than a physical force, in controlling the elements of political disorder; and that to give a certainty to the habit of education in towns, is to do for them that which has visibly raised the whole peasantry of Scotland, both in intelligence and virtue, above the level of any other population.

Chalmers, Thomas (1819). *On the System of Parochial Schools in Scotland and on the Advantage of Establishing them in Large Towns.* Glasgow, pamphlet.

6C                                                                          Glasgow, 1810s.

And his care and influence reached much further than in the bare provision of school-houses and schoolmasters. He took the liveliest personal interest in all the operations he had set agoing. 'His visits to my school', says Mr. Aitken, 'were almost daily, and of the most friendly description. In all states of weather and in every frame of mind he was there; depositing himself in the usual chair, his countenance relaxing into its wonted smile as he recognized the children of the working classes. Again and again, looking round upon them from his seat, his eye beaming with peculiar tenderness, he has exclaimed, 'I cannot tell you how my heart warms to these barefooted children!' One day, after sitting longer than usual, he left, saying, 'I expected to meet Major Woodward and his lady here. Be sure, should they call, to tell them these are the children of our working classes, they form so striking a contrast to the sights they are accustomed to in Ireland'. Sometimes he would enter the school buoyant and congratulatory, introducing the Bishop of ____, or the Lord and Lady of ____, developing to the visitors this or that other feature of his parochial system, and generally concluding with the request, 'Now just let us hear one class read a portion before we go'.

Hanna, Reverend William (1852). *Memoirs of Thomas Chalmers.* Edinburgh, Sutherland and Knox.

6D                                                                          Glasgow, 1840s.

It was under the influence of those feelings and convictions, which the facts now stated are so well fitted to produce, that the experiment I am about to describe was begun, and has been steadily progressed. Ever since I came to Glasgow, sixteen years ago, the kirk session and congregation over which I have the privilege to preside, have maintained, at an average cost of from 80*l.* to 90*l.* a-year, a large and flourishing school in the eastern part of the Tron parish. We now commonly call it the Bridgegate school, as it enters from that street. It is spacious and handsome; not equalled, certainly, in either of these respects, by any apartment in the Grammar school of the city. We had been long and deeply sensible, however, that the means of education, including the well attended Sessional school of the Established Church, in the same neighbourhood, were altogether inadequate to meet the wants of the district. Between King-street and the Old Wynd, no school of any kind was to be found. After much time spent in seeking, in that dense and crowded block of buildings, for premises suitable for our purpose, and within the reach of our funds, we at length succeeded in securing in the Old Wynd the very thing that we wanted. It had been a candle manufactory, but it had given little light, after all, to the dark district in which it stood. We hope it is otherwise now. Let it be told to the honour of that now degraded part of our city, that a son of the Wynd – now one of the most prosperous and venerable of our fellow-citizens – gave us a subscription of 400*l.*, to encourage us in our enterprise. Aided by other friends of a kindred spirit, and by a grant from the government education fund, we were enabled to purchase and fit up, at an expense of from 1100*l.* to 1200*l.*, the candle manufactory as the Old Wynd school. It was opened for the first time towards the close of 1848; and with its three commodious school-rooms, its excellent playground, its swinging ropes and other accommodations for the children, was at least one new thing under the sun introduced into that long neglected locality; a well dug in the wilderness, an oasis appearing in the moral desert.

Buchanan, Reverend Robert (1850). *The Schoolmaster in the Wynds: or How to Educate the Masses.* Glasgow, pamphlet.

6E                                                          Glasgow, 1850s.

During the last six years much precious fruit has been gathered from this field. Children of drunken fathers and heart-broken mothers have not only been blessed but made a blessing, carrying home the first real peace and prosperity for ten or twenty years. Others have come regularly, though attacked by their companions and beaten by their parents. One has brought eleven; another seven; several leave the sabbath school to plead with others at home to come with them to the evening service. Their love of mission work is most touching. One girl, now at work, in order to have something to give, lays aside her 'sugar money'. A little fellow came back with his mission card and tenpence he had collected, saying, I have nothing but my rabbit, and a boy in the close has promised me sixpence for it! Another little fellow, losing two fingers at his work, was carried to the Infirmary, but found he could still do something for Jesus. In the bed next to him was a little sweep, whose face had been sometimes seen in the meeting. Him he taught to pray, and for another in the same ward he searched passages from a large type Bible, and tried to explain their meaning. These children have not only their regular contributions for Foreign Missions, but for the sick among themselves, while a few of the older children give a penny a week to educate six poorer than themselves.

MacColl, Reverend Dugald (1867). *Among the Masses:
Work in the Wynds.* Glasgow, pamphlet.

6F                                                          North Britain, 1847.

In one of the volumes of Minutes of Committee of Council on Education, of which one or more now appears annually, we find a Report from one of the English inspectors on the state of education in Norfolk, and another from the pen of one of the Scotch inspectors on the educational state of the county of Haddington. The educational contrast of these two agricultural counties, lying within a few hours' sail of each other, is remarkable. The county of Norfolk is, like Haddington, a rich agricultural county. It contains not less than 750 parishes, more than two-thirds of the parishes in all Scotland. The average population of each of these 750 parishes is little more than 500 souls; and its parish churches lie so close to each other as to appear at every turn of the road or of the coast. In such a state of ecclesiastical sufficiency, one would have expected the intellectual and moral returns to have been amongst the highest in the kingdom, and that Norfolk would have been a great moral and intellectual garden. What says the inspector of the Church of England?

'Very few adults of either sex can read or write. An opinion prevails, that those who remain of the preceding generation more commonly possessed these acquisitions. A female has officiated as clerk in a parish for the last two years, none of the adult males being able to read. In another parish the present clerk is the only man in the rank of a labourer who can read. In another, of 400 souls, when the present school was established two years ago, no labourer could read or write. A Dissenting minister addressing a small congregation, was lately interrupted by a cry of "Glory be to your name!" He immediately repressed the cry, explaining such language could only be used to the Deity. The answer was – "Then glory be to both of you!" This, says the inspector, "I have too much reason to believe is a *characteristic* fact, the suppression of which would therefore disguise the truth". – *Minutes of C. of C. on Education.* 1840–41.'

We need not quote any part of the Haddington Report. Of no part, no rural part of Scotland, from John o' Groats House to the Mull of Galloway, could such an anecdote be told as a *characteristic* fact. The Church in Scotland has nowhere so failed in her great duty as the educator of the people. But let us rejoice with trembling . . . Low as the education of letters is in the county of Norfolk, not so is the education in those physical and social habits which preserve and promote health and home-happiness, and inspire self-respect. Of the habits of the poor Norwich weavers, very little, if at all, above the weavers of Paisley in the amount of their weekly earnings, the same inspector thus writes:–

'One marked and favourable peculiarity even amongst the poorest Norwich weavers, is their strict attention to cleanliness and decency in their dwellings – a token of self-respect and a proof of ideas and habits, of which the severest privations in food and dress did not seem to be able to deprive them. Their rooms might be destitute of all the necessary articles of furniture, but the few that remained were clean, the walls and staircases whitewashed, the floors carefully swept and washed, the court or alley cleared of every thing offensive, the children wearing shoes and stockings, however sorry in kind, and the clothes not ragged, however incongruously patched and darned. "Cleanliness and propriety", said one man, "are, in spite of our poverty, the pride of Norwich people, *who would have nothing to say to dirty neighbours*".' . . .

Whatever, therefore, be the superiority of our working population in the education of letters, we must not shut our eyes to the deplorable fact that this education of letters has been wholly unable to prevent the masses in our towns from sinking into a physical state in house and person which to an Englishman, even to a Norwich weaver, earning only seven shillings a-week, were unbearable. If England still wants schools for the education of letters, she has homes for the higher education of habits and tastes, and for nursing into strength the best feelings and sweetest affections of the human heart. The physical training of the Scottish population has been neglected. The education of degrading and every-day circumstances is proving more than a match for all the intellectual and moral advantages of the nation, and we are vainly imagining that school training is to counteract the training of homes and neighbourhoods, that are strangers to decency and comfort. If all Scotsmen get a smattering of learning, and are able to talk and dispute better than any poverty-stricken and fallen population in Great Britain, what avails it except to make them the more intensely to feel and resent their miseries? The schoolmaster has been abroad among the Scottish as he never was among the English masses – but what has he done to elevate the tens of thousand in our crowded cities and manufacturing villages in the scale of humanity? Has he trained them to wash their persons or to cleanse their dwellings – to prefer air and light to darkness and corruption? Has he made any homes to smile, or rendered the poor man's fireside the most attractive spot in all the poor man's world? If he has not cleansed even the outside of the man, how shall we hope he has elevated the inner man; and if has not been able to rouse him out of the filth, indolence, and apathy of his animal degradation, how can we hope that he is permanently elevated in his spiritual character?

'The State of Scottish Towns' (1847). *The North British Review*, 7.

6G                                                          Glasgow 1830s.

[Granny calls upon her daughter-in-law, Leezy. They discuss the new 'Infants' Training School', recently opened by David Stow and now being attended by Leezy's children]

*Leezy*: Now, Granny, ye're aye sae muckle in the *'preaching way'* whene'er ye meet a body, that ane can scarcely get a word o' plain truth about ony thing o' *importance* for ye. Ye speired at me what schule the weans were at. Now I'll tell ye, gin ye like. It's an Infant Schule, whar they learn hymns and sangs, counting wi' beeds, and clappin' o' hands, swinging on ropes, and bigging brigs wi' bricks, and heaps o' thae kind o' things.

*Granny*: And ca' ye that a schule, Leezy?

*Leezy*: Weel, our ain man – wasna – very – sure – about it – himsel'; but I wadna let him tak' them out for a wee, till we saw. Indeed, Geordie, wee laddie, wadna come out. He's now been there amaist a fortnight. He gangs half afore ten in the morning, and comes back at ane – then he tak's a bit o' bread, and aff like a whittrit again afore twa, syne, back at four-hours, just at the gloamin' time.

*Granny*: Leezy, Leezy, are ye acting right to let Mary and Geordie be sae muckle out o' your sight, and gang to a playing place like that, and ca't a schule? What gart ye send them there, ken ye?

*Leezy*: Weel, I'll tell ye, Granny. Ye see, twa-three o' the neebours' weans are at that schule, and enteeced them to gang ae day, and they plauged and deav'd my head a' the next day for siller, just to let them gang, for they got sic grand fun they said, marchin' and swingin' and singin', and I canna tell ye what a', that I was just obleeged to let them gang, their ain way – and when they gaed wi' the baubees in the morning, I was like to gang clean gyte (almost mad) wi' anger, for the maister sent them back wi' word to me to wash their faces cleaner by the afternoon; and now they daurna big ony dams, for they maun aye gang with clean hands and faces, and their hair weel kamed, neebor-like, ye ken. But – atween us twa, Granny – I hae na muckle objection to the change, for their bits o' legs and coat-tails are no sae aften draigled (thoroughly bespattered) as they used to be.

*Granny*: Ye have tauld me how ye sens them, but what gart ye send them to a place like that to be sae lang out o' your sight?

*Leezy*: Didna I tell ye, Granny, that they were amaist a' day playing down the wynd wi' the neebour's bairns, and they're nae mair nor that at the schule? And our Sandy, who has mair sense than me, speired about things the other day for twa minutes, and he finds they learn heaps o' things about perpetriculars and horizontails, which the weans sing, and point wi' the fingers, first straught up, syne straught afore them. Sandy found out as weel that ther was nae leein' nor swearin' in a' the schule, and that the true religion was learned there. At first, when he looked at them, he thought it was a 'gentle' schule; but the maister said, Wait a wee, and ye'll may-be see your ain just like the ithers. Syne the maister said (and Sandy thought it wasna far wrang), that cleanliness was neest to godliness.

*Granny*: I'm no just sure o' a' this wark, Leezy. The schule canna be the right sort, I'se warrant, when they hae sae muckle fun . . .

Stow, David (1860). *Granny and Leezy –*
*a Scottish Dialogue.* Glasgow, Longman and Roberts.

6H                                    Aberdeenshire, 1860s.

The greater number of the older schools were badly lighted and ventilated, and even in many of those of recent construction the light was admitted either at the roof or on the east or north side; showing that architects had not yet become sufficiently aware of the vast importance of affording the largest amount of sunlight and fresh air into schools, in order to maintain the health of teacher and scholars.

In most of the schools the furniture was objectionable: the desks were usually placed along the walls, or in parallel groups, in sufficient numbers to allow all the scholars, who were able, to write at one time; the seats were of uniform height, adapted to the size of children of twelve or thirteen years of age, so that those who were above that age had difficulty in disposing of their limbs, while those under it had their short legs dangling in the air, finding 'no resting-place for the sole of their feet'.

The small supply of educational apparatus was generally of inferior quality; the maps were old and tattered, and the blackboard had nearly become white. The books were ill adapted for elementary education. The infant classes were supplied with Primers containing the alphabet, and words of one syllable, which seemed more fitted to teach parrots to speak than intelligent children to read; while the further advanced had First and Second Reading Books, consisting of trash, sufficient to turn the appetite of the keenest scholar from the irksome task of learning to read . . .

The memory of the children was tasked with oral lessons in spelling and meanings of words nowhere to be found except in Butter's or Carpenter's Spelling Books. Copy lines of the largest size were given to the smallest children, with the shortest fingers; and no attention was ever paid to their mode of sitting or holding the pen. Indeed it was impossible for any teacher to regulate the movements of thirty or forty children seated at the writing-desk: so the writers were allowed to assume every possible ungainly attitude. Their arms spread wide on the table, their limbs as far apart under it, the fingers besmeared with ink, and the tongue protruding from the mouth, gave the idea that the performers were engaged in the most laborious employment.

The arithmetical books were generally far too difficult. Addition and Multiplication Tables were learned by rote, and sums in Addition were usually performed by a rapid process of counting the fingers, or dotting the slate with the slate pencil . . .

The ignorance of parents, and the want of a proper system, render long school-time necessary; and teachers, like donkey-drivers, know that the animals they overtask can only be made to perform their work by the infliction of physical pain; and if anything can excuse the frequent use of the taws, it is when the wearied scholar cannot be made otherwise to carry on his tiresome and hateful task.

Watson, (Sheriff William) (1863). *Elementary Education.* Aberdeen, pamphlet.


61                                                    Aberdeen, 1850/60s.


As you have asked me to write you my short biography, I will just begin. I was born in Aberdeen; my father was a weaver, but he deserted my mother, and she was left friendless. All that we hear now is, that he is married, and has a large family, and he is a photographer. When I was five months old, my mother had to go to her work, and my grandmother had to take care of me. At last I grew up, and thought myself very useful. I used to try and light the fire, but I found it rather difficult at first. My mother bought me a little tin mug: I was running round the house one day, when I fell, and the sharp edge struck my eye. I had to go to the doctor, and get a plaster on it. One night, at six o' clock, I went to meet my mother at the mill-gate, but I lost myself, and I began to cry, when a woman came to me, and asked what was the matter. I told her, and she took me home. I went to my aunt's room, and locked myself in; when they saw they could not get me out, they had to get a ladder, and open the window; at last I got out. After that we got a house down in Carmelite Street. I was put to a school down in Trinity Street, where I learned some of the letters. One day my mother gave me a penny to pay my teacher, but instead of doing that I went to the market and spent it. When I saw my grandmother, I ran and hid myself below one of the stalls. When I went home I got a whipping, and no dinner. I was six years old when I came to this school; I could neither read nor write, nor do anything. When I heard about geography, grammar, and arithmetic, I could not make out what they meant, but now I understand somewhat of them. I was at school one Sabbath, when a girl told me that my grandmother was dead. When I heard it I could not believe it. I went up to the house and found it true. Not long after her death my leg was hurt, which made me very unwell. I had to go to the hospital; I lay for a while there. At last I was obliged to get it cut off, to save my life. The day I left hospital I took the measles, and the dregs fell into my eyes; then I was quite blind, not knowing daylight from darkness. As I could not walk, I was very solitary, but for all I attended school. If it were not for our teacher and Dr. Pirie, I might have lost my eyesight altogether. All should be very thankful that they have every thing they need for their use. Some years after I lost my leg, my mother was washing a woman's floor, when a rusty needle stuck in her finger. She had to go the hospital, and she lay there ten weeks. Every Friday I went to see her, and she told me that it would grow no better, so she had to get it cut off. At last she came out, and a few months after she was back to her work. At school we play till nine o'clock, and we get our breakfast, and the little ones goes into the playground, and play till ten o'clock, and then we come in and get on our pinafores, then we all go to our proper seats, we sing a psalm, and then repeat the Lord's prayer; after that we read a chapter. When it is done we have to answer all the questions, and if we do not answer them we are kept in at night. On Monday and Thursday we get our arithmetic. On Tuesday we read our history books; after we read them, we have to write the outlines in our own words. Wednesday we get our grammar, and on Friday our geography. On Saturday we have to repeat the catechism, and a few verses out of the Bible. At twelve o'clock the oldest ones clean the school-room, &c. At one o'clock we get dinner, then we go home for the day, but on other days it is after 6 p.m. before we go home.

'A.H.' in Watson, (Sheriff) William (1864). *Autobiographies of Industrial School Children*. Aberdeen, pamphlet.

My beloved Instructress [mother] no doubt drew genuine satisfaction from seeing that her boy showed real anxiety about learning to read. She lost no time, but forthwith began her labour of love. As good luck would have it, our old friend, John Duncan, who was with us at Walton, had by this time recommenced work in my father's shop. He sympathized entirely with my mother's endeavours to instruct me. They held an educational counsel together, and resolved that my next lesson should be the 2nd chapter of the Gospel according to Matthew. Thirty years after this, John Duncan told me that by the time I had completed my sixth year, I was able to read fairly well in the New Testament . . .

It was now resolved that I should be sent to a Dame's School in Maver's Court, Holburn Street. The dame's name was Nannie Thomson. I got little good there, however. The school-room was small and Nannie smoked, not a short, but a long, black pipe that lay on the cheek of the fire as they called it. We often saw her lift the pipe and walk out, no doubt, to indulge in the weed. When she took me near her I smelt tobacco and didn't like it. She was very industrious, and to eek out her income Nannie knitted stockings, and while she was listening to our lessons she drove her knitting wires briskly. The only attraction about this seat of learning to me was that Nannie was a dealer in poultry as well as a teacher and stocking knitter. She kept the live-stock in the same cellar that she put her scholars in when she considered it necessary to imprison them for bad conduct. I was frequently detained in this house of correction, and on one occasion remember being able to make my escape by setting two hens to cackle so terribly that Nannie thought they were being killed, which led her to come and drive both me and the hens out of the cellar.

My next teacher was Johnny Bremner. His schoolhouse was in the middle of a row of red-tiled cottages at the south end of Hardgate. Like Nannie, he had to carry on his teaching operations in one room, but it was of considerable size. There were double writing desks round three sides of the room, and on both sides of the fireplace there were shelves for the school books, and a large jar with ink, which Johnny made himself. He was a picturesque figure was Johnny Bremner, for that reason alone I took to him at once. He dressed quite in the style of the period, in corduroy knee breeches with navy-blue stockings, a

buck vest, and blue coat with long swallow tails and gilt buttons, and a
dark orange-coloured napkin, adjusted about the neck after the fashion
of the parsons of that period, with a watch and chain from which was
suspended sundry gilt trinkets. On his head was a 'lum-hat' of which I
think it would be safe to say that it had seen

> 'Yon weary winter sun
> Twice twenty times return'.

The curriculum at Johnny's school consisted of lessons in reading in the
Proverbs of Solomon and in other parts of the Bible, and in the first and
second collections. For arithmetic, Gray's was the book used; and, in
writing, Johnny wrote fresh lessons in our writing books daily. There
were no steel pens then, and he made, himself, all our quill nebs as he
called them. The mode of dismissing the school on Saturdays was in its
way unique. About a quarter of an hour before the time for leaving, the
school door was thrown wide open and each boy had to go up to the
master bonnet in hand, and for the last thing he had to do, say the
Lord's Prayer. It generally happened that he began near the master's
desk with 'Our Father', and from there moved backwards towards the
door, which, when he reached, he commonly wheeled round, shouting
'Amen' as he left. In the winter time we each took peats with us for the
school fire. Towards the afternoons the poor old man frequently got
drowsy, and seated in his chair, he would fall sound asleep. On such
occasions he often got a rude awakening. The boys usually had some
powder about them, and they would make a hole in a piece of peat and
by means of a string attached to a bit of red hot wire pull it down on the
powder, with the result that need not be described. On such occasions
Johnny would belabour the whole school without distinction; at such
times he was very impartial. He had a habit of throwing his leather strap
at a boy when he wanted to whip him, meaning that the boy should
carry it to him and submissively accept the consequences . . .

I think it right now to record my belief that Johnny Bremner, as a
teacher, made the very best of the means and equipment that were at
his disposal, and that he managed to turn out boys grounded in the
three Rs better than is frequently done now under our modern system,
with its magnificent and expensive appliances.

My next move was an important one for me. There were half-timers
in those days. I was engaged as message boy in the autumn of 1830 to

a shoemaker. My wages was 1s. a week with shoes free, and I was allowed three hours' absence each day for school. The Lancastrian school in Blackfriars Street was chosen for me. The headmaster there was Mr Peter Robertson, who afterwards became the chief of the West-end Academy . . .

The plan of our school lessons was this: – The school consisted of nine different classes. The first class learned the alphabet by tracing the letters on sand by the pupil's finger. This had the double advantage of imparting a knowledge of the ordinary Roman letters and the letters used in ordinary writing as well.

When the work of the school was in full operation, the classes were broken up into groups; the monitor who was the pupil-teacher of that period, stood in the centre of each section with a pointer in his hand, to which he drew the attention of his pupils to the lesson of the day. It might be on the blackboard, written with chalk, or on a large board on which a printed sheet was displayed. While this was going on either Mr Robertson or the chief monitor made a tour of inspection from class to class . . .

I soon afterwards left the Lancastrian school, and undertook the duty of reading the Aberdeen newspapers, namely the *Aberdeen Journal* and *Aberdeen Herald*, to the men in my father's workshop. Previous to this they read turn-about, but when they found that I could read fairly well they offered me a small sum weekly for reading to them – that arrangement suited my taste and saved their working time . . .

In connection with our daily readings in the shop, there was now another great treat preparing for me. The men had been considering for some time whether they could afford to take in the *Weekly Dispatch*, the great Radical London weekly paper of the day. A writer of that time said of it the *Dispatch* addresses itself chiefly to the operatives and artizans, to whose feelings and comprehensions its strong, rough, unceremonious mode of dealing with principles, potentates, and powers that be, seem peculiarly appropriate. With the two Aberdeen papers and this great luminary from London I thought our intellectual stores very ample.

Lindsay, William (1898). *Some Notes:
Personal and Public.* Aberdeen, privately printed.

1821–90: involved in radical local politics and general campaigns for workers' rights; journalist and newspaper proprietor.

# 7 BOARD SCHOOLS AND BURGH ACADEMIES

*School Days Forty Years ago in the Calton*:
George Henderson, 1912
*Second Report by Her Majesty's Commissioners
apointed to inquire into the Schools in Scotland*: 1867
*The Tenth Annual Report and Remarks of the School Attendance
Committee*: William Mitchell, 1883
*My Seventy Years*: William Haddow, 1943
*The Woman Question*: Educational News, 1899
*Presidential Address, EIS Annual Congress*:
William Blackstock, 1899
*As I Recall*: John Boyd Orr, 1966
*The Clacken and the Slate*: Magnus Magnusson, 1974
*Address at prize-giving, Glasgow High School*:
Sir Henry Craik, 1889
*Opening of Insch Public School*: Sir Henry Craik, 1890

Figure 12. **Harris Academy, Dundee: Infant Department, 1916** If the classroom aids –
the abacus and improving prints – speak of traditional attitudes, the 'action song' indicates a
willingness to experiment with a more child-centred approach. *Dundee City Libraries*

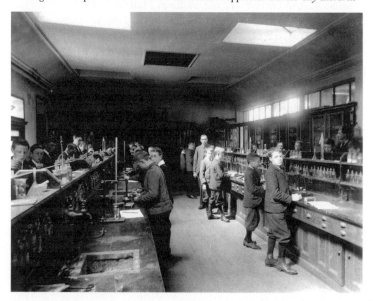

Figure 13. **Harris Academy, Dundee: senior boys' science class, 1916** Further up the
school, the boys are at work in a laboratory where the equipment is intended to enable this
'Higher Grade' school to offer a credible academic alternative to the 'Higher Class'
secondary, such as the nearby Dundee High School. *Dundee City Libraries*

The Education Act (Scotland) of 1872 declares that 'the means of procuring an efficient education may be furnished and made available to the whole people of Scotland'.

The noble simplicity of these words pledged, after decades of patchwork voluntary effort, of sectarian schemes and private ventures, the instatement of a truly national system. Much, however, would depend upon the precise application of that 'efficient', and what was to be understood by the 'whole' people.

The legislators had been guided by a series of official inquiries. Known collectively as the *Argyll Commission* (1865–68), reports were made on the 'Lowland Country Districts', 'Hebrides', 'Glasgow', 'Burgh and Middle Class Schools'. The separating of Glasgow from the Lowland rural parishes demonstrates the division that had evolved between the established agrarian communities and the newly industrialised districts, while the label 'burgh' and 'middle-class' points to a further differentiation, one that was based on a, by now, institutionalised sense of social class.

In the cities, few could now look to send their children to their burgh school. The level of fees, a starting age of, typically, nine, a single sex intake and a syllabus that emphasised the classics rather than the practical, all served to exclude any but the relatively well-to-do. Not only that, in the larger, more economically complex manufacturing centres, the inhabitants had become increasingly stratified, both with regard to district and to occupation. The *Commission* noted that the landed aristocracy had got into the way of packing their sons off to the improving atmosphere of an English 'Public' school, while the labourer's offspring was likely to squeeze into the church 'Session' school or to pay his twopence-halfpenny for a week's letters at some backstreet venture place – or, simply while away the days on the streets or at menial under-age employment.

Certainly none of that class was present in October 1824, when, amidst the crescents and the squares of the New Town, Sir Walter Scott had declared the privately funded Edinburgh Academy open. Gathered before him was the first intake of young gentlemen – the sons of mercantile figures, doctors, lawyers and military officers.

*The Scots Magazine* approved: the elegantly classical building housed 'a greater number of educational advantages than any similar institution in this part of the United Kingdom'. The placing was important: if the Academy was meant to be a national adornment, it was also one that would take as its reference points Westminster, Charterhouse, Eton.

Eighteen months on, *The Scots Magazine* reported another academic arrival in the city. 'The New System of Education' is what the title announces – but this exemplar is no Academy. In this case, the challenge is not to polish manners and accents; rather it is to persuade the intake to come at all – and thus forsake 'the embryo blackguards prowling our streets, with lawless desires brooding in their breasts and horrid swearing in their mouths'. For this is no porticoed West-end edifice but St George's, a church-run district school, crammed into one of the darker recesses of Scotland's capital city. Its curriculum will be based on practical objects, meaningful to the labouring classes.

In these two buildings, less than one mile apart, is mapped out the pair of institutional traditions which were to pervade the urban scene: the downmarket district elementary, embattled within its grid of unsympathetic streets; the salubriously located West-end establishment, where stately lines and collegial ethos reflect, not confront, the residences that stretch out on either side.

As with the Academy, the urban schools built by mid-century philanthropic and ecclesiastical effort were designed to project a consistent tone, but reformatory rather than developmental. Their pupils were to be encased within a specifically constructed environment of rectangular regularity and vigilant control. The fact that economy was an important factor consolidated these intentions. Schools had to be so arranged as to enable the greatest quantity of children to be processed with the maximum dispatch and uniformity of outcome.

What this represented was, in fact, the industrialisation of teaching. Thomas Markus in his 'The school as machine: working-class Scottish education' (1982) has demonstrated how the very architecture of the school plant and the configuration of its classrooms, with their tiers of iron-bolted desks, combined into a total expression of mechanistic regularity. They were compounds where the values of deference, discipline and conformity were to be stamped upon the raw human material from the massed tenements.

The extent to which, as the century moved on, this was so may be glimpsed in an account George Henderson gives of his days at a Free Church school on the eve of the Education Act (**7A**). What strikes him, as he recalls the strict geometrical lines of his own schooling, is the completeness with which the outside world is shut out. The young George daily walked to school through a vibrant mix of street life and industrial activity. But, within the classroom walls, there was no natural science, no art from life, only a geography based upon the remotest corners of the Empire. This was a place where the master ruled according to a Calvinist distrust of human nature, especially in its unreconstructed childish forms.

George Henderson's place was, however, far from being the worst that Glasgow could offer. When it turns to the 'Private Venture School', the *Commission* makes spectacularly grim reading (**7B**). Clearly, the term covered a great range of institutions which, in quality and ethos, were related to a market which was demarked by social class: in contrast to the nether regions of Calton, for example, the 'rich and fashionable' Blythswood is listed as having 22 private schools – all 'good' – and an almost 100 per cent attendance rate. In any case, the private sector only accounted for 19 per cent of the Glasgow school population as opposed to 36 per cent at the kind of church session institution which George Henderson went to. The *Commission* has devoted its lurid eye-witness to these grotesque, but minority, examples in order to drive its conclusion: 'We can only say, for the sake of all concerned, teachers and taught alike, that the sooner private venture schools for the lowest classes cease to exist the better'.

The imaginative power, however, which the official description carries is such that its example spreads beyond the immediate strategic intention. The inner city schools, and the unnamed ragged hordes who cram its spaces or roam the streets and vennels in its stead, are to be associated with the worst maladies of nineteenth century urban existence- dirt, smell, overcrowding, lawless poverty and – most frightening of all – an uncontainable, swarming anonymity. If this depiction gave impetus to the reformers' case for a publicly controlled system, the Problem of the City was being projected in ways that would play upon its social divisions and set a limit upon the solutions which would be sought for their treatment.

The specific measures of the 1872 Act promised well enough: locally elected School Boards permitted to levy a rate to finance accommodation and staffing; mandatory attendance from ages 5 to 13. The Government would award annual grants to individual schools to secure proper standards. Its team of inspectors would monitor these matters; they would be employees of the 'Scotch Education Department'.

If the powers of the Church and the magistrates had now been swept away, the old parish pattern still remained, since the new Boards would be based upon their divisions. There were now 987 of them but the largest by far was Glasgow. At its first meeting, the Board had elected the self-made businessman, William Mitchell, as Convener of its Attendance Committee. In 1899, when he came to his twenty-sixth and final report, he felt entitled to boast of all that had been accomplished in that time. When he came into office, the attendance rate was 40 per cent; now it was 89. The Board had inherited 200 buildings – 'the majority bad' – with room for 53, 796 children; the city now had accommodation for 110,000.

To get to that point, they had first transferred, leased, patched and improvised property; then they had built, built and built again. By the time of Mitchell's valedictory report, Glasgow had 57 new public schools. It was an epic achievement which was replicated nationally: by the end of the first decade of the new era, Scotland possessed 970 of them.

The Glasgow Board had also persuaded the people to attend them. It had been done by the deployment of Attendance Officers and a regime of fines, but also by visiting deprived homes and by turning the schools into a sanctuary of care and warmth. It is a theme which Mitchell returns to repeatedly in his annual reports (7C).

In the face of such multiple deprivation the concept of universal education began to expand. Thought began to move from the simple provision of places to the means of ensuring that all the children would be able to benefit from the opportunities now being offered them. Awareness of the wretched state of young working-class health was further aroused by the level of rejections of Boer war recruits. The nation suddenly discovered that it could not expect to breed an Imperial race from undernourished children subsisting in slums. Physical education entered the curriculum. The Government's 1908 Education (Scotland) Act gave Boards extensive powers of medical inspection and treatment.

School meals became widespread; in many areas, the supply of clothes, footwear, even fresh air holidays, was put in place, sometimes through charitable effort (a mid-day bowl of soup at a halfpenny), increasingly by the Board itself. In retrospect, these developments might seem to be inevitable features of the modern industrialised state. But, at the time, many saw the extension of the school into a welfare agency as an affront to the nation's respect for personal responsibility, as founded on Presbyterian self-governance. A later Glasgow Board member, William Haddow, gives a rich account of the struggle to persuade Church and philanthropic prejudice. (**7D**).

A further challenge was teacher supply. In the larger parish school it had become common for the 'dominie' to be assisted by an infant mistress and, perhaps, a 'pupil-teacher' who, again, was frequently a young female. It was this gender which was to enable the now universal system to 'man' the Board schools. The network of training centres was extended into all the cities. Its intensively utilitarian two-year courses began to produce the required numbers; the teaching force became feminised. By 1911, only 30 per cent of its certificated members were male – but their average salary ran at double (£145 to £72) and their chances of promotion at considerably more than that. Mrs. Skea's election represents a rare, and characteristically contentious, moment of female triumph (**7E**).

Elsewhere, by the First World War, the peace had been won. The legislation was in place; the Glasgow Education Department alone had a staff of 16 medical officers, a team of dentists, oculists, 72 nurses, a dermatologist, mental health consultants and was handing out 25,000 hot meals a day, as well as the morning bottle of milk.

The purpose behind such technological modernity was to counter the social problems that bedevilled children's home lives. All that was to be cleansed away by the new city architect designed, purpose-built school blocks. Like the municipal hospitals which were being assembled at the same time, these were put in place to contain the deserving, the unwashed and the unruly alike, within the same four-square arrangement of solid, stony design. Such buildings were also required to respect the ratepayer's purse. Two, three storeys, came to be standard, with accommodation for upwards of one thousand inmates.

It was all undeniably, enduringly impressive. One hundred years later, many of the new Board schools were still in use, still standing as island fortresses within enclosures of waist-high wallings, the tops implanted with a line of pointed iron railing, an acre of asphalt playground behind. Inside, the classrooms were ordered into a hierarchy of floors – Infant to Junior to Senior – which ran round the great central hall, useful alike for morning assembly and weekly drill.

If the circumstances had been more relaxed and spacious, the Board system could have planted, into each district, a school which would have been welcomed as an intimate part of its communal life. But now, instead, it erected buildings which reared hard-faced above it, there to act as a place of dutiful attendance and daily sabbatarian discipline. In this, it expressed the sense of institutional mission which had fired the clergymen, the university professors and the public-spirited businessmen who had sat upon the early Boards and who had had to grapple, not only with the abrupt arithmetic of demand, supply and local rates, but also an intake so unversed in the civilised, hygienic ways that they could only be dealt with as the savage young of a dark and unreclaimed territory.

They built their schools to formalise the differences rather than to enter into a communal intimacy. The School Board era was one of great, even heroic advances. The schools it built, the schemes it introduced, the values it implanted constituted an experience which drove deep into the formative consciousness of generations of young Scots. Given such a role, it is not surprising that the attitudes which it provoked should be so ambivalent. For those who, like the President of the EIS in 1899, could recollect the chaotic days before, 1872 brought in a new era of social justice and individual fulfilment (**7F**); to an idealistic young man like Boyd Orr, the unremitting regimentation only further dispirited the existences of his young charges (**7G**).

Meanwhile, the example set by Edinburgh Academy had also taken hold. Boyd Orr's reference to 'the system' points to an educational structure which had become more, not less, deterministic and socially divided since 1872. Although the Act had set up a network of schools which all could attend, its provisions had also recognised the role of a superior category of public school, one which would be expected to operate to the same standards as those attached to the host of independently funded establishments which, by now, had sprung up in imitation of the Academy's refined model. A select group of 'Higher Class Public Schools' were to be singled out – the Grammars of Aberdeen and Paisley were among them, alongside both Edinburgh and Glasgow High Schools – which could be regarded as supporting an advanced 'Secondary' curriculum. The designation and the selectivity indicate that the Scotch Education Department wanted the people to think of the ordinary Board School as being confined to a more basic 'Elementary' schooling.

In the coming decades, the SED would admit further numbers to the 'higher class' Secondary ranks – but, by 1918, they still numbered no more than 56. Meanwhile the Edinburgh Academies, augmented by the transformation of most of the old charitable 'Hospitals' for poor and orphaned children – Robert Gordon's, George Heriot's, Hutcheson's – into fee-paying establishments, patronised by the urban bourgeoisie, continued to cultivate their own corporate magnificence. During the years when the Boards were struggling to put together bricks, pupils and disinfectant, the school in New Town Edinburgh was taking on all the adornments of an English, not a Scottish, public school (**7H 1, 2**).

That this was the company which the SED wished its own centres of Secondary excellence to keep is shown by the exhortations which its Secretary handed out, along with their prizes, to the young gentlemen of Glasgow High (**7I**). The following year, he travelled up to Buchan to preside over the opening of a new village school (**7J**). But Insch was to be an 'ordinary' example, one that had to be judged by its capacity to impart the three Rs, the utilities of manual work – and the facts of a geography which, despite the location in his anecdote, he insists on pronouncing 'Colonial'.

7A                                                         Glasgow, 1860s/70s.

Chalmers street, where our school was situated, is a little street connecting Anderson street and Claythorn street, and parallel to the Gallowgate. The school consisted of a two storey building at right angles to the street, with an annex a single storey in height on the street line. There was a direct entrance to the playground on the west side of the school, and on the east side access was attained to the first floor through a small court by a door on the left, while an enclosed outside stair on the right led to the second floor. This was the advanced school of my day. The school buildings thus formed adjacent sides of a rectangle, of which the remaining portion was completed by the playground. On the sides of the rectangle not bounded by the school, there were various buildings, the most important being a 'sweetie' factory. This, needless to say, was a most satisfactory arrangement . . .

Anderson street was always an interesting street to me. On the left was a dyework and on the right a forge, where, like many a child before and since, I

> Looked in at the open door
> And loved to see the flaming forge,
> And hear the bellows roar
> And catch the burning sparks that flew
> Like chaff from a threshing floor.

Horse-shoeing and fastening the iron tyres on cart wheels were responsible for long delays both going to and returning from school.

Opposite the school, also, there was a lime-kiln which enabled us on our own account to make slaked lime without knowing what we were doing. It was sufficient for us that we transformed the 'sivers' [drains] into live volcanoes, while we watched with never-failing interest the whole mass heaving like a miniature Vesuvius.

It is strange that I can recollect no information vouchsafed to us on natural science, as one might have expected where illustrations could have been had at our very door. Of course nature study then was not, and the 'three Rs' ruled with an iron hand . . .

My first school book was what we called the 'Sixpenny'. I recollect yet some of the stories with corresponding illustrations, the one uppermost in my memory being the veracious record of the mouse freeing the lion from captivity by gnawing the ropes which bound it.

I had, however, long before school time dabbled in books on my own account, an illustrated copy of Bunyan's works having been an early favourite of mine, when I was wont to lie prone on the floor, following the story by aid of the pictures as well as I could. I soon became familiar, not only with the 'Pilgrim's Progress', but also with the 'Holy War', by the same author. As a vivid picture of the Commonwealth and its opponents, it is, doubtless, a valuable contribution to the literature of the period, but, needless to say, this did not trouble me then.

There was another copy of Bunyan in my father's house which I think I must have got read to death. It had little wood-cuts, in which the devil and the devils were realistically rendered. There are no plates such as these now, with their quite impossible little fiends.

The schoolmaster, during my first experience of the upper school, belonged to that type, now happily dead, who were wont to convert school hours into a time of weeping and wailing, a lurid, and as some may think, a fitting background to the Shorter Catechism and the joys of the elect . . .

Of the methods of teaching in my time, while it might be claimed that the head master was able to exert his influence more powerfully than at present, through his being brought more constantly into contact with the senior pupils, yet this advantage was largely neutralised by a total lack of appeal to their observation. We were drilled in the elements of grammar, geography, reading, writing and arithmetic in a way that would have pleased the practical mind of Mr Gradgrind.

Music and drawing came in as interludes. In music the constant use of the modulator was excellent practice for the ear, but drawing failed for the general reason already given that there was no appeal in its teaching to the world outside. Consequently, we were forced to content ourselves with making more or less fair copies of intricate ornamental forms without getting any insight into its use in making the hand the servant of the eye in all that we saw around us, and thus we failed to get an acquisition which would have been of great service to most of us.

Writing was another part of the curriculum which caused us 'dule and sorrow'. We were supposed to take a certain time to each line, and under threat, we were not supposed to begin another line until 'next line' was called. This led to endless dissimulation. In my anxiety to get done with a disagreeable task, I generally contrived to get the line done in the fourth of the time, the remainder being spent in make-believe, or, if it were absolutely necessary to avoid trouble, in beginning and ending another line . . .

Perhaps the most successful subject in my experience was arithmetic, not because the methods of teaching it were better, but that, being a distinctly mechanical subject, the simple rules were capable of being firmly inculcated by persistent drill.

> Henderson, George (1912). *School Days*
> *Forty Years ago in the Calton.* Uddingston.

A personal advocate for working-class self-improvement, Henderson was speaking to his local Library Association.

The school-room is on the area floor, and is reached from the street by a long stone stair. When visiting the place we found the master engaged, assisted by some of the bigger boys, in 'flushing' the pavement with water. On entering the schoolroom, we were well-nigh suffocated with the noxious smell. In a room 27 feet by 21, and with a very low ceiling, 170 boys and girls were jammed together. It was with great difficulty a passage into the interior could be obtained; and the heat and the effluvium were so overpowering, that before we could attempt anything like an examination, it was necessary to turn more than a half of the school into the street. On inquiring of the master, with a natural air of surprise, how he could tend classes where he had not room to turn his foot, he pointed to a corner, where, by displacing its occupants, he could acquire a couple of square yards of room, and in this nook, we endeavoured to make ourselves acquainted with the instruction communicated. And, as might be expected, it was sorry enough. The master had been unfortunate in business, and betook himself to his present occupation, as the only one within his reach, for which his inclination and abilities qualified him. He admitted he could not do the children justice in so confined a place, and with not even a monitor to aid him. Nevertheless, he has struggled on for several years, the number of his scholars only being limited by the extent of the accommodation. He was satisfied, he said, that, if he could afford a better schoolroom, he could gather three times the number of children he now takes charge of. Notwithstanding they are of the most ragged order, and hail chiefly from the neighbourhood of the Saltmarket, he has no pupils (he assures us) paying less than 3d., while nearly a half pay 4d. a week. This is one of the cases which illustrates the necessity of an education that will reach such children as attend this school. Swarms of them are growing up without instruction to fit them for occupations above hewers of wood and drawers of water, or to give them a taste for reading, and make it other than a drudgery and a task. We may not estimate the importance to the country and the benefit to themselves, were these hordes of neglected children – a representative section of which we have now described – reared in the knowledge and practice of virtue, of which a sound education forms so essential and pervading an element.

Education Commission (Scotland). *Second Report by Her Majesty's Commissioners appointed to inquire into the Schools in Scotland.* (1867).

In many rooms no furniture at all; and the families, including men and women, and children, huddled together at night on such straw or rags as they can gather. This bareness of any kind of furnishing enables the occupants to flit about from one house and one district to another with the greatest possible ease, and there is a constant fluctuation going on, enabling the inmates to thwart the School Board Officers at every turn.

The houses are close and unhealthy; no conveniences existing for the ordinary decencies of life without going down long stairs to back courts, and from this and other causes the rooms are frequently reeking with malodorous stench. In certain buildings no provision for such purposes exists at all, even in the lanes or courts below. Separate conveniences for women and children are all but unknown.

The stairs, closes, and lanes leading to these houses are very often dark and filthy. I entered more than one large tenement over a dung-heap lying at the entrance. An abominable practice may be observed on the stair-landing, where the jaw-box [sink] is made the receptacle of all the liquid filth from the numerous houses adjoining . . .

As to clothing, the miserable character of this may be seen at certain Schools where the lowest class are to be found, the absence of shoes and stockings being a common feature, but a large number are kept back from School for this very reason, that they have no decent clothing or shoes. If they have they are not infrequently in pawn to supply the pressing wants of the family, or to provide strong drink for the parents. Cases have been reported where the clothing of such Children is never taken off, and other cases where only the ragged outer garment is laid aside at night. As to washing, either of skin or clothes, this is too often omitted altogether. The Officers report broken-out heads as a frequent consequence of this state of things, and the abundance of vermin need not be surprising

Poverty, grinding poverty, meets us at every turn. What pale, pinched faces have many of these poor Children, whom we must compel to go to School. Scores of times have they been brought before us when they have scarcely broken their fast, and when their little bare feet have been led to the defaulters' meetings along the frosted streets, exciting more pity for their want of food and clothes than for their want of Schooling . . .

Is it to be wondered at that the Children so fed, so clothed, so lodged and flitting about, as they do, from house to house, and district to district, should be irregular in their attendance at School, or tardy in reaching the Fifth and Sixth Standards? I confess I am filled with amazement when I consider the number who do attend with a fair amount of regularity.

Mitchell, William (1883). *The Tenth Annual Report and Remarks of the School Attendance Committee.* Glasgow.

7D                                    Glasgow; Edinburgh, 1900s.

The first centre we visited was one in the Anderston district. There was a small hall – situated over a disused public house – a nice environment for children! It was a cold, snowy winter day, and a crowd of poorly clad and bootless children were queued up waiting for the hour of twelve to strike, when the door would be opened. The plight of these children was a sight never to be forgotten and even my very conservative colleagues were evidently horrified. But Scene 11. was just as bad.

When we climbed up the dirty, rickety wooden stair, we found a filthy room where soap and water had been strangers for many months, if not years. Backless forms were ranged in rows on which were tiny bowls of soup, a metal spoon and a piece of bread. As the children entered the hall they knelt down on the dirty floor in front of a basin of soup and eagerly supped the contents. It was not a pleasant sight, and it was quite evident that the other members of the Committee were shocked at what they saw . . .

Before the Bill was introduced in Parliament, the Secretary for State sent a draft copy to School Boards for their criticism, and a Conference was held in Edinburgh for that purpose. And what a meeting! All the Ministerial Chairmen of various denominations and all the Free and Auld Kirk Elders were present in full force, all wanted to air their views, and soon the meeting was a battle of tongues and a rabble of disorder – so much so that I told them they would disgrace a Dockers' Meeting.

By the time the Chairman and Secretary were appointed, speeches made explaining why the meeting was called, and the first few pages of the Bill was passed without very much comment, it was one o'clock and an adjournment was made for lunch. We trooped over to the

Caledonian Hotel, on the invitation of the Edinburgh School Board, where we found a magnificent six or seven course meal.

By two o'clock we found our way back to the Conference Chamber, and then the fun, or rather the riot, started. By a curious coincidence, the first clause on the Bill to be discussed was the famous Clause Six giving power to feed, clothe, and medically inspect school children. The newly well-fed Ministers and Elders would have none of it. Everybody seemed to be on their feet at once wanting to make speeches. They yelled and shouted at the poor Chairman and the whole Conference was in a state of pandemonium.

Amidst the babble of voices one could hear such phrases as 'Breaking up the Homes'; 'Taking away Parental Responsibility'; 'Pauperising the Children'; 'Socialism'; 'Charity could do all that was necessary'. Then religious bigotry crept in. Many said that they might accept the clause if it applied to Protestant Children but Roman Catholic Children must be excluded.

Haddow, William (1943). *My Seventy Years*. Glasgow, Robert Gibson and Son.

1865-1945: founder member Independent Labour Party and prominent in Glasgow politics; from his base on the Board, campaigned for range of welfare issues affecting children and working-class amelioration.

7E                                                    Aberdeen, 1899.

A joint meeting of the Aberdeen and Kincardine O'Neil branches was afterwards held to nominate a member for the General Committee of the Institute . . .

Miss WALKER, Free Normal, in the name of the women teachers of Aberdeen and vicinity, nominated Mrs Skea. Their reasons for supporting the canditature of a woman were three. In the first place, the interests of women demanded it. While she frankly and fully admitted that men are the best judges of classical and scientific subjects, she as fully maintained that women are the only persons capable of bringing about much-needed reforms in the teaching and examining of what might be called the domestic subjects – cookery, laundry, needlework, to say nothing of kindergarten work, infant school life, and the physical education of girls. Secondly, the grievances of women teachers cried out for it. Setting aside the burning questions of salary and the pension scheme, she held that the grievances under which so many women are now labouring, in the remote and outlying districts especially, which arise either from the laziness and selfishness of headmasters, or from the intolerance and ignorance of illiterate, narrow-minded, members of School Boards – (hear, hear, and laughter) – would be reduced to a minimum were there only one or more large-hearted, prudent and sympathetic women on the committee, to whom their timid, retiring sisters might unburden their wrongs. And, in the third place, the welfare of the Educational Institute required it. The necessity of the presence of a lady on the committee having been thus demonstrated, Miss Walker submitted that the claims of Mrs Skea to the appointment were overwhelming.

Mr FORBES seconded the nomination.

Mr J. C. ANDERSON moved the re-election of Mr D. V. Lothian. Mr Robb, King Street, seconded.

Mr R. M. LITTLEJOHN moved the election of Mr George Fenton, and Mr Johnson, Broomhill, seconded.

Mr FENTON nominated Mr J. C. Anderson, but Mr Anderson declined (Applause).

Amid some considerable feeling – to an outsider, inexplicable – the meeting proceeded to the vote . . . The result of the vote was smartly announced as follows –

Mrs Skea–69 votes
Mr Lothian–39 "
Mr Fenton–36 "

Then, amid considerable applause from the ladies, arose the cry of 'another vote'. Another vote was taken accordingly between Mrs Skea and Mr Lothian, with the following result:

Mrs Skea–69 votes
Mr Lothian–65 "

By this it appeared that 10 'male' votes had been dropped – Mrs Skea's vote remaining the same as on the first occasion. The Secretary, in reference to some murmuring, said the scrutineers had faithfully and accurately summed the vote. The only explanation was that ten members had abstained from voting.

Mrs SKEA thanked her supporters, declaring she would go to Edinburgh as the ladies' representative. She was not one that would go there and not argue their cause – (hear, hear) – she only hoped she would be discreet enough not to spoil it. (Applause).

This was all the business.

'The Women Question' (1899). *Educational News*, 4 September.


7F                                                          Greenock, 1899.


We began school in a weaver's shop, which had been converted to educational purposes simply by the substitution of desks for looms. It had an earthen floor, a stove at one end, which received each morning a contribution of slate pencils and slate fragments, that we might enjoy their crackling during the only quiet portion of the day, the time of prayer; and at the other end was a lofty desk, with a formidable cane lying over it; for our master had a terrible proneness to pass *verbis ad verbera* [from words to blows]. The street-boys, who enjoyed that freedom from the restraints of school cruelly denied to us by our parents, kept in evidence at our windows, hooted at our door, and led us a wretched life, when, like a Highland torrent, we sailed forth at intervals to play in the public street, our only playground. The roaring din of that school, three or four classes shouting at one time, is in our ears still. We advanced from class to class, we know not how, picking up crumbs of knowledge without explanation or aid from the teacher who, like Dryden's Alexander, 'Sate, aloft in awful state', and merely punished us if ever we ceased to roar. The din was reckoned the measure of our progress. We believe this condition of things prevailed in the adventure schools throughout the land. Any place was good enough for a school . . . And any one was good enough to set up as schoolmaster. The halt, the maimed, the lame, the 'stickit minister', took to teaching as an unfailing *dernier ressort*.

No doubt the Parochial and Burghal Schools and Schoolmasters occupied a higher plane; but, unfortunately, we had no experience of these. Yet, to them, also, vast changes have come, all in the way of educational advance. Even Greenock was no Paradise for the teacher; and, by implication, school would not have many Elysian features for the scholars. We find the Grammar School rector, John Wilson, saying of his work – 'I am compelled to bawl myself hoarse to wayward brats; to cultivate sand; to wash Ethiopians – for all the dreary days of an obscure life' . . .

The primary schools which now, like the night-lamps of our towns, light up the vista alike in the quiet country road and in the busy city thoroughfare throughout all the land, are unrivalled in architecture, in equipment, and, we venture to say also, in educational results, among all the nations of the world. Teachers are for the most part well trained for their work - the physically, mentally, morally incompetent being carefully excluded. How sweet and easy is discipline now, compared with what it once was! The obstinacy, the trickery, the disorder and noise that used to prevail are known no more. For the young child, school has become a Kindergarten. The attempt is made to realize the poet's fancy: 'Heaven lies about us in our infancy'. Our girls are being well prepared in sewing, cooking, laundry classes, for the life-work before them.

Blackstock, William (1899). Presidential Address, EIS Annual Congress. *Educational News*, 7 January.

7G                                        Glasgow; Saltcoats, Ayrshire, 1900s.

Immediately after graduating in 1902 I applied to the Glasgow School Board for a job and was given one in a school in the slums. The playground was a small area laid with concrete. The rooms were overcrowded, and the children were ill-clad. Looking back now, I realize that the majority of them were obviously suffering from malnutrition and some of them from actual hunger. Some came to school with no breakfast, and others with only tea and bread and butter. Going round between the seats one could see the lice crawling on their heads and on their clothing. We were supposed to teach them grammar, arithmetic and all the other subjects in the educational curriculum. I went home the first night feeling physically sick and very depressed. I had another look at the school the next day and came to the conclusion that there was nothing I could do to relieve the misery of the poor children, so I sat down and sent in my resignation. I returned home to work in my father's business where I could make £3 a week instead of a little less than £2 a week which was the remuneration of a university graduate school-teacher at that time. The work was much more enjoyable than trying to forcibly feed education down the throats of children who did not want it and received little or no benefit from it.

132

After three or four months working with my hands I thought it was time to go back to teaching for a bit to give some return for the scholarship, and was appointed to the Kyleshill School in Saltcoats about seven miles from where we lived, which meant I was able to stay at home. This was a school in the east end with children from the poorer part of the town. I was given the senior pupils aged from twelve to fourteen years. Nearly all the children came from poor homes and were compelled to start work as soon as they left school at fourteen, or earlier if they could get exemptions. As none of them was going to university or even a secondary school there seemed little point in teaching them formal grammar, higher arithmetic and other subjects needed for examinations. The more common sense view seemed to me to give them as pleasant a time in school as possible and not set them home lessons which could not be done properly since the only table in the whole house was the kitchen table.

Although these children were all from the lower income groups they were by no means inferior in mental ability to the children from better-off families. At one of the local teachers' meetings – which I seldom attended – I heard some disparaging remarks made about the poor school I was in, and wondered what could be done to show that these children were as clever as those in the other schools, including the fee-paying schools. I discovered a way through an endowment which gave six bursaries to school children in the area. I picked out four of my cleverest boys, told them to send in their names for the bursary examination, and then kept them in after school hours for about half-an-hour for three weeks before the examination teaching them the subjects I should have been giving them if I had adhered to the curriculum. The boys obtained the first, second, fifth and sixth places in the examination. This result gave an increased feeling of self-respect to the senior pupils and to the teachers in the school. It was obvious that the system of primary school education at that time lost the country the services of many potential first-class leaders from the poorer ranks of society.

Orr, John Boyd (1966). *As I Recall*. London, MacGibbon and Kee.

1880–1971: soon left teaching for medicine; became internationally famous nutritionist; Nobel Peace Prize 1949.

**1)** Even a bare summary of what he [R. J. Mackenzie, Rector Edinburgh Academy, 1888–1901] achieved during those thirteen years of reconstruction is staggering:

He successfully launched the Preparatory School.
He built a science laboratory and made science compulsory.
He established an Upper Seventh, and encouraged pupils to enter the Academy earlier and leave it later.
He enforced a system of promotion by merit, reducing the size of classes, and reorganised them into A and B levels.
He started the school Boarding Houses.
He made sports a compulsory part of the curriculum.
He bought a new playing-field, New Field.
He built a gymnasium, and started gymnastic displays.
He introduced a system of school prefects, and called them by a Greek name, *Ephors*.
He created a new sense of discipline inside and outside the school – parents had to conform to it, too.
He insisted on an official school head-dress.
He started a school choir and sang leading roles in it himself.
He started a school orchestra.
He composed the music for the school song, *Floreat Academia*.
He launched *The Edinburgh Academy Chronicle*.
He revived the school library.
He started a school museum and established a fund to maintain it.
He established regular productions of Greek plays in Greek.
He started regular Academical Reunions involving the school.
He fostered enthusiasm and loyalty amongst Academicals, helped revive the Academical Club, and urged the establishments of an Endowment Fund . . .

**2)**

## FLOREAT ACADEMIA

*The Text*                              *The 'Crib'*

1. Floreat Academia,                    1. Floreat Academia,
    Mater alma, mater pia:                  Mater alma, mater pia:

*134*

| | |
|---|---|
| Huic paremus, hanc amanus, | Love and homage we are bringing, |
| Ergo fortiter canamus | Eager to be loudly singing – |
| 'Floreat Academia'. | 'Floreat Academia'. |

| | |
|---|---|
| 2. Domi suboles est nota, | 2. Sons afar her fame are telling, |
| Atque loca per remota: | Sons at home her glory swelling; |
| Hic et illic gloriantur | Each one proud that he was reckoned |
| Quia nostri nominantur . . . | As a 'geit' or as a 'second' . . . |

| | |
|---|---|
| 4. Hi complexi sunt honorem | 4. Some achieved respected stations, |
| Pacis imponentes morem, | Dealing law to conquered nations; |
| Indulgentes hi virtuti | Some, whose cry for glory's louder, |
| Signa Martis sunt secuti . . . | Yield themselves as food for powder . . . |

| | |
|---|---|
| 7. Foruit, florebit usque | 7. Like a stately tree she'll flourish, |
| Artibus virtutibusque, | Generations yet to nourish; |
| Arbor ferax et natura | While her sons, in all directions, |
| Rite fruges repensura. | Gather fruit from her perfections. |

| | |
|---|---|
| 8. Venit vox a Solis ortu | 8. Hark! from regions near and distant, |
| Redit a cadentis portu | East and West, a cry insistent – |
| 'Nos te, Mater, salutamus': | 'We salute thee, gracious Mother!' |
| Ergo fortiter canamus | Loud then brother sing with brother – |
| 'Floreat Academia'. | 'Floreat Academia'. |

'Verse 4' originally ran 'Some cut quite respected figures/Dealing law to conquered niggers', a version long since disowned by everyone concerned.

Magnusson, Magnus (1974). *The Clacken and the Slate. The Story of Edinburgh Academy 1824–1974*, London, Collins.

1929– : distinguished Academy FP; Icelandic-born journalist, broadcaster and historian.

**71**  Glasgow, 1889.

But the task which lies before a school of this sort remains essentially what it has been in the past. The task of our burgh schools is to train, in the most comprehensive sense, the best and most promising of our youth to be good citizens . . . You are to remember that now, by some circumstance or other, you are held worthy of more than the education that falls to the common lot. I do not suppose that you will be so foolish as to see in this any ground for self-appreciation or self-conceit. But if you are wise, you will undoubtedly see in it something which imposes on you a severe and high responsibility. If one thing is more certain than another in education it is this: That before long the world will insist that no greater time be spent on education than is spent with absolute profit. Boys will not be allowed to spend time at a higher school simply because circumstances seem to render it convenient that they should go there. Education has, no doubt, other aims besides those that are merely practical, but practical, at least, it must be; and the more we organize and develop our secondary schools, the more certainly we shall say, 'these schools are for those who have brains and the industry to profit by them, and for them alone. They must not be open to those who prolong their school course only because they do not wish to enter into the drudgery of work, or who fancy that they may get a certain credit from having been pupils in a secondary school'. We must train only those who are worth training in these schools; and the rest must get betimes to such work as the elementary education (which is the indisputable and indefeasible right of every boy) may enable them to do.

You then, in this school, are already in a select class, and it is for you to justify the selection.

Craik, (Sir) Henry (1889) at prize-giving of the
High School of Glasgow. *Scots Magazine*, 4, September.

1846–1926: High School FP; first Secretary of Scottish Education Department; influential in establishing its traditional policies with regard to firm central control and academic excellence, founded on bipartite 'Secondary/Elementary' schooling; became Tory MP in later career.

7J                                                      Insch, Aberdeenshire, 1900.

I have said it before, and I will repeat, that as far as I am able to judge, in the ordinary schools of the country, we have no need to be ashamed or afraid of being outdone by any other country. (Applause) . . . I was speaking the other day to a lady not belonging to Scotland, and not actually either within the bounds of England or Scotland, but an English lady. She told me, with some pride, that her son on his first visit to Germany had visited some German schools, and that he had been enormously struck with their advance, and their very high state of efficiency. I asked her what he found they were learning. She said they were having a lesson in geography, and he was struck particularly with the fact that, when the name of Alaska was mentioned in a lesson, the most of the children seemed to know a great deal about it, and where it was. (Laughter). Well, I told her that if her son had taken the opportunity, which I do not think he ever did, of visiting any of the schools either in England or in Scotland, he would have found that such prodigies in information were not unrivalled even in Scotland, and I think that our friend Mr Walker [Headmaster, Insch Public School] might have had something terrible to say if he found a class studying Colonial geography having no knowledge of Alaska. (Laughter and applause).

Craik, (Sir) Henry (1890) at Opening of Insch Public School, September 1890. *Educational News*, 7 October.

# 8 THE COUNTRY MATTERS

*The Schools and Schoolmasters of Banffshire*:
William Barclay, 1925
*Circular 374*: Scottish Education Department, 1903
*Rural Schools*: James Beattie, 1903
*The Second Reading of the Scotch Education Bill*:
Lyon Playfair, 1872
*James Ramsay MacDonald: Labour's Man of Destiny*:
J. Hessell Tiltman, 1929
*Education in Nineteenth-Century Rural Scotland*:
Sydney Wood, 1991
*William Cramond MA, LL.D., Schoolmaster at Cullen*:
Alexander Cormack, 1964
*The Scottish-Farm Labourer*: Alexander Gordon, 1889
*Bondagers*: Margaret Paxton, 2000
*The Late Dr Grant: Educational News*, 1895
*Robert Lindsay and his School by one of his Old Pupils*:
Anon., 1906
*The Brave Days*: Neil Munro, 1931
*A Memoir of 88 Years*: Sir Alexander Murison, 1935

Figure 14. **Echt Public School, Aberdeenshire, c. 1900** Although a 'school's-out' shot, the dress and poses indicate that the photographer's visit to this small rural village was treated as a special – and parochially proud – occasion.

Figure 15. **Kirkcaldy High School, 1958** The school gave this the title 'Homeward Bound'. The scene captures the new post-war world of glass-and-concrete schools erected on green-field sites, replacing the old nineteenth-century era of centrally located burgh and parochial institutions. *Kirkcaldy High School Souvenir, 1958*

When, in 1925, the local branch of the EIS brought out *The Schools and Schoolmasters of Banffshire*, its intention was to do more than recount localised history. It is, according to the Foreword, a chronicle of 'character, heroism, both humble and brilliant, enterprise, adventure, romance and humour'. These are the ingredients of a Walter Scott novel: the aim was to make romantic celebration of the nation's academic tradition – and to campaign against its willful suppression.

It opens with a scene of homage (**8A**). And the grand symmetry of the narrative is rounded off, in its final pages, with the lineage of the Ogilvie dynasty, from modest Rothiemay: five brothers, four Doctorates, a spread of Chief School Inspectors, of Rectorships and, in Joseph, the founding Principal of the Teacher Training Centre at Aberdeen. These were men whose devoted work enabled Banffshire's 'country lads' to 'struggle with toil and penury' and so rise up 'to do a great work for country and the Empire'. But then, in words which turn loving retrospect into battle-cry, the editor, William Barclay, sounds out his warning (**8B**).

Twentieth century communication and social development had, however, transformed his Banffshire. And that was not all. Since its inception in 1885, the SED, from its Whitehall offices, 600 miles away, had been pursuing its goal of rationalisation. As in the towns, but here for additional logistical reasons, its officials wished to encourage only a select number of well-placed centres to be properly Secondary and the wastefully little, out-of-the-way schools to revert to the Elementary role that, in any case, was all that most pupils could manage. When, in 1903, it explained its position (**8C**), the slighting of the all-purpose school was seen by rural districts as a 'destruction' of each local lad's birthright chance to take the higher studies necessary for success in the universities' annual bursary competitions.

The old Scotland refused to go quietly. The great problem which the SED had in carrying its arguments was that it was attempting to engage with two different conceptualisations of nationhood: that which was ready to ride cosmopolitan, modernising enthusiasms, and one that remained rooted in the native soil of inheritance and local independence. And it was the latter which was able to present its views

*141*

as the more deeply felt and vividly substantiated. In the very year of '374', the *Educational News* published a key-note article by James Beattie MA of the High School, Oban (**8D**).

This was the kind of mytho-poeic composition which, with its insistent blend of topography and moral force, Barclay was later able to exploit. In the Preface, he declares that his is 'a county that may be taken as in many ways representative of the conditions throughout Scotland'. This reference to a fifty by thirty mile wedge of land, almost exclusively rural and with no centre of population greater than 5,000, is, on the face of it, a conceit. But his Banffshire holds, within its terrain, the glens, farmlands, fishing communities and pure shining rivers which correspond to the 'Scotland' of its pastoral recollection, if not to any urbanised present.

Developments in communication, the growth of the tourist industry and the popular travelogue had only served to heighten this perception. This was the quintessential Scotland of the imagination and the eclectic visitor that Lyon Playfair seized hold of when he sought the conclusion with which to stir his parliamentary colleagues in 1872 (**8E**).

Constructions such as these were not for export only. In the event, the centralising policy failed to penetrate as deeply as local sentiment feared – the demographic realities of a sparsely populated countryside, and the support of their local Authorities, meant that many small centres did retain a Secondary top. But they were also assisted by the extent to which they were able to appropriate the country's increasingly varied educational record in the name of a parochially 'democratic' Scotland, in which each ancient parish should maintain its own academic centre.

It was at this time that exemplary biographies of local heroes began to appear. By 1930, peasant Scotland had produced a lad of parts who had ascended his way to the very office of Prime Minister, and to the accolade of *James Ramsay MacDonald: Labour's Man of Destiny*. That its subject was the illegitimate son of a farm labourer, and was brought up in a but-and-ben behind the fishing village of Lossiemouth, has obvious dramatic potential. To this is added a scene-setting through which the relatively mild climate of the Moray Firth, with its gently sanded shorelines, is transfigured into a stern, character-building landscape (**8F**).

His experience was, however, hardly typical. When the Argyll

Commission investigated the country's famed parochial system, the conclusion was that the lad of parts was the rare chosen one and that his advancement depended upon a privilege of position which gave him the master's special attention – while the ordinary rest were left to get on with it. The Commission demonstrated what a very small figure they comprised – according to its volume, *Report on Education in the Country District of Scotland*, only 5.25 per cent were taking Latin and even fewer, 0.63 per cent, were taking Greek, and they usually came from the village's middling class:

> [I]n those old-fashioned parish schools which we visited, we found, not infrequently, a class of three or four boys in Latin, two of them perhaps the minister's sons and one the teacher's, about a fourth part of the school able to read well, and to write in copy-books and to do a little arithmetic, but the other three-quarters unable to spell.

And though the grateful recall might elevate, the recorded particulars could point to something more earth-bound. The individual school-logs, which it was now incumbent upon each head teacher to keep, open up the day-to-day actualities. The North-east historian Sydney Wood has sifted the records from Forgue, an upland parish which straddles the hills between Huntly and Inverurie. They reveal preoccupations remote from Latin conjugations or the higher reaches of Euclid: attendance, rough weather, inaccessible footpaths, measles and diphtheria, the counter attractions of markets and fairs, the struggle to extract fees from parents who value the labour of their children more than they do their education, the problem of persuading the Board to lay aside £2 a year to relieve the teacher of having to clean the building himself. In an era when the teacher's income is largely dependent upon the good maintenance of the roll, these rear up as the true burdens of the day. Sometimes, John Catto who, during the 1870s, with one young female assistant was responsible for the academic nurture of some 105 rural souls, would give way to logbook despair (**8G**).

On their own, the weekly summaries can quickly pall into a series of repetitive domestic irritations – a drawn out list of snowdrifts, scarletina, royal birthdays, absences to assist at the neeps, of recalcitrant parents and ill-kempt, odorous offspring. But, when attached to a whole life, these terse phenomena take on a poignantly human significance. *William Cramond MA, LL.D. – Schoolmaster at Cullen* uses the teacher's own log records, in tension with personal recollections by ex-pupils, to achieve exactly that (**8H**).

Cramond graduated with First-Class Honours in Classics at Aberdeen in 1866 – 'a remarkable attainment for a boy who had little intellectual background at home and who had to climb up that steep pupil teacher ladder to the university, teaching in a parish Kirk School from age 13'. In 1904, he took early retirement from his headmastership of Cullen Public School, on the Banffshire seaboard – the consequence, it was said, of thrashing a pupil with such severity that the police were called in. In between those dates, he passed away nearly forty years enclosed within the same small fishing port, master of a school of some 400, assisted by a staff of one qualified assistant and, usually, a quartet of pupil-teachers.

He appears to have derived little joy from this lifetime's service. The log-book entries grumble about frequent pupil absconsions to go to the fishing, to a ploughing match, to see a circus arrive; there are running concerns about the cleaning of the school privies, the rain coming through the roof, the reluctance of parents to stump up fees. And there are long weeks when the spring farm work or the autumn herring rob him of pupils, of his public authority and his grant money; on occasion, he has to organise the scholars into a room-sweeping party, or when the 'offices' are running high, await a sure black mark in the annual report of an Inspector whose vigilant nose for such matters has earned him the tag of 'Privy Counsellor'.

Yet, all this while, Cramond was building up an alternative existence as a local historian of some note. In 1893, he brought out *The Annals of Banff*; the previous year he had been awarded an honorary LL.D. by Aberdeen University. The scholarship was undoubted. What most pupils recalled, however, was a precise little man, socially aloof, exacting, prone to outbursts of harsh temper. 'His method of running the school was based on force and compulsion through bullying the teachers and belabouring the pupils.'

Dr William Cramond's long servitude in his little Banffshire corner suggests the habitation of two separate and unequal worlds; a fringe of private scholarship and due academic honours, against the vastly grey hinterland of bureaucratic frettings and a local indifference born of the absolutes of land and fish.

The lonely, resentful history of William Cramond MA, LL.D. is a reminder that, beyond the fabled stories of a book-hungry peasantry, the true priority remained the rooting around for a living (**8I**). While the analysis here is of the adult, it was often on the young that the denial of education fell most heavily. Usually, the farm-labourer's child, of whatever ability or aspiration, was rushed into work as rapidly as possible – and this was an imperative that continued deep into the following century (**8J**). The gender of this witness shows the persistence of another familiar rural destiny: the pushing of the daughter into domestic service, first at home, then some richer person's scullery.

The disparity between such raw testimony and the native legend could only be maintained by the force of stylised description. The writing stance adopted in *Schools and Schoolmasters of Banffshire* is that of the relayer of epic tales in which the virtues of the lone scholar-hero are set amidst the elemental grandeur of an enduring Scottish landscape. Against the circumstances of modernity, the perspective becomes self-consciously backward-gazing, an elegiac summing up of moribund splendours. By 1895, the obituary prose-poem has become a standard feature in the *Educational News* (**8K**).

Pastoral piety, community paternalism, simple virtues which broaden out into the publicly honoured funeral, the nearest factory chimney a hundred miles and another generation away: these are also the basic ingredients of the group of writers – commonly accepted as J. M. Barrie, Ian Maclaren and S. R. Crockett – who came to be termed the 'Kailyard'. It is no accident that the 'Late Dr Grant' was penned within a year of the appearance of Maclaren's collection *Beside the Bonnie Briar Bush* and its pasteurised tale of the village dominie whose fabled ability to spot and bring on the county's next Chief Bursar finds its consummation in the achievements of a humble local boy at the university. The name accorded to the former – 'Domsie'- provided the title; that bestowed on the wondrous peasant scholar gave Scottish education a defining term- 'the lad o' pairts'.

The Kailyard authors have been criticised as the meretricious exploiters of a turn-of-the-century publishers' phenomenon, one that fed upon a whipped-up taste for homeland nostalgia. Their embarrassing success has often been located in the marketing skills of the London book market which, it is alleged, was catering for a non-Scottish or an expatriate's stereotyped view of a land quaintly distant in both time and social custom. That, on the contrary, Maclaren and his colleagues were engaging with an indigenous need is shown, not only by many of the contributions to be encountered in the EIS's own journal but also by the eagerness with which its members took up the title 'lad o' pairts' as a slogan in their campaign to retain the inherited 'democratic' ways. The named three, moreover, quickly generated a line of imitators, many of whom deployed the school and its locally venerated teacher as chief movers in their popularly sympathetic portraits of auld lang syne (**8L**).

The bringing together of school, land and fading past to form the preferred expression of native identity, and to do so with an emotive regard that blurs the distinction between non-fiction and literary study, inevitably, as the modern age moved in, pushed its imaginative location towards the country's more highly coloured margins. The combination is shown in Neil Munro's 'autobiographical' evocation of his schooling in an Argyll crofting community (**8M**).

The writing has a ripened sweetness which appears to dwell in a land that is completely alien to the harshness of 'Bondagers' or Dr Cramond's tartly indifferent Cullen. If, within the opposition of the pastoral epilogue and the documentary exposure, we wish to seek out the constants, it should be among those biographies, which offer a less heated version of rural schooling. In 1935, the posthumous memoirs of Sir Alexander Murison appeared. In outline, his story fits into the conventional pattern of 'one who, born in the wild hinterland of Aberdeenshire of very humble and poor parents, and once a herd-boy on the hills, rose from the shieling of a dreary countryside to high distinction as a scholar not only in Great Britain, but all over Europe and America'. The citation, however, comes from the 'Editor's Note': the personal account which follows is that of an evenly balanced commentator, able to draw upon a remarkably well-stocked memory and not at all in need of the traditional adornments.

His opening pages take us back into the educational environment of the mid-nineteenth century, the very period when the wider reputation of his region's schools was being stored up. Murison was the son of a joiner whose home was in New Deer, in the midst of what was now becoming one of Scotland's great farmlands, fanning out west and north of Aberdeen. After a spell at the nearest Dame's school, he entered the parochial school at Whitehill. The teacher was Mr Alexander Greig MA, a true graduate dominie. But the man himself had ten children to feed; he was forced to wear himself out doubling and trebling up as Elder, Registrar and Inspector of the Poor. The effects upon his class-teaching are judiciously appraised by Murison's detail (**8N**).

The writer turned out to be one of North-east Scotland's authentic lad o' pairts, a brilliant linguist with an international standing. Later, he moved on to Old Deer where he really did encounter a dominie hero in Robert Wilson, whose skill and devotion were such that, at fifteen, and after a finishing year at Aberdeen Grammar School, the prodigy was able to win top bursary at the annual Aberdeen University Competition. But, Murison recognises, his experience was exceptional: 'The Master was far ahead of his time'.

The impression, overall, made by this account is not so much of his Aberdeenshire schooling as being a privileged intellectual adventure but of physical encounter. The rural environment is palpably there, for him, as an immediate, prosaic and minutely insistent presence. The boy is absorbed in the wheel of the seasons, seen with the eye of the farmer. The description which ends the extract has the rhythm of pastoral invocation but the detail is flatly agrarian: the North-east of Murison is, after all, a place of ordinary habitation, not a cinematic vista of mountainous crags and scholars' lairs. Mud, not the sparkle of granite, is the dominant element.

The country school itself merges into the plainness of the landscape – bare walls, musty odours, the rough feel of unvarnished deal benches and the hard rectangular spaces where the red-faced teacher pounds the floor. Syllabuses are recalled but as repetitive events that leave their mark on the memory traces, not as mental explorations. It is the physicality of the experience which protrudes: lists of rivers and of kings drilled into the skull, tables and rules and lexicons hammered into the consciousness, the teacher's jabbing finger ever in motion. To the children, the indignities involved seem no more than another fact of their lives, part of the texture of the day that will encompass the long trudge home across the turnip fields and the itch of home-woven underwear against the skin.

Certainly, there was the possibility of getting on. But so much depended on the quality of the teacher and his willingness to separate out a small minority of candidates and devote spare hours to their coaching for the hazard of the annual bursary competition. Even more rested upon the economic circumstances of the family and the social expectations which had become fixed within the consciousness of the community. Murison, blessed with an exceptional linguistic gift, serenely sailed through it all – but, at each crucial stage, he found that his artisan – not labourer – background was able to finance the move to a better placed school. At no point does he mention that he shared these experiences with the sons and daughters of the lairds who owned the land on which his parents lived and toiled.


8A                                                    Keith, Banffshire, 1921.

At the Grange, Banff Road, Keith, on November 13, 1921, died Mr Charles Mair. He was aged 84. Mr Mair was a man of high intellectual ability as well as of rare force of character. While he was engaged in business, he was at the same time of a scholarly turn of mind, and during his retirement in later years, took an intelligent interest in place-names, and it is a surprising fact that taking up in his old age the study of Gaelic, he could with ease translate any part of the New Testament from that language. He was for over thirty years in business in Grange as a country grocer, carrying on a small farm at the same time; he was a devoted member of the Parish Church there, for long an elder, and for some time a Sunday School teacher. At the funeral the chief mourners were his seven sons. It will likely long remain a unique feature on such an occasion that there should be round their father's grave five sons all First-Class Honours graduates of the University. One son was Rev. John Mair, Spynie Manse, Elgin, who at Aberdeen University won the Black Prize for the best Latin scholar and the Aberdeen Town Council Medal for the most distinguished student at the termination of his Arts course. Another son was Charles, cattle-dealer, Fife-Keith. A third was James, of Coats Higher Grade School, Cambuslang, and a fourth was George, flesher in Keith. A fifth son was Alexander, Professor of Greek at Edinburgh University, who at Aberdeen University won the Simpson Greek Prize, the Liddel Prize for the best Latin or Greek poem (in four different years), and the Ferguson Scholarship in Classics, open to the graduates of all the Scottish universities, while in England his academic successes included a First Class in both parts of the Classical Tripos, the Gold Medal for Greek Epigrams, the coveted Craven Scholarship, and the Chancellor's Classical Medal. A sixth son was Gilbert, headmaster of Spiers School, Beith. The seventh was Robert, like others of the

family, a First-Class Honours graduate of Aberdeen; a graduate in Law
of Edinburgh University, the winner of a Military Cross in the war,
and, in 1923, when clerk and treasurer to the Forfarshire Education
Authority, appointed clerk to the Education Authority of Lanarkshire.

Barclay, William (1925). 'Introductory', The Schools and<br>Schoolmasters of Banffshire. Banff, Banffshire Journal.

8B                                                        Banffshire, 1925.

The system, for good or ill, has been destroyed. The policy of
concentration of pupils at a few centres may in the days that lie ahead
find someone to praise a beneficence and a prescience that, to the
minds of some, have not yet become apparent. It is sufficient for the
present purpose to say that even in the smallest rural schools in
Banffshire under the old and well-tried regime, sons of the county
were so trained in the classics as in homely moralities that in after life
Banffshire was proud to acclaim them as her children. They passed to
the big world outside, played their part in the life in a way that brought
abounding credit to the county of their birth, and brought ever-
renewed renown to it as a training place of ambitious youth.

Barclay, William (1925). As above.

8C                                                             SED, 1903.

'My Lords are of the opinion, from a careful consideration of the facts,
that the tendency . . . to make one and the same school with one and the
same staff serve many different functions is the weak point of educational
organization in Scotland compared with that of other countries . . . they
are satisfied that increasing division of function as between different types
of school is an essential condition of further educational progress'.

Scottish Education Department (1903). Circular 374, 16 February.

8D                                                    Oban, Argyll, 1900s.

It is not going too far to say that the rural household is the touchstone
of national character. The vital force that invigorates the city has its

genesis in the country. The enterprise of a people, whether in developing the resources of their own or other lands, depends ultimately upon the industry and intelligence of a peasantry. The staying power of a nation lies in the physical, intellectual, and moral well-being of its rural population. Thus the rural home, naturally the greatest of all influences for good or for evil, determines the success or failure, the growth or decay of an empire.

In a lesser degree the same may be said of the rural school, which, so far as the training of the young is concerned, is but an expansion of the rural home. It is indeed an auxiliary of the home. It aims at deepening the impressions made around the family hearth, at fixing the good habits formed in the routine of household duties, and sometimes, too, at counteracting the evil influences of a vicious upbringing. Moreover, it provides for that which is beyond the resources of the home, the systematic development of mind and body through methods of instruction that are in harmony with the best thought and ripest experience of the time. Its highest purpose is to aid the home in so training the youth that they may grow up to be alert, sober, thrifty, diligent, generous, pious men and women, ready to work out the ideals of a useful and honourable life wherever their lot may be cast, whether in the village workshop, or on the farm, in the turmoil of the city or in the forest clearing of some distant colony . . .

[T]he rural school must be equipped for the best all-round training of mind and body that the State can afford to give, so that our children who remain for the work of the fields may in still larger measure be possessed of those virtues of intellect and character that have for centuries distinguished the Scottish peasantry while our children who go abroad may exalt the *perfervidum ingenium* [ardent character] of their native race in the uttermost corners of the earth . . .

Scotland has been blessed in the past with excellent rural schools. Here and there, as for instance, in the counties of Aberdeen, Banff, and Kincardine, they have achieved a fame that still excites the envy of other countries besides our own. Elsewhere, too, there are rural schools doing magnificent work, but it will be my purpose to show that they are fighting against heavy odds, and that unless their conditions be modified they are destined to fall behind in the educational race, and then woe betide Scotland's educational prestige!

Beattie, James (1903). 'Rural Schools'. *Educational News*, 17 January.

8E                                                                              Westminster, 1872.

Many of my English friends, on both sides of the House, know
Scotland well, for they have stalked the deer on its rugged hills, and
wandered over the heather in search of grouse and of health. Have
they ever wondered – when they have followed their sport in the
mountains or glens, or fished in the rocky rivers – what could make
such a country peaceful, prosperous and contented? They know that
it is restricted in area, barren in soil, and possesses only in one small
portion of it the elements of mineral wealth. Then they would find it
difficult to give any other explanation than that its inhabitants are, on
the whole, an educated and God-fearing people. That our education
has deteriorated is true, or this Bill would not be now before us. But its
peculiar characteristics remain as of old, and it is the duty of all
Scotchmen to see that they are maintained. We have had a glorious
inheritance from our fathers, and we should transmit it, not only
unimpaired but improved, to our sons.

> Playfair, Lyon (1872). 'The Second Reading of the
> Scotch Education Bill'. House of Commons, 7 March.

1819–98: from high-achieving Angus family; after distinguished academic career
in chemistry, as MP played prominent role in range of public issues including
promotion of scientific and technical education.

8F                                                                  Lossiemouth, Moray, 1870s.

At Lossiemouth Nature sounds a perpetual challenge to the adventurous. It is impossible to picture 'the lover of soft paths' coming from
such a spot. Inland there rises a spur of the mighty Grampians, snow-
capped for half the year and lifting their heads to Heaven above the
dark forests of their slopes, 'like huge creatures squatting on some
coast in the earliest of early days'. And facing the hills the sea, which is
never quiet. Life in that region is hard, but it is also sane and
wholesome; untouched by the forces of modern industrialism yet
intensely, vitally alive . . .

Young James Ramsay MacDonald was not only born *in* Lossiemouth; he was *of* it. His forebears had lived and died in the district for
over two hundred years. His father was a Scottish farm labourer; his

mother a remarkable woman, who, in the poverty into which he was born and in which he was reared, remained 'undaunted by Fortune's frown'.

Few men destined to great things have begun with such heavy odds stacked against them . . . His interest in books was reflected in his prowess as a scholar at the local elementary school. There young MacDonald's remarkable ability was soon perceived, and there, despite his poverty, he was able to secure better education than would have been possible at that time for a lad so poor anywhere else but in Scotland.

Writing about his schooldays, Mr MacDonald has given us an unforgettable picture of a Scottish Board School at that time:

'The work done in the school was of an old order now. It was a steady hard grind to get at the heart of things. We turned everything outside in, pulled everything to pieces in order to put it together again, analysed, parsed, got firm hold of the roots, shivered English into fragments and fitted them together like a Chinese puzzle, all by the help of Bain's Sixteenpenny Grammar (which the Dominie's pupils must remember in the same way as they do the Shorter Catechism), and wrestled with "deductions". Then every bolt in our intellectual being was tightened up. One of the dominie's generalizations was: "You must master: that is education: when you have mastered one thing you are well on the way to master all things" '.

. . . The school days of the poor were not unduly protracted, and at twelve years of age young MacDonald nearly went the usual way of the Lossiemouth lads, namely, to sea in one of the fishing boats which provided some of the local men with a scanty living. He actually did leave school and earned his first few shillings 'howkin' tatties' (lifting potatoes) in the fields.

At the first crisis in his life, however, there was a man who detected that bigger things than potato lifting might be waiting for young MacDonald if only poverty could be overcome. This was his Dominie. The old schoolmaster already looked upon MacDonald as his most promising pupil, and by making him a pupil-teacher and remitting his fees, he was able to start him on the road to a professorship or a pulpit.

He did even more. He encouraged young MacDonald's reading; he interested him in mathematics and the classics, and when his pupil-teacher showed a preference for science typical of a mind which has always hunted for the truth in all things, this very real friend still helped him as far as he could. The friendship thus begun continued to his death, and to this day the Dominie's most distinguished pupil still wears the gold watch which his old master left to him.

Tiltman, J. Hessell (1929). *James Ramsay MacDonald: Labour's Man of Destiny*. London, Jarrold.

8G                                     Aberdeenshire, 1870/80s.

[School log-book entries]
In this secluded district where the minds of children come in contact with but few people, the children's intelligence is long of developing, . . . I fear that in a district like this where anything like intelligent talk at home may be seldom if ever engaged in if even heard, the intelligence of the pupils is at a very low ebb, everything must be put in before it can be drawn out and when that has to be done I fear the process approaches close upon cramming instead of educating . . .

Apart from bad weather and miserable roads, the home influence here is in the majority of cases of a very low order. Most of the children lead two lives – a gross, vulgar, semi-barbaric one at home, and a civilized one in school . . .

Wood, Sydney (1991). 'Education in Nineteenth-Century Rural Scotland – an Aberdeenshire Case Study'. *Review of Scottish Culture*, 7.

8H                                     Cullen, Banffshire, 1890s.

'He had a habit of biting his nails when listening and irritated. One boy near him, petrified with fright, as we all were, could not find the genitive of puer. With an 'ett', Cramond impatiently flicked the boy's cheek with his fingers whereupon a startled 'pueri' burst forth. It was the only time I ever saw Cramond smile' . . .

Dr Cramond was treated by the community with the respect that the Scot of 1890 accorded to learning. Yet schoolmastering must have been purgatory to such a scholar. But the parents had no illusions about his ability as a teacher. The fisher boys came or didn't come as they cared . . .

Another former pupil of the period 1896–1903 from age 5 to 12, who graduated MA 1912, has supplied the following admirable assessment of Dr Cramond in his last 7 years at Cullen School. 'My mother, who was a former pupil, always spoke very well of him. I can still picture him, passing through the classroom; in school. He wore a velvet smoking cap with tassel (as both my schoolmaster uncles did) and had a little trim reddish beard; he walked with a quick purposeful step, head tilted a little to right, left hand slipped into his coat pocket, thumb outside always, while his right arm swung smartly with his step. Outside school, he always wore a bowler of the old early brimmed type, probably very smart then. I can't remember his interfering with any of our class work in the junior school. It wasn't until I reached Standard 6 that I actually came under his rule – and that only for a short time, as I left Cullen School to tramp daily to and from Fordyce about 1903. Promptly at 8.50 each morning he used to hurry up Seafield Street from the Schoolhouse in the Square to his work. Promptly at 11.5 he passed down again to partake of 'elevenses' which, rumour had it, consisted of biscuits and cheese, washed down with a glass of ale – and very nice too. I can recall Mrs. Cramond as a tall, quiet lady, handsome and dignified, probably overshadowed by the intellectual brilliance of her husband. The daughter Minnie had inherited all her mother's good looks and carriage and was blessed in addition with beautiful golden hair from her father. Davie, the elder son, also took after his mother, while Willie, my contemporary, followed rather the build and appearance of his intellectual and less handsome father. I remember them as a very happy and worthy family, which didn't mix much with the tougher and less genteel elements of the town . . . We never thought that Dr Cramond was a good teacher; he just was not cut out for teaching boys and girls; he was too short tempered and impatient to explain things and to wait for things to sink in. Only those pupils who were very 'gleg in the uptack' found favour with him; otherwise he raged and fumed at our mistakes, dismissed the class for the time being and made us return to the lesson after four o'clock, Meantime I suspect he was either writing up some of his antiquarian treatises, or reading them in the Elgin Courant. He always got the Elgin Courant; it was a little more sophisticated than the bucolic Banffie of those days, I feel. The Dr probably contributed lots of articles to the Courant, but I am not sure. His rather irascible nature led partly to his early retirement from Cullen. In those days there was no keen sense of humour in the make-up of the Schoolmaster, pupils or parents. Life was real, life was earnest.'

Cormack, Alexander (1964). *William Cramond MA, LL.D.: Schoolmaster at Cullen.* Banff, Banffshire Journal.

## 8I          North-east Scotland, 1880s.

The adult farm-labourers of the present day are the product of the old state of things. It may be thought a paradox, but nevertheless it is pefectly true, that they are one and all absolutely illiterate, and yet none are without a smattering of education. They are able to read and to write; they have been drilled by the schoolmaster to a certain extent in grammar, geography and history; some have been even indoctrinated in the rudiments of Latin; but the bucolic influences to which these agricultural labourers have been subjected since leaving school, have driven from their memories the greater portion of their slender education. Untouched by the spirit which is at work in the urban centres, social, political or religious questions have for them no interest, and the sole remaining part of the primary culture which was instilled into their minds by the loquacious pedagogue is this simple ability to read and write. In their own way they discharge the simple duties of life, but to nearly everything that is beyond the scope of primitive natural affection they are blind and callous. The rising generation are now sent to school in obedience to requirements of the Education Code, at the latest, at the age of five; but, in the olden times many of the children of the agricultural toilers did not appear in the schoolroom till the ages of seven, eight, or nine. They were, in addition, most irregular in their attendances, and the cases of young men and young women of sixteen, seventeen, and eighteen who were unable to read a difficult sentence, to write legibly, or to spell with any degree of accuracy, were numerous, and as a consequence, there were always – especially in the wintertime – several big, burly young men, and stalwart young women to be found in attendance at country schools. The help of such persons was, of course, in great demand, during the summer and autumn, for turnip-hoeing, peat cutting, harvesting, potato ingathering, and such like, and the hard pressed, struggling parents were compelled to send their sons and daughters into service, in order to eke out the means of a scanty livelihood.

Gordon, Alexander (1889). 'The Scottish Farm-Labourer', *Scottish Review*, October.

8J                                                                    Roxburghshire, 1910s.

Ah left school at Yetholm. Ah wouldnae be very long at the school there when ah left. Some o' the girls in ma class jist went tae service. That wis common. Ah know one, she went tae Edinbury, and oh, she wis homesick. And she'd tae get up at five o'clock in the mornin', she told me, and black leid the range and have the breakfast ready at eight and make the porridge and have ham and egg, ken, a' ready for their breakfast. And, oh, she couldnae sleep at night, jist homesickness. But she stuck it, and wis there for seven years at the finish. Oh, long hours, and she wis supposed to go to church on the Sunday. She got a day off every fortnight. Ah can remember her tellin' me – she wrote a letter and told me all about it. She didnae get very much money. But ah wid have went tae service, oh, ah wid.

As a girl, well ah'll tell ee what ah wanted tae be – a nurse. Ah like-ed, ee ken, ah like-ed tae look after children. Ah had younger brothers and sisters, that wis it. Ah had tae keep an eye on them. So as far back as ah can remember, ah wanted tae be a nurse. When ah left school – that wis when ah wis fourteen – ah could have stayed on, but, well, ma father worked in the dairy and ma mother used tae help him. It wis never discussed that ah could maybe go to the High School. So ah thought ah wid jist leave at fourteen tae help ma mother wi' the other children. It wis jist expected ah would leave when ah wis fourteen. Well, ah wis disappointed in a way that ah wis jist at home lookin' efter the other children. That wis fairly common among girls in these days, the older girls stayed at home, when they left school and helped their mothers. And, ee ken, it wis jist ye left school at fourteen. It wis jist like that. When ye came fourteen ye left.

Paxton, Margaret (2000). *Bondagers. Eight Scots Farm Workers.* 'Flashbacks No. 10', Ian MacDougall (ed.). East Linton, Tuckwell Press.

8K                                              Banffshire, 1895.

On Saturday the 2nd of February the grave closed over the remains of
one of the most notable figures in the northern half of Scotland – Dr
James Grant, headmaster of the Keith Combined Public School.
Three score years and ten were the measure of his days, but who
shall measure the effect of his fifty years' work among the hundreds
and thousands of pupils that were privileged to feel the influence of
that strong and vigorous personality moving among them? . . .

Among us in our beautiful Highland glens he arose like a prophet, and
he was a voice crying in the wilderness. But the wilderness was quickly
transformed. He himself was wont to look back to these early years with
kindly remembrance of the sincere and lofty respect which his attached
disciples paid to his commanding influence, and which ennobled master
and pupils alike. He has been heard to say that he never had better
material to work upon than he found in his own native glens. This was
characteristic of the modesty and generosity of the man, who, as usual,
forgot himself. It was not the material, it was that the hour and the man
had come. Fair-haired, rosy-cheeked, healthy little shepherd boys there
were in plenty, who could bound over the heathery hills with the
fleetness of the deer, or climb the tall pine trees with the agility of
squirrels, or contest with the others the possession of the treasures of the
silver streams, but these formed the sum of their accomplishments. This
was the uncultivated material that filled the glens when a large, burly,
somewhat ungainly figure, full of the fire of genius and the fervour of
youth, strode in to reclaim it. This was Mr Grant, and he roused such an
enthusiasm as forty years have not sufficed to allay.

Mr Grant taught successively in Kirkmichael, Glenlivet, and To-
mintoul, and so long as he remained in these parts, neither distance,
nor mountains, nor flooded stream formed any obstacle to the hardy
youths whose souls he had set on fire. Wherever he was there they
gathered. It was not the cold and formal teacher that *he* was to his
pupils; they were his friends and companions, and not even Socrates
himself could have been rewarded with a more devoted admiration
than they rendered to him. Far and wide over the globe these pupils
are scattered, and some of the most brilliant of them, alas, have gone
before him, but to those that remain his death will come as a great
shock, and his loss will remain as a lasting sorrow.

'The Late Dr Grant' (1895). *Educational News*, 9 February.

8L                                 Kincardineshire, 1830s/London, 1906.

When last I visited Maxie Hillside I found her small hut still there, with another lone old woman as its occupant. Rob's school, however, had entirely disappeared, The whins had been uprooted, and a field of stunted oats had taken their place, so that all the beauty and the attractions of the Hillside for me were gone. I turned my back on it and looked not towards it again. Visions of the past, however, rose in my mind as I slowly made my way to the nearest railway station. Rob and his bairnies, Jeanie Crabb, Jean Ross, the little lammie [lamb] with the pretty spot, its last resting-place, now obliterated by the plough, and, above all, Mary Craigie and our four years loving companionship, all came back to me so vividly and with such a sense of reality, that until I heard the whistle of the approaching train I was for a time Rob's little schoolboy again.

> *Robert Lindsay and his School by one of his*
> *Old Pupils* (1906). London, T. Foulis.

*The Bookman*, February 1906 – 'The little school stood on a hillside of the Grampian range; the little book stands just as separate. It is like "Rab and his Friends", a simple chapter in the homelier life of Scotland . . .'

*Dundee Advertiser* – 'A little book rich in the promise of becoming a classic. The author writes with simple charm, quaintly beatified by many an old homely word, and the interest of the story is more appealing as sympathetic imagination has been only occasionally resorted to where memory has failed . . . So intimate, so pathetic, and so loving by revealing the life of other days, as that is brought back in fireside reverie. The little book seems sacred. It is one that might make Barrie himself feel both ware and humble, and one can hope that it will reach many readers to instruct and inspire them.'

> 'Some Press Opinions' [published in third edition of above] (1908).

8M                                                       Argyll, 1870s.

The snow will be deep in Glencaldine today; it is just such weather as we loved in March when we had to put on an extra waistcoat and carry a peat through the drifts to old John MacArthur's school. But there is neither school nor dominie up the glen now, and on all the Scottish mainland – doubtless also in the islands – youngsters no longer carry a peat on winter days for the schoolroom fire. The school satchels which the late James Coats, jnr., distributed so lavishly through rural Scotland were not designed to accommodate peats, and in any case it is forty years since the Scottish Education Department, with an utter lack of sentiment, proscribed the diurnal peat of winter, and put the cost and cartage of fuelling on the rates . . .

Probably Whitehall was unaware of what rural sentiment was attached to the peat; its long traditions, its sacred associations with the old parochial schools when school boards were unknown and codes were a horror undreamt of. It had more of romance than the ancient horn-book, or the spelling-book of the ingenious Mr. Butters, for it had been the readiest of missiles in hastily organized morning skirmishes, and on a wet day especially it had a singularly soothing, squashing sound when it struck the ear of some unbreeched enemy disposed to bully on the strength of superior age and a seat in the fivepenny class . . .

The smell of peat-reek all winter pervaded John MacArthur's schoolroom. It was the first thing missed by James Chalmers (*Tamate*), the martyr-missionary of New Guinea, on entering his first academy on his first visit home from the mission-field. Chalmers had trudged the glen in snowdrift weather with his peat in his oxter, as stormy a lad as the rest of them, redoubtable in morning skirmishes up the river-side.

He had hoped to confirm his dreams of Glencaldine and his boyhood, but Whitehall had robbed him of the opportunity.

Munro, Neil (1931). The Brave Days. London, Porpoise Press.

1863–1930: writer of historical romances and humorous tales ('Para Handy').

8N                                        Aberdeenshire, 1850/60s.

On a bitterly cold morning, probably in March, 1854, I started from home and marched to my father's workshop, then in John Falconer's field. There I was joyously taken in hand by a band of half a dozen youths from the 'Cottages' and thereabouts, who perversely rejected the easier route through the woods of Brucklay, not perhaps without special attractions on the longer route; and they undertook solemnly to deliver me safe and sound at the school door. They despised roads, and ploughed in a bee line through the snow-bound fields of three or four farms. On the last farm we stopped for refreshment at a plot of vegetables, and I was ordered to partake as the rest did. A parsnip fell to my share.

As for the school: in the middle was a clear space for marshalling a class on foot; on each side of this space was a long and broad table, with forms alongside; on two sides of the room the desks sloped from the walls with forms in front of them. Our average number would perhaps be about 50 – boys and girls. In the morning we stood out for the Bible or the Catechism: I was soon able to repeat the whole Catechism – even the definition of 'Effectual Calling' – with literal exactness; but fortunately nobody ever enquired how far I understood it; we got no explanation. General reading and history: spelling, but no explanation. Our history was Goldsmith's 'History of England': and one day a yokel, improving the slack winter days, read 'Thus died George I', pronouncing 'I', not as 'the First' but the personal pronoun. Not a word of explanation. Geography: the little text-book said – 'London, the capital of England, on the river Thames', and so on; and so said all of us. But, for all the maps we had about us, never were we shown England or the Thames or London, and the lesson was but a repetition of meaningless terms. What geography we did learn we learnt apart from book or class, by puzzling each other to discover the various names on the wall maps before us. That is how I came to discover Woolloomoolo, Timbuctoo, Kamchatka, and other resounding places. Writing: we copied the copper-plate lines of our writing-books as best we might: not a word of instruction, nor of comment (when we showed up) except in the grossest cases of slovenliness . . . Arithmetic: we were left to struggle with our text-book. Those that failed to cope with the text-book came for help to some of us that could enlighten them; and, when the better arithmeticians were stumped, they took their slates to the Master, and he worked out the refractory sum quickly, laid the slate pencil on the side of the slate, and handed over the apparatus – with a gruff 'There!' perhaps, but without a word of explanation or encouragement. I was very soon able to do any sort of sums ranged under the title of Arithmetic, and then the Master produced from his desk several more advanced books, which I devoured in succession. Of the multifarious contents I remember only two titles: 'Strength of Materials' and 'Practical Gunnery'! This for a child not within sight of his teens! Euclid was never even named. Latin: I seem to remember Ruddiman's 'Rudiments'; and I remember distinctly how I laboured at home, weak in inflexions and destitute of a dictionary, to turn Gray's 'Elegy' into Latin! Where was the science of Education, or a hint in season to a bewildered and groping child? . . .

Nearly all our clothes were home-made: underwear of wool, thickly woven by my mother, rendering over-wear all but indifferent. It was long before I succeeded in getting those wonderful peg-top trousers so temptingly exhibited in Mr. Wallace's window. Not till I was 17 did I ever wear anything that could be called an overcoat: and then I was enthralled by an 'Inverness cape' in my first winter at University. Boots and shoes did drive us to the shoemaker; but from the last bitter day of one winter to the first perishing day of the next winter I ran 'barfit' (barefoot), and had almost to be thrashed ere I would confine myself in foot-wear.

Yes, a delightful time. The school was no source of trouble whatever. Out of school, it was a charming world: brown under the plough and the harrow, yellow with the waving corn, green with the lush grass, white under the sheet of snow – sunshine, rain, snow – singing of birds, lowing of cattle, wimpling of the burns, rushing and howling of wind – all alike enjoyable in turn.

Murison, Sir Alexander (1935). *A Memoir of 88 Years*.
Alex and Sir James Murison (eds). Aberdeen University Press.

1846–1934: after triumphant student career at Aberdeen University, became noted European scholar in languages and in jurisprudence, from his base at University College, London.

# 9 A TERRIBLE EFFICIENCY IS BORN

*The Story of my Boyhood and Youth*: John Muir, 1913
*Octobiography*: Helen Cruickshank, 1976
*The Code*: T. M. Davidson, 1892
*As I Recall*: John Boyd Orr, 1965
*Third Schedule (Needlework)*: Code for Day Schools, SED, 1906
*A Family in Skye*: Isobel Macdonald, 1980
*A School in South Uist*: F. G. Rea, 1913
*Our Public School Curriculum*: James Clark, 1905
*Robert Millar of West Linton*: *Educational News*, 1909

Figure 16. **Moray House Training Centre, Edinburgh, 1880** The latest batch of young female teachers in training to meet the needs of a workforce greatly increased by the 1872 Act. *Scottish Life Archive*

Figure 17. **Aberdeen College of Education, 1968** This press photo appeared under the headline, 'Headmasters, here we come!' – suggesting that, although fashions and constraints had changed since 1880, sexist assumptions still lingered on. *Aberdeen Journals*

In 1913, in the midst of the sweetened reminiscences of pastoral schooling, an autobiography appeared which plunged the reader back into a different nineteenth-century Scotland. This was *The Story of my Boyhood and Youth* by John Muir. Its author had long since been more famous in America, to where his family had emigrated in 1849. There, he had become known as 'the father of conservation', an impassioned student of the great wildernesses of Alaska, California and Oregon.

His first eleven years had been spent in Dunbar. The opening chapter pulses with hectic descriptions of how he and his friends, 'red-blooded playmates' all, roamed the hills, burst into gardens to plunder apples, scoured rockpools for eels and crab. For more organised sport, they would stone cats, cheer on dog fights, watch squealing pigs being butchered at the abattoir. 'Wildness was ever sounding in our ears and Nature saw to it that besides school lessons and church lessons some of her own lessons should be learned' (**9A**).

Yet John Muir was no offspring from some deprived home: his father was a devout churchgoer and Army man, head of a family sufficiently well-to-do to employ a servant to wash and dress the children before they hared off to school each morning. The house was large, with a cultivated garden, in the spruce seaport of Dunbar. When they were aboard their emigration ship, the captain invited the Muir children to his cabin where he quizzed them on their schooling. He 'seemed surprised to find that Scotch boys could read and pronounce English with pure accent and knew so much Latin and French'.

Muir's account thrusts the reader back into a rural Scotland which was more savage, more naturally free and less socially ordered than anything to be met with in the Kailyard. The education of the day, fiercely administered by 'old fashioned Scotch teachers' is of a piece with this sense of unregulated independence.

In 1976, the poet Helen Cruickshank's *Octobiography* appeared. Born a half-century after Muir, her early days were also spent in a rural setting, also beside a well-endowed East-coast burgh, Montrose. The background was similarly comfortable, for her father was the manager of the large mental asylum serving north Angus. As a child she also became immersed in the natural world: on the hospital farm she would watch the cows at milking, would be allowed to assist in the piggery. At twelve, she passed the Qualifying and entered the upper stream at Montrose Academy (**9B**).

These are very different recollections from those of John Muir. His are wild with the sensations of a boyhood that is free and instinctual; hers are watchfully accumulative, domesticated by their steady adherence to the ordered family round – two separate sensibilities at work. Yet the contrasts cannot be fully explained as the distinction between the embryonic civil servant and the future explorer of the West. He went to school in the 1840s, she fifty years later. Between these two dates, Scotland itself had changed and, with it, its schooling. What we are catching through the blaze of John Muir's memory is a rural society that is based on a scatter of small and isolated communities, self-sufficient in their manners, free to act out their existences as an unquestioned part of the teeming natural scene; two generations onwards and the small country town has become subject to a less intimate and more publicly ordered culture.

Sixty years of administrative development lay behind the transformation. The Act of 1872 was far from marking the government's entry into the management of the nation's education. In 1833–4, parliament had embarked on a system of annual grants to encourage the building of new schools throughout Britain. Six years later, the Education Committee of the Privy Council was set up to administer what was fast growing into a full-scale regime, with schoolroom resources, teacher training and methodology now within its orbit. Her Majesty's Inspectors of Schools then began its work. Grants became ever more specifically targeted: a notorious mechanism of 'payment by results', awarded against individual pupil performance, was imported from south of the border. '1872' itself was part of a whole sequence of mid-century legislation that sought to regulate health, policing, poor relief and housing standards. The trail of codified requirement and institutional organisation grew ever longer and more winding. Montrose Academy became a civic institution divided into departments, in which those who taught no longer behaved as a force of nature but as properly monitored subject specialists.

They worked within a curricular framework which matched the regularised character of the building that enclosed them. The explanatory memoranda, the mandatory regulations and the inquisitorial visits, which the SED spun out of the 1872 Bill and by which it earnestly strove to institute an efficient mass education system, had reached into every little classroom (**9C**).

The Department was now issuing a yearly Report of more than one thousand pages; the 'Code for Day Schools' comprised one hundred of them. Teachers were instructed to maintain a log-book, but refrain from including any 'reflections of a general character' within it, to keep a portfolio of official letters, 'numbered in order of their receipt' and adhere to an agreed timetable. They were also required to have ready

> a record of work done in each subject . . . in such detail as shall show the previous course of instruction at any time throughout the year. Any examination of a class which an inspector may institute at any of his visits in order to satisfy himself as to the efficiency of the work, shall be based upon this record.

John Boyd Orr's curricular crime, (**9D**), was easily proven: the requirements for every subject, from Infant Needlework to Higher Greek were clearly laid down (**9E**).

In the early decades of the nineteenth century, Lord Brougham, anxious to propel the nation towards a universal system of education, had launched his cry, 'the Schoolmaster is abroad!' Now at its end, with that ambition achieved, it appeared that it was the School Inspector who had gained the triumphant ubiquity. He had become the Department's enforcer: empowered by statute, armed with the latest Dover House documentation, he was the monitor of all that he surveyed.

The result was as intended: standardisation of curriculum and attainment, which brought accountability to all the academic outposts of the land. Increasingly, the character of biographical memory shifts from intimate stories of self-willed dominies, giant-sized in their pedagogic freedoms, to retracing laborious journeys across the time-table's endless foothills. From Helen Cruickshank's anglophone Angus, right across to the Celtic west, the Scottish syllabus came to share the same regularity of feature. When Isabel Macdonald, the Big House factor's girl, worked her way through the 1890s in Portree School, Skye, she did so by direction of the SED's Standards, not as an expression of her working relationship with the dominie. Hoisting the children through the Six Standards required an anxiously mechanistic pedagogy in a strange tongue; promotion beyond Standard 2 depended upon its mastery (**9F**).

Indeed, it was in the Highlands and the Islands that the Department's drive to regularise became most marked. Historically, this was the region that had always confronted Scottish education with its greatest difficulties. Problems of access, shortage of local resources, absentee landlords, the far-flung layout of the parishes and the absence of any significant middle class, had all combined to militate against a system which depended upon effective parochial organisation. Above all, there was the Gaelic.

A range of charitable and Church initiatives – most notably the efforts of the Society for Propagating Christian Knowledge – had been at work, but it was the parents themselves who had striven to band together to provide a precious basic schooling for their disfavoured young: as recent scholarship has shown, the legend of a Celtic wasteland cannot be sustained. By 1860, most of the gaps had been filled; thirty years on and the SED was bringing the blessings of uniformity to even the most remote of Hebridian outposts. For places like South Uist this meant the imposition of the English language and, in 1890, the arrival, as their teacher, of George Rea – from Birmingham (**9G**).

With standardisation, came a sense of a universal government provision, one that, statute by statute, was reaching into areas traditionally left to the responsible parent and his tightly-knit Presbyterian parish. As the twentieth century advanced, the feeling that the local school was no longer a familiar and intimate presence, that bound teacher and home into a commonly understood purpose, began to broaden into dismay at the ways of the young citizens who were its products.

When, in 1905, a local headmaster directed his concerns to the Falkirk branch of the EIS, he furnished the *Educational News* with several pages of grumbled lament that had to be extended over two issues (**9H**).

To a large extent, the painful sense of rupture was a matter of system, not, as alleged, of morality. Over the preceding seventy years, Scotland's educational provision had grown in both complexity and coverage. What, in 1905, now confronted the long-serving teacher was far removed from the intimate, free ways of small classrooms where strode single-handed dominies and venture dames. The 'school' was now compulsory and it was prolonged. Whereas in the past, any lack of interest in its ways, or preference for child employment, could be simply expressed by a brief and fitful attendance, registration returns were now demanded for all the days of a career which stretched out to age 14. Once, health, clothing and nutrition had been regarded as privately domestic concerns; now, extensive welfare schemes were operating, exposing parental incapacities which had always been there.

What Mr Clark was really complaining of was 'the modern age' itself. Alongside the anguish occasioned by a disturbingly new Scotland, the *Educational News* found space to offer up its accounts of the recently departed. The years around the turn of the century were when those who had entered service under the former parochial system were now slipping from the scene. In the tributes represented by **9I**, it is a whole world that is passing.

The laments and the warnings were to be repeated many times in the decade that followed and, always, it is the ideal of a former, less encumbered and more astringently pure Scotland that is deployed as the guiding value. Hooliganism, now sufficiently visible on the streets to occasion the *News* leader of March 1909, is viewed there as the consequence of 'the breaking down of the last vestiges of parental responsibility' and a nationwide 'reaction against the traditional views with regard to religion and morality'. And, characteristically, it is seen as the product of the towns, not the old rural Scotland. Six months later, the same journal reports that similar observations were filling the agenda of the AGM of the Secondary Education Association. In the keynote address, Dr Maxwell posed the question, 'What is the secret of Scotland's greatness?' The answer he gave was 'Freedom', and, as its most powerful expression, the old parish school where the master had the 'freedom to educate the lad o' pairts as he thought best, in such subjects as he loved most himself'.

It was a construction that inevitably implicated the educational settlement of 1872 and, as its chief agent, the SED. The Act had erected 'a big educational machine' and 'the liberty and the independence of the teacher' had become stultified by statute and inspection. The old intimacies of the parish schoolroom had been ossified beneath the parliament-directed regime and its 'deadening', ever modernising Departmental hand. It was here that the criticisms of the age and of its newest systems sounded their deepest emotional note: the Board School was an intruder, the universalisation of its presence was driving out the native character of Scotland's educational experience.

The new was the alien. To those who had been brought up in it, it was not the past which was a foreign country but Scotland's twentieth-century present.

9A                                                                    Dunbar, 1840s.

An exciting time came when at the age of seven or eight years I left the auld Davel Brae school for the grammar school. Of course I had a terrible lot of fighting to do, because the new scholar had to meet every one of his own age who dared to challenge him, this being the common introduction to a new school. It was very strenuous for the first month or so, establishing my fighting rank, taking up new studies, especially Latin and French, getting acquainted with new classmates and the master and his rules. In the first few Latin and French lessons, the new teacher, Mr Lyon, blandly smiled at our comical blunders, but pedagogical weather of the severest kind quickly set in, when for every mistake, everything short of perfection, the taws was promptly applied. We had to get three lessons every day in Latin, three in French, and as many in English, besides spelling, history, arithmetic and geography. Word lessons in particular, the wouldst-couldst-shouldst-have-loved kind, were kept up, with much warlike thrashing, until I had committed the whole of the French, Latin and English grammars to memory, and in connection with reading lessons we were called on to recite parts of them with the rules over and over again, as if all the regular and irregular incomprehensible verb stuff was poetry. In addition to all this, father made me learn so many Bible verses every day that by the time I was eleven years of age I had about three fourths of the Old Testament and all of the New by heart and by sore flesh. I could recite the New Testament from the beginning of Matthew to the end of Revelation without a single stop. The dangers of cramming and of making scholars study at home instead of letting their little brains rest were never heard of in those days. We carried our school books home in a strap every night and committed to memory our next day's lessons before we went to bed, and to do that we had to bend our attention as closely on our tasks as lawyers on great million-dollar cases. I can't now conceive of anything that would enable me to concentrate my attention more fully than when I was a mere stripling boy, and it was all done by whipping – thrashing in general. Old

*170*

fashioned Scotch teachers spent no time in seeking short roads to knowledge, or in trying any of the new-fangled psychological methods so much in vogue nowadays. There was nothing said about making the seats easy or the lessons easy. We were simply driven point blank against our books like soldiers against the enemy, and sternly ordered, 'Up and at 'em! Commit your lessons to memory!' If we failed in any part, however slight, we were whipped; for the grand, simple, all-sufficing Scotch discovery had been made that there was a close connection between the skin and the memory, and that irritating the skin excited the memory to any required degree.

Fighting was carried on still more vigorously in the high school than in the common school. Whenever anyone was challenged, either the challenge was allowed or it was decided by a battle on the seashore, where with stubborn enthusiasm we battered each other as if we had not been sufficiently battered by the teacher. When we were so fortunate as to finish a fight without getting a black eye, we usually escaped a thrashing at home and another next morning at school, for other traces of the fray could be easily washed off at a well on the church brae, or concealed, or passed as results of playground accidents; but a black eye could never be explained away from downright fighting. A good double thrashing was the inevitable penalty, but all without avail; fighting went on again without the slightest abatement, like natural storms; for no punishment less than death could quench the ancient inherited belligerence burning in our pagan blood. Nor could we be made to believe it was fair that father and teacher should thrash us so industriously for our good, while begrudging us the pleasure of thrashing each other for our good . . .

Notwithstanding the great number of harshly enforced rules, not very good order was kept in the school in my time. There were two schools within a few rods of each other, one for mathematics, navigation, etc., the other, called the grammar school, that I attended. The masters lived in a big freestone house within eight or ten yards of the schools, so that they could easily step out for anything they wanted or send one of the scholars. The moment our master disappeared, perhaps for a book or a drink, every scholar left his seat and his lessons, jumped on top of the benches and desks or crawled beneath them, tugging, rolling, wrestling, accomplishing in a minute a depth of disorder and din unbelievable save by a Scottish scholar. We even carried on war, class against class, in those wild, precious minutes. A watcher gave the alarm when the master opened his housedoor to return, and it was a great feat to get into our places before he entered, adorned in awful majestic authority, shouting, 'Silence!' and striking resounding blows with his cane upon a desk or some unfortunate scholar's back.

Muir, John (1913). *The Story of my Boyhood and Youth*. New York, Houghton Mifflin.

1838–1914: USA naturalist of literary eloquence and pioneering advocate of conservation; regarded as father of modern environmental movement.

## 9B                                                    Montrose, 1890s/1900s.

On my first day at the Academy, that ancient seat of learning founded in 1815, I was somewhat overawed as I climbed the shallow flight of steps leading to the Trance – the entrance – and was directed to the Rector's room. My brothers, however, shared the ordeal and we soon settled down to our respective curricula.

The main building of two storeys was crowned by a dome, which has been quite recently and rather incongruously gilded by a charitable donor. This building housed the English and foreign language departments, while two detached annexes on either side of the main building contained departments of the other subjects taught. The janitor rang his bell at hourly intervals and we all scuttled about, changing classes as required. I always enjoyed this brief dash into the open air, as I never liked being cooped up too long in one room.

I enjoyed learning new and unfamiliar subjects including Latin, French and German. We were encouraged to read verse aloud in all three languages. Oddly, and sadly enough, I now realize we had a better elementary grounding in poetry in these languages than in our own . . . In the English class, so far as I can now recollect, we had no vernacular poetry except for a smattering of Burns, and none of our classics. Dunbar, Henryson, Alexander Hume, Alexander Scott and the like were closed books to me till I discovered them in adult life.

Apart from these omissions in Scotland's classics and its history, in mature retrospect, I have nothing but praise for the teaching I got during my five years 'under the Dome'. The favourite teacher of many of us was John Yorston, a graduate of Edinburgh University who taught Latin and

Greek and after my day became Rector. He was an inspired and inspiring teacher, not only for Latin but of a rounded way of living, and with his wit and humour his classes were always something to look forward to. He was a keen botanist and angler, and learning of my father's evenings at the river he often asked me about 'the fishing'.

I was astonished to find that one of my teachers, Mr Crockett, had taught my mother handwriting. When he discovered me carving my name on my desk, and, worse still, flicking ink-laden pellets up to the ceiling, he wagged his long grey beard at me and said sadly, 'O, Nellie, Nellie, your dear mother would never have done this'. I wasn't so sure of that . . .

When I reached my last day at the Academy and came home with ten prizes strapped on the back of my bicycle, all my father said was: 'If you go on like this you'll break your strap'. He made sure that his only daughter and the youngest of the family should not suffer a swelled head from any over-praise from him. How Scottish!

But I wasn't to go on like this. Although I won first or second prize in every subject at school, I said firmly that I didn't want to be a teacher. I incurred the Rector's displeasure, as he wanted me to go to the University and 'bring honour to the school'. But there were no grants available, unlike conditions today, and my father was already paying lodgings for the two boys away from home. He couldn't afford to send me to University. So it was imperative that I began to earn my living as soon as possible . . .

In Dundee I sat an examination for the local post office and took first place but not the appointment, as I was merely marking time till I was old enough to sit a higher-grade exam that would take me to London. I sat this three-day exam at Marischal College in Aberdeen, eventually taking seventh place in a competition that attracted several hundred entrants. Even then I had to wait another six months before taking up my appointment in the Post Office Savings Bank in West Kensington.

So again I had to mark time at home. I worked in my father's office, learned to type and file invoices, took private lessons in conversational French and somehow got myself elected a member of the Montrose Artisan Literary Association. Often I was the only female present.

Once I revisited the Academy on the prescribed visitors' day, to call on the Rector. He received me coldly and when I asked about my classmates, several now University students, and especially about one Charlie Johnston who used to walk part of the way home with me, the

Rector's acid reply was: 'Oh, he's another pupil gone wrong. He has entered the Civil Service'. I never called at the school again.

In July 1903 I got my 'call-up' and set about my preparations to leave home for the first time and earn my living. I was then seventeen years of age.

Cruickshank, Helen (1976). *Octobiography*. Montrose, Standard Press.

1886–1975: passed her working life as civil servant in London and Edinburgh; poet, Nationalist and supporter of Hugh MacDiarmid.

9C                                                              Dundee, 1892.

## THE CODE

A little book, with an innocent look,
Is the Code, the Code, the Code,
Which 'My lords' have writ – it is full of wit,
This innocent book, the Code.


From morning till night, as the hours take flight,
I think of the Code, the Code;
When I take to bed with an aching head,
I dream of the Code, the Code.


When teachers meet each other they greet
With the Code, the Code, the Code;
Charming topic its 'subjects specific',
A topical book the Code.


One day a week, with club and a cleek,
I fly from the Code, the Code;
But the talk on the green, the strokes between,
Is the Code, the Code, the Code.


Six weeks a year for a holiday clear
I seek a Highland abode;
But dry or wet, I can never forget
My holiday friend the Code.

When I'm laid aside, 'My Lords' will provide,
From the Code, the Code, the Code,
A gratuity nice – Oh Paradise!
I'll have leisure to read the Code.

Davidson, T. M. (1892). 'The Code'. *Educational News*, 21 May. [extracts]


9D                                        Saltcoats, Ayrshire,1900s.


As I was very fond of singing, a good deal of time which should have been spent on academic subjects was devoted to chorus singing of Scottish songs which the children enjoyed. By this time, however, the school inspectors instead of coming once a year for a one-day examination had taken to popping in unexpectedly at any odd time. One day the inspector came in when we were singing and wanted to know what should be taught at that hour according to the curriculum. As a matter of fact I was not sure. I told him about the kind of homes the children came from and the sordid lives they lived with no prospect of any employment other than that of their fathers, and I said that I thought it was a good idea to give them as good a time as possible in their last two years at school. Fortunately, the inspector, a decent fellow, was himself fond of singing and got us to sing some of the songs we had learned. He left, saying that he had enjoyed the music but warning me to adhere to the curriculum or there might be trouble in his report on the school.

Orr, John Boyd (1965). *As I Recall*. London, MacGibbon and Kee.


9E                                              Whitehall, 1906.

THIRD SCHEDULE
NEEDLEWORK.
GIRLS' AND INFANTS' DEPARTMENTS
**The materials used, and the stitches of the exercises performed before the Inspector or in the garments shown to him, should not be so fine as to strain the eyesight of the children, and the presentation of needlework of too fine a character will be considered a defect.**

*175*

## *Infants*

1. Needle drill. Position drill.
2. Strips (2 inches by 2 inches) of soft, loosely woven calico to be hemmed with coloured cotton: – 1. Red 2. Blue.
3. Knitting-pin drill.
4. A strip knitted on two needles (12 inches by 3 inches) in cotton or wool, or four small squares (3 inches by 3 inches).

### *Girls – Junior Division*
### GROUP A

1. Hemming, seaming (top-sewing), felling. A small untrimmed garment, or other useful article, showing these two stitches.
2. Knitting on two needles, purl and plain, e.g., cuffs, vests, strips for petticoats, & etc.

### GROUP B

3. Pleating, sewing on tape strings: a simple garment, e.g., pinafore, apron, petticoat, etc.
4. Knitting, four needles, plain and purl, e.g., cuffs, welts of socks, & etc.

Nos. 1 and 2 (Group A) to be required from the lower part of the Junior Division; Nos. 3 and 4 (Group B) from the upper part of the Junior Division.

'Third Schedule', *Code (1906) for Day Schools*. London, H.M.S.O.

9F                                                         Portree, Skye, 1900s.

Towards the end of April I went to school for the first time, and loved it. It was the old school under Fingal's Seat, a small massive building of grey granite quoined with red sandstone, now ruthlessly demolished to make way for a blank-faced structure of glass and concrete. The old stone building grew from the wild landscape of moors and heights that rose behind it: its impressive but useless tower and its gothic-arched sash windows suggested the dignity of learning. The A.B.C. class and the first two Standards were all taught in one long room with rising tiers of wooden desks and an iron stove, where dear Miss Robertson was infant-mistress, helped by boys and girls in their teens who were training as pupil-teachers. We found these rather dull, except dark-eyed gay Muriel Gillanders, the headmaster's daughter, whom we adored; it must have been a hard day's work for Miss Robertson to train them as well as teaching us. Her face was strong and tender, in ivory contrast to dark hair going grey; she had dark blue eyes with a hint of green in them and a humorous twinkle. She could comfort and encourage in Gaelic the little souls who came to her knowing no other language, but they had to pick up English before they moved on to the next room where Standards Three and Four were ruled by Miss Mackie who came from Aberdeen, knew no Gaelic and stood no nonsense.

There were little chairs and tables; no pictures on the walls; no fun with water or clay or poster-paint. Our education was confined to the three Rs and religious knowledge. We began the day by saying the Lord's Prayer together. I had not met it before, and was full of awed delight in its words and its rhythm. Then we settled down to sums on slates, or to copy-books where pot-hooks and simple forms like *a* and *o* led our clumsy little fists to looped cursive script lines which proclaimed – 'Aberdeen, the Granite City', or 'Inverness, the Highland Capital'. I made short work of our reading-primers with their big print and bright pictures of apples or pussies or children at play, but sums and writing were more discouraging . . .

In mid-October I was advanced to Standard III, and moved into Miss Mackie's room. Children did not go up by years in the primary department of Portree school; they were moved when their teacher thought they were ready. I spent two years with Miss Mackie; Alasdair only six months. She was the most elderly and the least interesting of our teachers; pale and portly with grey hair done up in puffs, a high-necked blouse and a voluminous skirt with a broad leather belt where they joined. She kept good order and drilled us well, but her methods were repetitive and monotonous: when an Inspector walked in one morning and gave us a lively lesson about the countries round the Baltic sea it was like rain in the desert. I came home full of conceited glee. 'The Inspector was telling us about the Laplanders, and he asked what animals they kept, and all the children said, "Polar bears", but I said; "Reindeer", and he said I was a clever little girl, and oh! he was such a nice man!'

Teachers had to be versatile in those days. I remember elderly Miss Mackie giving us lessons in Swedish drill. We were lined up on the classroom floor and she stood on the top step of the desk-tiers doing energetic arm-movements or stooping and straightening with a will while we followed her count. When she taught the girls sewing she had to keep a stern eye on the boys who were doing sums on the other side of the room, and ply the tawse at the first sign of disorder. Sometimes tattered books were handed round for 'silent reading', which would give her a breather. We had to take these books as we were given them and no arguing: there was one story about a little girl who stole a plum which all my friends said was wonderful, but it never came my way.

Macdonald, Isobel (1980). *A Family in Skye 1908–1916*. Stornoway, Acair.

Relatively privileged upbringing – father was Lord Macdonald's factor and mother a trained teacher.

9G                                                    South Uist, 1890.

The scene of the children of all ages entering at the doors, each with a piece of peat which was deposited on the floor near the fire, was quite novel. Though it was winter time none of the children wore shoes or stockings and all the boys with the exception of a few of the biggest wore kilts of home-spun cloth. Most of them, boys and girls alike, looked hardy and weather-beaten. Many curious but shy glances were cast on me as the children proceeded to their places, and an occasional smile from me evoked no answering smile from any of them.

While the lessons, given in Gaelic, proceeded, I read the log-book, and recorded therein the fact that I had that day taken up duty. I then followed as far as possible the instruction that was being given, went round overlooking those who were inscribing in books or on slates, and making mental notes for future guidance. There was no break in the session from ten o'clock in the morning till dismissal at three o'clock in the afternoon. Before the children dispersed I addressed a few words to them which they met with solid silence. It was getting dark, so retiring to the house, feeling none too cheerful after the first day's experience of my new school, I set to work planning how best to cope with matters. While I was so engaged there was a tap upon the sitting-room door; it was opened, and a voice said: 'Teee'. I went to the kitchen, but my housekeeper had disappeared as before, so I had my meal of boiled salted ling and potatoes, the latter with their skins on.

The rest of the evening I spent in preparation of school work; and after a supper which was a duplicate of that of the night before, I went to sleep while thinking of my plans for the future.

Matters in school were a little better next day. I gained a 'Yess' or a 'Naw' from my student teachers, now and then, in answer to my questions – probably they had thought over their conduct of the previous morning. But they astonished me by the way in which they had memorised the chapter of history I had given them to study; page after page they reeled off, absolutely word perfect; and this faculty they evinced throughout the whole course of their subsequent study. This, of course, was very valuable, but apt to prove embarrassing when I wanted them to reason things out for themselves as in mathematics, or from causes to effects.

I myself took charge of the top class throughout that day but could get no English from them except when they were actually reading English from the books. The next day or so it was the same, and it was fully a month before I began to get any response in English. I knew that mutually we had difficulties. Theirs lay in shyness of trying to express themselves in (to them) a foreign language; that they had never had a man teacher before; and that his pronunciation of fairly familiar words was different from any they had ever heard before; so that it was not easy for them to grasp the exact meaning of what I said. Above all, I believe that they had an acute fear of ridicule from each other. My difficulties are fairly obvious, I think. However, by a combination of patience, perseverance and sympathetic consideration for them, before many weeks were over I had overcome much of these difficulties and established a modicum of mutual confidence.

Rea, F. G. (1913). *A School in South Uist. Reminiscences of a Hebridean Schoolmaster 1890–1913.* John Campbell (ed.). London, Routledge.

Was in charge of Garrynamonie School 1890–94 and 1904–13 before finally leaving for post in Birmingham. At that time, the parish had 5,821 inhabitants of whom 3,430 spoke Gaelic only. By all accounts popular and esteemed – though he never did learn any Gaelic.

Stirlingshire, 1905.

It is a melancholy confession to make, but any teacher of an upper division who keeps his mind alert to what is passing around him in the daily work of the classroom, is driven to the conclusion that in the multiplication of subjects which has taken place in the curriculum the 3 Rs are fast being thrown into positive neglect, and boys are reaching supplementary classes, lamentably deficient in spelling or ready facility of expression. Spelling is taught in a haphazard, unsystematic fashion, and rules are seldom given for the guidance of the pupils . . . 'Sweets is sticky' is not an exaggerated specimen of the introductory sentence in a fourth class's essay on confections. The sentence itself is certainly not a confection, despite its alluring alliterative sibilants . . .

We have now got to the stage where too much is free; when parents are too much encouraged to shirk all their moral responsibilities, by relieving them of some of their financial responsibilities. What a man does not pay for, he seldom appreciates, and the granting of one concession makes him all the greedier to covet another.

This shirking of responsibility by parents suggests to me another view of our professional labours, an aspect of our work so well referred to by our Inspector, Mr Millar, but a few weeks ago. Parents now shirk much of the responsibility which should be theirs in inculcating by example and precept moral training on their offspring. In the home circles there is too much mollycoddling, and too little of the sterner discipline which turns out men. Parents to a very large extent have thrown up their hands, and it is not an uncommon remark, though certainly a very sad one, to hear a parent confess that Johnny has got beyond him. Yes, the responsibility for the moral upbringing of the young is being largely thrown upon the teacher and parson. Parents say tacitly, it is the business of the minister and the dominie to make good men; the father has enough to do to mind his work, as if this were not the most serious part of it; and, again, the minister and the schoolmaster are well-paid to do it . . .

The good example of the parent is the first influence to mould the young mind at its most impressionable stage, then come those of the teacher and minister. These must seem to work in harmony, else the young child will soon sneer and scoff. But, I fear, the home influence is in many cases most pernicious in this respect; children are encouraged to set at naught the discipline of the schoolroom, and to carry complaints to the family board; the etiquette and virtues inculcated in the classroom are frequently ridiculed in the home circle, and then when the parents go down the street and meet rude boys, or hear profanity, they stand in holy horror, and say, at least inwardly, and often openly, 'I wonder what you are taught in school' . . .

I should like to say a word on the excessive waste of both time and money in the craze for sport, and particularly football, among the youth, ay, and old age of this country. I suggested earlier that the spirit of play was rampant in our curriculum. Of eighty per cent. of the male population the topic most engrossing in conversation is that of sport. It is the one great subject of discussion at bench, anvil and desk. The *Referee* is better known than any novel, the most fascinating that ever came from the pen of author.

Clark, James, Public School, Denny (1905). 'Our Public School Curriculum', Parts 1 and 2, *Educational News*, 24 June.

91                                          Peebles-shire, 1909.

**Robert Millar of West Linton:** The last week of January has seen the grave close over the remains of one of the most widely known of the rapidly-diminishing band of 'Old Parochials'. Robert Miller, whose death we regretfully record, came as parish schoolmaster to West Linton in the early sixties, and although a good many years have elapsed since he retired from the active duties of his office, he never ceased to take a keen and living interest in all things affecting the educational welfare of Peebles-shire and, indeed, of Scotland. Mr Miller belonged to the philosophic type of schoolmaster. In his quiet village home at the base of the Pentlands, he had, as the years rolled on, thought out his own views as to the place of man in the great scheme of things, and his ideas on education fell into place as part of a well-ordered harmony. And so to him teaching was a great calling, and its highest purpose was ethical. He delighted in the 'lad o' pairts', but character stood first of all, and never was precept founded on nobler or more abiding example.

The most outstanding feature of Mr. Millar's work as a school-master – a feature we would earnestly commend to every young teacher – was perhaps the extraordinary interest he continued to take in all his former pupils. He was never more genuinely happy than when tidings came of the well-being of some one of his old boys and girls, and scores of them- the writer among the number – have to thank the 'Maister', not only for their 'first push', as he called it, but for wise counsel and kindly help given time and time again . . .

And now he sleeps! No more shall we wander by his side with rod, or gun, or golf-club, sharing his delight in the open air, and his child-like love for all living things; no more listen to his apt quotations from the Aeneid – for well he knew and loved the Latin poets, and, most of all, the Mantuan; no more his cheery optimism and faith in the universal good shall put our unworthy doubts to shame. One of Nature's truest gentlemen has gone from us. May Scotland still have many such to educate her youth!

'Robert Millar of West Linton' (1909). *Educational News,* 29 January.

1918–2000

# 10 A GENERAL GROUNDING: PRIMARY SCHOOL EDUCATION 1918–65

*Scottish Traditions*: Lord Haldane, 1917
*SED internal memorandum*: George Macdonald, 1920
*Voices from War*: Eddie Mathieson, 1995
*A Privileged Boyhood*: Alexander McRobbie, 1996
*Shoes were for Sunday*: Molly Weir, 1970
*Jennie Lee, a Life*: Patricia Hollins, 1997
*Message to Edinburgh Education Week*: William Taylor, 1936
*Look after the Bairns*: Patrick McVeigh, 1999
*That Golden Age Again*: Winnie Carnegie, 1996
*Crowdie and Cream*: Finlay J. Macdonald, 1982
*The Winter Sparrows*: Mary Liverani, 1976
*Education Pamphlet No. 4*: Scottish Education Department, 1939
*Schemes of Work for the Primary School*: Aberdeenshire, 1953

Figure 18. **London Road School, Glasgow: primary class, 1914** Bolted desks, tiered flooring and sixty pairs of eyes firmly trained on the one teacher. *Glasgow City Archives*

Figure 19. **Bonaly Primary School, Edinburgh, 2001** Today's pupils encounter the past: visit by a local school to the classroom preserved at the Museum of Education, London Road School, Edinburgh. *Museum of Education, Edinburgh*

Ten days after the armistice which ended the Great War, a new Education (Scotland) Act became law. Although it laid out a number of important administrative changes – principally the absorption of the 947 School Boards into 38 county authorities – the Bill was notable for its spirit of inclusiveness and expansion. The leaving age would be raised to 15; Catholic schools, whilst retaining their own denominational character, were welcomed into the public sector; secondary education was established as a universal right for the able; a systematic progression from 5 to 18, with continuation classes for the non-academic, was envisaged.

The Act promised to fulfill the hopes for 'Educational Reconstruction' which had been sounded out in the latter stages of the war, as the politicians looked forward to converting the people's sacrifices into a socially just peace. The words of Lord Haldane (**10A**) demonstrate the current spirit: there must be a truly national system that would serve each one of his fellow Scots.

In the event, as the EIS *Centenary Handbook* put it, 'the vision of a world fit for heroes faded into the light of common day'. Brutally soon, it became apparent that the economic realities were against them all; from 1923 onwards, education was at the forefront of the sequence of public spending cuts by which the Exchequer struggled to steer Britain through the Depression years. The more ambitious of the 1918 proposals were aborted – it was not until 1947 that the leaving age would finally be raised.

Just as influential to the slow progress of Scotland's education over the next forty years – and with a second war to be endured – was the cautious management of an SED which proved determined to continue its old policy of separating out the latter stages of schooling into an academically orientated 'secondary' provision for the intellectually able few, while the ordinary rest would continue on their 'elementary' way. This meant that their primary years were simply to be topped up with two years or so of practical pre-employment course-work (clerical, manual or housework), uncompromisingly labelled 'Supplementary' or, later, 'Advanced Division'.

Its thinking, in this respect, is exposed by an internal memo its

Deputy Secretary circulated in 1920 (**10B**). In public, the Department continued to deploy two distinct Codes – one Secondary, the other Elementary – by which to regulate a strictly dual-track provision. The strategy aroused hostility. Critics, led by the EIS, saw it as a betrayal of the democratically open education as enshrined in the common parish school. Yet, as Haldane's phrasing reveals, that inheritance was also founded upon a divisive notion of intellectual merit. His 'equality' is to be one not of provision but of opportunity: if of 'character', an 'aristocracy' still.

In laying down two routes, the SED could, therefore, claim to be offering an authentic, indeed, progressively efficient, interpretation of the country's educational heritage. The practical consequences of this policy may be glimpsed in the experience of Eddie Mathieson (**10C**). Clearly able but, as the son of a poorly paid paintmaker, locked into an environment of two-room tenancies and raw council house schemes, at five, he finds himself entrant into a regime of limited expectations and repressive discipline. When he moves on from the Primary stage, he proceeds, not to academic Leith Academy, but to Albion Road, an establishment not yet entitled to the name 'Secondary'. There, his 'Advanced Division' syllabus, though tricked out with 'useful' activity, fails to engage his interest. A future joiner, he chips away disconsolately at a 'woodwork' based on patronising, set-piece model-making.

For this Edinburgh lad, the curriculum, from the basic Infants up to his pre-apprenticeship adolescence, has been the perpetuation of an authoritarian rule that clamps down upon both creativity and character alike. Yet, although his is an alienation that is echoed in a number of working-class accounts, there are others which, from the same setting, offer a version that is so different as to constitute a second, alternative model of the typical Scottish Elementary Education – parental solicitude, not individual oppression.

For Alexander McRobbie, Gove Street School acted as a refuge from a disordered existence within a grimy and overcrowded Cowcaddens tenement (**10D**). It is a response shared by his contemporary Glaswegian Molly Weir. Her descriptions convey an almost rapt immersion in the secure minutiae of the classroom regime. Indeed, her fond references to the utilisation of Grannie's sponge and Father's tobacco tin take the identification with the ethos of the local school a stage further, as the routines of the slate join with other, earlier episodes of the daily round – the Vere Foster handwriting, the chants that 'The Battle of Waterloo was fought in 1815', the playground skipping games – to form a logical, comfortable extension of the domestic economy to which she returns at 4 o'clock within her own vigilantly respectable wee tenement home (**10E**).

Each instance is alike, however, in its election of a special teacher as the key. Weir's roly-poly, bespectacled Miss McKenzie, described earlier, acts as a maternalistic counterpart to McRobbie's glamorously dynamic Miss Moyse. And it is significant that for each, Scottish education's grading machine, which is already at work in the weekly rankings of the class into top boy and bottom girl, into dux and dunce, has singled them out for prominence. When, at 12, they each have to take the 'Qualy' that will determine their Secondary or Elementary destinies, they can do so confident in the sense of their own academic worth which the system has tutored into them.

Nor are they held back by their families' poverty. For each, the vigilant, favourite teacher seeks out a scholarship scheme. But these were the minority beneficiaries of a regime which punished the less able and the irredeemably poor. Jennie Lee was to discover its double-handed nature from both sides of the desk. Although she grew up in a Fife mining community, she benefited from being the only child of a 'decent', politically conscious family, one that introduced books and the piano to her as treasured possessions. Having risen by scholarship to Edinburgh University, Lee returned as a teacher, determined to spread these values to the least favoured children she could find. The result was personal calamity, a breakdown in the very orderliness which had guided her own advancement (**10F**).

One of the features of pronouncements by politicians and officials of the interwar period is their up-beat message of educational progress. Buoying up their audience with references to the inherent superiority of their Scottish tradition, but aware of its reputation for austerity, they are satisfied to contrast an enlightened 'modern' provision with the harshness of the past (**10G**). While the 1930s did see some infusion of new equipment and accommodation, for the generality of pupils the experience of hard-won minority success and widespread frustration continued. Some did find a correspondence between the insistent orderings of the classroom and their own ambitions; many others, once the basics were mastered, struggled to locate any relevance there to the condition of their own working-class lives. For them, the grim child-fearing pedagogy to which they were daily subjected only served

to complete the sense of victimisation, which their domestic deprivation had begun.

It was a pattern that was repeated in the rural lowlands. Patrick
McVeigh's account of his village schooling in the soil-rich Lothian
farmlands is embittered by a consciousness of social bondage which turns
the classroom detail into a political indictment (**10H**). Where Molly Weir
surrounds the ritual of slate-cleaning with a moist nostalgia, he recasts it
as calculated stigma. The running sore of the rubbed out elbow joins the
threadbare Woolworth's bag and cheap mass-consumption bread of the
home table to expose the mockery that lies behind the promise held out
to them by the revered figure of the lad o' pairts.

As in the case of their urban counterparts, there were, however,
others who could look back on their schooldays as an integral part of a
way of life that was simply there to be accepted, along with the weather
and the encirclement of the northern seasons. Nurtured within the
Buchan 'farmtouns', Winnie Carnegie recreates a picture of her nine
years Elementary education at the one plain, three-teacher school,
which views it as a homely centre to a life governed by thrift and hard
endeavour (**10I**). Its timetable of facts and drills is to be placed
alongside the playground games and the trek back amongst the village
fields as a binding childhood routine.

But whatever the location, running through these extracts is an
irresistible sense of the system at work. For Finlay J. Macdonald, it
bears an unmistakable political stamp, one whose imperialistic colouring is made all the more stark by being so arrogantly aloof from the
subtle textures of his own Hebrides culture (**10J**). For him – as
elsewhere in *Crowdie and Cream*, he recounts the expulsion of his
native Gaelic from the Infant classroom – its chief weapon is language.
In this, he is at one with Patrick McVeigh. But if Macdonald is
prepared to regard the submission to English as an inevitable part of
growing up within the modern British state, the Lothian man is fierce
in his denunciation of the schools' acquired contempt for the people's
tongue. He sees the insistence on a standardised English as an exercise
in social control, one whose aim is to keep the first-named of Lord
Haldane's 'peasant and peer' in his place, and to recruit the more
compliantly able of them to act as agents in that process.

But, in the end, it is to the detail of the day-to-day curriculum that
these witnesses return us. Like all those painful lessons on speaking
'properly', the weight of facts to be shifted into the memory requires

an inculcation so remorseless as to demand a nerve-laden, minute-on-minute testing (**10K**). The early morning's mental arithmetic, the endless lists of history's dates to be chanted out, the *Royal Readers'* merry couplets, the capes and the bays of all the British isles made up an obligation so insistent as to become at one with the basic facts of the young Scot's life. Not only that, it had an inescapable substance which loaded the Elementary timetable with a body of knowledge so immemorial that, for generations, the Scottish curriculum remained unchangeable and unchanged.

Although the SED would periodically exhort its teachers to clear out the 'lumber' which cluttered their work, its officials would always return to the codified syllabus as a daily task which was solidly, reassuringly there (**10L**). And when, in the coronation year of 1953, the Education committee of Winnie Carnegie's Aberdeenshire came to revise the Primary School Syllabus in line with 'post-war developments', the thirty-two teachers who formed its working party could do no other than to repeat the grids and the lists handed down from earlier versions (**10M**). After all, these made for what she would have recognised as a 'good grounding'.

10A                                   Edinburgh, 1917.

Lord Haldane said the nation was in the final rounds of a great struggle – a struggle for liberty and a struggle for life, in which it became all of them to concentrate their first efforts. After the War there would come another struggle, a peaceful struggle, none the less a serious struggle, for this nation and this people. The question would be which of the countries of the earth was able to hold the foremost place in the great rivalry. What this War had made apparent was that the basis of victory in the struggle was mind . . . The democracy of this country was profoundly touched by the problem of education. He did not believe there could be a real democracy in this country unless there was an educated democracy. (Applause). They could not shunt education into a water-tight compartment. They could not lock it off from the other concerns of life. There were people who talked as though by a complete system of education you would make men equal. You would not. Nature issued her edict against it. Nature sent into the world some with physical and mental endowments superior to their neighbours.

There would always be an aristocracy in this country; but, from the point of view of democracy, let it be an aristocracy not of rank but of character. (Applause). You could not educate all men equally, because they had not the same capacity of absorbing it equally, but you could give to every boy and every girl in the country, whether they were the children of the peasant or peer, the labourer or the professional man, at least a chance of getting what was the best and highest in education. Equality of opportunity in education seemed to him to be the great maxim for democracy (Applause).

For the realisation of these ideals they must have a thoroughly thought-out and established national system of education, that would reach the whole nation without distinction of rank or caste . . . He had recently read some articles asking the question whether Scotland stood where she did, and whether England was not getting up on her education. The writer pointed out that in some respects the English system had gone forward very fast. He quite agreed that England had done more in recent years, because she had more to do to make up leeway. (Laughter and applause) . . . The substance of education north of the Tweed, however, was to his mind incomparably better than the substance south of the Tweed. (Applause).

> Lord Haldane (1917). 'Scottish Traditions', speech to Workers' Educational
> Association of Edinburgh. As reported in *Educational News*, 5 October.

1856–1928: Edinburgh Academy-educated judge and member Liberal and wartime Coalition governments, with interests in philosophy and social issues.

**10B**                                          Scottish Office, 1920.

They have ignored the fundamental fact that the school population falls into two parts – the majority of distinctly limited intelligence, and an extremely important minority drawn from all ranks and classes who are capable of responding to a much more severe call. It is vital for the body politic that each of these should have the very best education which it is possible to devise, but the education must be adapted to their capacities and matters will not be helped by ignoring the differences between them. The type that is best for one is not necessarily the best for the other, and attempts to establish equivalence may result in harm to both. I am sure it would be far more profitable to admit the difference, to attempt to discover what was the most suitable course of training for each, and then to spare no pains to make these courses as good as they possibly could be.

> Macdonald, (Sir) George (1920), Deputy Secretary Scottish Education Department. SED internal memorandum, Scottish Records Office files, ED/8/3.

Secretary SED 1922–28; noted archaeologist and classicist who had taught in independent sector and at Glasgow University.

10C                                                      Edinburgh, 1930s.

When we moved to Lochend I went to a school called Hermitage Park, which was a fair bit away from Lochend. It was at the bottom of Lochend Road. There were actually three schools there: Hemitage Road, Saint Anthony's – a Catholic school we played at football – and Leith Academy.

I hated school. I hated every minute of it. I hated every school I ever went to, every school. It worries me now that it might have been my intelligence – incapable of learning you know. But, on the other hand, I could write in these days, a fair wee composition. I used to get quite good marks for composition. My spelling was pretty atrocious and remains so to this day. I don't want to knock the education system then. I think they were dedicated people in the schools, even in these days. But they did believe in usin' the strap in the schools I was in. And I got my fair share of that. I got belted all over the place, because I was incorrigible really. I was in all sorts of mischief. I used to play truant as well quite a lot. In the summertime particularly, I roamed up Arthur's Seat. I knew every nook and cranny of Arthur's Seat and used to play cowboys and Indians up there. It wasn't just myself, oh no. I had a good mate that did the same. Him and I got thrashed stupider, but we used to do it just the same. It was this being cooped up in the classroom: I just couldn't bear it. I was an energetic laddie and I liked to be out in the fresh air . . .

I was an assiduous reader. I read and read and read as a laddie. I went to McDonald Road library, at Leith Walk, which was a long walk away. I would go home with three or four books. I've read all my life, and still do. I gobbled up just about everything: boys' stories, adventures, some o' that, but I read the theory of evolution when I was about sixteen. I very early on formed an opinion that religion

*193*

was a load of rubbish. I couldn't swallow the stories out of the Bible . . .

After I left Hermitage Park primary school I went to Norton Park secondary school – it was called Albion Road School then – and that's when the horror began for me. The teachers there were tougher, harder and more prone to use the belt! I have no happy memories at all about that school. Again, it was the discipline, and my work was going wrong. I was a keen reader – but mathematics, oh, terrible. My spelling wasn't too good. Though, mind you, my spelling could have been better then than it is now. I had two good subjects. One was technical drawing and the other one was art. I developed a bit of flair for the technical drawing. Everybody hated it and I thoroughly enjoyed it – strange. But it wasn't that that led me to think of becoming a joiner. I actually got woodwork at school and I never finished a model yet! I was hopeless. The woodwork teacher hated me, of course, and I hated him. He used to throw lumps of wood at me for talkin' when I should have been workin', or puttin' a chisel down in the wrong way or whatever. He always had a lot of wee bits of wood on his desk and he was a dead shot! He would get you on the skull wi' this wee lump o' wood. I hated joinery work. I used to make all these daft wee tooth brush racks and pipe stands – everybody smoked pipes in these days. But I never finished one of them. I certainly hadnae any intentions at school o' becomin' a joiner. I just didn't have any ambitions at the school. All I ever thought about was getting' away from school! That was all that was in my mind.

I left school, I think it was a month or two before I was fourteen. I couldn't get out of the door quick enough. Of course, a few years later I looked back with regret and thought, 'Why did I . . . ?', you know.

Mathieson, Eddie (1995). In Ian MacDougall, *Voices from War. Personal Recollections of War in our Century by Scottish Men and Women*. Edinburgh, Mercat.

1924– : after harrowing war service in Burma, became militant trade unionist (Amalgamated Society of Woodworkers) and worked in further education.

## 10D                                                  Glasgow, 1930s.

Unlike many children, I loved going to school. It meant an escape from a cramped existence in a house that always smelled of boiled cabbage, Lysol disinfectant (to control the bugs) and where the cheap furniture was usually covered with a film of coal dust from the bunker under the food cupboard.

At school, things were clean. Even the lavatories were much cleaner than the communal toilet we shared with five other families. More importantly, at school I had my first experience of people who actually seemed to care about their charges. At home, we were never a demonstrative family. From age five, I never dreamt of kissing my mother, nor can I remember her kissing me. Kissing was reserved for babies or very wee bairns. At five, and going to school, I was a 'big boy', especially as I was the oldest child. Big boys didn't cry, suck their thumbs, or expect to be kissed or praised for their small successes . . .

At primary school, all my affection was directed towards, and returned by, two of my teachers and my one close school chum. A major reason I liked school was because I was always at the top of the class, or second from the top. My best friend, and the only boy I had anything in common with, was also the only English boy in a school where all the other pupils were Scottish.

Lionel Watson lived in quite a good part of Glasgow. His English parents brought him to Scotland when he was two, but because of their influence, he didn't 'talk Scottish' like the rest of us, but always spoke with an English accent – as 'if he had a plum in his mouth', my mother sniffed.

People who tried to 'talk posh' were scoffed at in our circle where everybody spoke in the unmelodious Glasgow vernacular. To speak English properly was regarded as putting on airs. However, in the classroom, most pupils tried to talk posh when speaking to the teacher. In the playground they reverted to the Glasgow patois . . .

Part of the bond between Lionel and me was because we alternated as top or second top of the class, which meant we always sat alongside one another. In those days, each oak and iron-framed desk seated two pupils. The top boy sat at the top right hand desk with the second top boy next to him. The rest of the boys sat in declining order of their scholastic merit, with the class dunce in the front row right under the teacher's eye. It was a co-educational school, but the girls were segregated and sat on the left hand side of the classroom, in the same hierarchical arrangement. There was an aisle about six feet wide separating the girls' side from the boys'. This ascended in a series of steps, leading to the five levels on which the desks were arranged, and let the teacher keep an eye on pupils at all levels.

It was down these steps that we descended fearfully when summonsed to the front to receive the leather strap, or 'tawse' as it was called in Scotland. Lionel and I rarely received the strap, which consisted of three or more whacks to the outstretched palm. Apart from being well-behaved, we were 'teacher's pets' because we grasped things immediately. In examinations, our good marks helped lift the class average . . .

Our most favourite teacher was Miss Moyse, a red-haired woman in her early twenties. She was very attractive and I think Mr Douglas was keen on her. Miss Moyse was the only daughter in a very wealthy family who lived in a three storey mansion in the Great Western Road. Her father was an important executive in a Clydeside yard at a time when the yards were in their heyday. Later, through her father, she helped get a job for my father when he was unemployed.

Miss Moyse had a beautiful speaking voice, with only the faintest Scots burr. I intensely disliked the Scottish accent in females, especially the harsh Glasgow accent. I made an early resolve that when I married, it would be to an Englishwoman, one who spoke English properly . . .

I'm sure Miss Moyse could easily have taken a job at one of the city's fee-paying schools, but she seemed to genuinely like working at a Glasgow Corporation school in a slum area. She also went out of her way to encourage her brighter pupils. In 1938, when I was eleven, the Empire Exhibition was held in Glasgow and Miss Moyse took Lionel and myself to visit it. She paid for everything, including our meals and snacks, and led us round every exhibit, explaining things we didn't understand.

The Empire Exhibition was the last of the international trade fairs to be held before World War II began. It was staged at Bellahouston Park from May until October, and during that period it had 12,500,000 visitors from all over the world . . .

What we saw at the Exhibition was a graphic portrayal of the British Empire at the peak of its influence – 'an empire on which the sun never sets'. To me, it was a mind-expanding experience to see a replica Victoria Falls in the Rhodesian pavilion; red-coated Royal Canadian Mounted police on horseback outside the Canadian exhibit; rubber tree tapping in Malaya; sheep being shorn in the New Zealand pavilion, and real live kangaroos in the Australian exhibit. That day, I decided I was going overseas as soon as humanly possible.

McRobbie, Alexander (1996). A *Privileged Boyhood*. Glasgow, Richard Stenlake.

1926– : wartime service in Malaysian jungle and Singapore; left for Australia where undertook hike right across its land-mass, thus becoming one of the continent's most famous immigrants. 'Privileged' because his father always insisted that a boyhood in the Empire's Second City was just that.

10E                                                         Glasgow, 1920s.

Unlike the teacher with her blackboard, we didn't have velvet pads for wiping the slates clean. Hideously smelling damp sponge or damp flannels were kept by each of us in little tin boxes, usually discarded tobacco or sweetie tins, depending on whether they'd been begged or borrowed from dads or grannies. These cloths were supposed to be damped with water before we left home, but as often as not we forgot. Then there was many a surreptitious spit to get them wet enough to wipe our slates, and they must have harboured germs by the million. In the course of time the damp contents rusted the insides of the boxes, and the smell was awful. Somehow one grew used to the peculiar odour of one's own sponge when the lid was opened, and it was only when the nose twitched at the whiff of a neighbour's box that the pungent aroma seemed revolting. I remember my favourite tin box was a beautiful pale blue which had once held Grannie's Christmas butterscotch, and Grannie allowed me, as a special favour, to cut off a piece of our soft new sponge to match this splendid container, instead of the wee bit flannel clout I usually carried. With what pride I flourished my box as I drew it from my desk each morning, and I was convinced it was the envy of the class.

I loved my slate.

Weir, Molly (1970). *Shoes were for Sunday*. London, Hutchinson.

1920– : became well-known actress on television and radio as well as freelance writer. Her 'Trilogy of Scottish Childhood' paints a warmly nostalgic picture of interwar tenement life in East-end Glasgow.

In September 1926 schools re-opened and Jennie began work. Her notebooks record interminably dull hours of sums on slates, sewing lessons, a day in the life of an Eskimo interspersed with a day in the life of an owl. She had never wanted to teach, but it was her only means to a degree. She wrote despondently to Suse advising her to take a secretarial course, a cookery course, or a hairdressing course, anything other than teaching. 'I am teaching this week & feeling like Hell – only a cold grey hell with all the hot stuff burned out. What a life'. It was drudgery. However, during her teaching practice, head teachers had found her 'bright, alert, keenly interested in the work', her discipline 'very satisfactory, sympathy the keynote' . . .

Fife's Director of Education had been careful with her. She was the well-known daughter of a well-known family. On graduation, he offered Jennie the choice of a local school, and she chose Glencraig, requesting a difficult class, confident that she could win them round. The school was some two miles from Lochgelly, its eight classrooms painted a depressing pea-green, the view from its windows blocked by a slag-heap that towered over the school. In it huddled some forty to fifty children, known to be something of a problem class:

> restless, nervous and not inclined to settle down quietly. It was my job to keep them interested and orderly. Every morning at nine o'clock we valiantly began the day. The first hour went quite well. But, before the end of the afternoon, I was hanging on for dear life in a losing struggle to maintain some semblance of order.

> I had no bent for this kind of teaching. I was too impatient; too much at war with my whole environment. I did not believe in what I was doing. I did not believe that there was any good reason why the children or myself should come to terms with life as we found it in that bleak mining village.

She exhausted herself. Her hair fell out. Discipline was usually maintained by the threat of corporal punishment, but Jennie had renounced the strap. The children tested her. They fought, they spat, they tore books, and Jennie broke. By her account, she gave the leading troublemaker two strokes of the strap. He laughed and threatened to throw his slates at her. She struggled with him and then spanked him.

Hollins, Patricia (1997). *Jennie Lee, a Life*. Oxford University Press.

1904–88: disillusioned with teaching, entered politics, becoming Labour MP at 24; with husband Aneurin Bevan acted as formidable advocate of full-bloodied socialism; became Britain's first Arts Minister; instrumental in setting up Open University.

10G                                               Edinburgh, 1936.

The work of the Committee has not been rendered any easier in recent times by the constant social and economic changes. Despite the difficulty of the times, however, it may fairly be claimed that definite progress has been achieved. One has only to contrast the dingy and cramped premises of some of the older schools with the spacious, well-lighted, and ventilated schools of the present day.

In the appointment of teaching staff, however, upon whose capability the success or failure of the whole system depends, the Committee find their most difficult task. Each step demands accuracy and patience. In the result the community may well congratulate itself, for in no other country is there such a high percentage of staff who prepare themselves by University and other studies; and in the methods of teaching, our Scottish Schools are constantly held up as an example.

Taylor, William (1936), Chairman of the Education Committee.
*Message to Edinburgh Education Week*. Edinburgh.

10H                                               East Lothian, 1920/30s.

Coarse and inarticulate farm boys, the butt of every venomous school teacher for their total inability to speak English, became transformed when they sat on the seat of a reaping machine or held the reins of a pair of horses at the plough. This was their delight; then they became kings, and the misery and humiliation of school were forgotten . . .

*199*

There was nothing of the romantic tradition of the Scottish 'lad o' pairts' amongst the children of these rural proletarians. They had little love of learning and they could not, as fee'd workers and tenants of tied houses, indulge in the luxury of personal opinions or independent thought. They were hired by the year, often by an arrangement which included the labour of their children and wives, and they were miserably underpaid . . .

The farm children who came to our school then were mostly poor, as we were of course. They were often verminous and, although they worked on some of the richest land in Britain, they ate white factory bread and margarine and cheap jam and they were often underfed and sickly. Most children in those days had a runny nose both summer and winter, but especially in the cold, called by that graphic Scottish word a 'snotter'. Most children also had a great mark on their right sleeve which was their substitute for a handkerchief. Sometimes the more caring and despairing mothers would even sew buttons on this part so that wiping the nose was painful; then the mark would be transferred to the other sleeve.

We were taught our lessons using slates, and each child was supposed to bring from home a clean rag soaked in fresh water. Usually a large part of the class were without rags, and cleaned their slates by the simple expedient of spitting on them and rubbing the surface with the elbows of their jerseys. Thus elbows too were almost invariably marked or rubbed clean through.

In the old school we sat at long benches which were fixed to the battered desks by an iron frame. Schoolbags of a sort were obligatory, and Woolworth's store in Edinburgh had a special line in these at a sixpence each. They were made of a sort of stiffened cotton and bound at the seams with a black stuff. Once the fabric got wet they lost all shape and little round black flecks came off the binding and stuck to what was our solitary schoolbook. This was a first reader with the unlikely title of *Chicken Locken Goes to School* . . .

The determining difference between the farm children and the village children was that the farm children arrived at school and were immediately expected to learn in a language, the English language, which was completely and utterly foreign to them . . .

At five years of age, these little, cold and poorly clad and fed children would be herded into a classroom and immediately bawled at by some spinster, herself trying to claw her way out of the working class, in a language which was as foreign to them as French or Italian. It was common for some poor child to look around the room in bewilderment and, if he was lucky, some helpful and bilingual classmate would whisper a translation before he or she was faced with the feared 'tawse'. 'She wants to ken whit name yer ca'ed', the translator would mutter, and relief would spread across the simple face of the questioned infant.

Then came the problem of a reply, and in many cases it would be a problem which remained with the farm child until he was eventually released from the purgatory of school or had slowly sunk to the dunce's section where he could, if lucky, spend the rest of his days in bored oblivion . . .

We would, of course, never be real English; that was accepted and understood. We were, however, taught in English and taught moreover to despise our own tongue. Later on, as we 'progressed' into higher school, we were taught the history of England, with Bannockburn thrown in. We were given English poetry and literature to read and, with luck and if we were bright enough, we could finish up like our schoolteachers, conscious of having achieved a good third-rate education and without any sense of identity and national pride.

McVeigh, Patrick (1999). *Look after the Bairns*.
'Flashback No. 8'. East Linton, Tuckwell Press.

Brought up in large impoverished farming family at Longniddry, near Edinburgh. His book offers vivid testimony to the hardship of place and period, and also of the agricultural way of life common then to most of lowland Scotland, but now gone.

101                                                          Aberdeenshire, 1920/30s.

There were three rooms at Tortie, the infant room, taking bairns from 5–7 years, the junior room, and then when you reached the ripe old age of 11, you moved with great trepidation into the 'dominie's en'. Each room looked alike, yellow distempered walls surrounded by dark wooden panels, desks which held two pupils, with a slit for your slate and a groove for your scalie, and woe betide anyone who lost their scalie or had a bit that squeaked on their slate. That was enough to merit a clout on the lug. The junior room excelled itself, there was a picture on the wall showing two cups crossed out, and two cups brimming full, and underneath was the caption:–

'Run away coffee, run away tea,
Milk and cocoa come with me.'

Such words of wisdom, but such frivolities for a school room!

We started each day with the Lord's Prayer, 'Our Father chart in Heaven', followed by one of the beautiful old Scottish psalms or a hymn. Our favourite hymn was undoubtedly 'Childhood years are passing o'er us, Soon our schooldays will be done'. We would glance at each other and secretly clap our hands under the desk. Little did we know or even think where our future paths might lie, and we would have scorned any grown-up who tried to tell us that these were indeed our happiest days.

Although the building was drab compared to today's modern glass structures, we had a very good grounding in the three Rs. There were different age groups in each room, and the teacher had to arrange the work accordingly. We were never allowed to slack nor talk to each other. I was firmly convinced that Miss Barclay told the truth when she said she had eyes on the back of her head. I had a favourite aunt who was a teacher in Aberdeen, and I always longed to search her thick hair to see where she hid her second set of eyes. The strap – or tag – lay permanently on the table, and if anyone did speak or giggle, or shuffle their feet it flew through the air and miraculously landed on the culprit's desk. The unfortunate one was told to 'bring that out here' and was duly chastised.

We learned most of our lessons by repetition, spellings, tables and history dates. During the geography lesson we stood in a half moon circle round the map which was hung on the back of the door. We repeated all the countries and towns with the pointer working overtime. Unfortunately this door was the only escape route into the playground from both the infant and junior rooms. Each time, and that was fairly often, when an infant wanted the wattery, the map had to be removed to let the door open. The pass word – oh yes, we were taught manners as well – was 'Excuse me, may I get past', but one five year old when confronted by the words

'What do you say?' could only stumble out 'Wull I win bye' before nature took its course.

We had a ten minute interval in the forenoon when we all raced outside into the playground. The youngest bairns played 'Chuckenies' where a tinkie wifie had to come and steal the chuckens. The older and rougher ones played Bush, a type of taki, when we all joined hands as we were caught and chased each other round about. If anyone tumbled on the stoney playground there was always a kindly lass ready to wash their wounds with cold water and blue and white marble soap . . .

Dinnertime was from 12.30–1 p.m. and again in the summer months we'd play across the dutch and eat our piece, unless we had previously eaten it at the 11 o'clock playtime. In winter we got a tin bowl of soup, and never did soup taste so good. The more affluent pupils carried tin flasks of cocoa to school and we were allowed to place them round the fire in the corner of the room, and so enjoyed a hot drink after their soup. When the soup season was coming to an end, we had a memorable feast of mince and tatties. This was looked forward to for days ahead, and there were few absentees on that important date.

In the winter, if a blizzard blew up, there was always a row of welcome horses and cairts waiting outside to give us a hurl home. We'd sit on the floor of the cairt and put our quytes over our heads and sing our playground songs. 'Down in Yonder Meadow' or 'Bobby Bingo'. If the cairt had been to the station, we might be lucky enough to find a locust bean or two, and these were bitten into and shared around.

On fine afternoons after school, our nearest stop would be a neep field and there we'd take our pick, and chap it on a pailing post and nibble its inside just like a rabbit. We knew where the best sooricks grew, which scrapie the teuchat had favoured for her eggs, and whether the mavie's gorblins had flown. We knew all the wayside flowers and berries, especially the edible ones, and we dug in the banks for 'R' nuts [pig nuts] . . .

Looking back, I am sure we had a better grounding in the three Rs than many of the children today. The pity was that the great majority of these dear bairns left school the day they were fourteen, either to hud the ploo' or to become kitchie deems. It is good to know that some who were able to tak' further learnin' went on to become doctors

or teachers, or made their mark in other spheres. Part of our heritage is
gone for ever with so many country schoolies closing.

> *dutch* – ditch; *quytes* – coats; *soorick* – sorrel; *teuchat* – lapwing; *scrappie* –
> hollow; *mavie* – songthrush; *gorblins* – chicks.

Carnegie, Winnie (1996). 'That Golden Age Again',
*Ugie Pearls*. Peterhead, Buchan Observer.

1916– : became civil servant and, in retirement, noted celebrant of North-east
Aberdeenshire life.


10J                                                      Harris, 1920s.

*The Royal School Series* (that was the umbrella title) consisted of two
Infant Readers and six Junior School Readers, all uniformly bound in
sedate dark blue covers sporting a large crown motif to remind us,
presumably, that, away in the outmost Hebrides, we were still the
fortunate denizens of the great power whose domains were splurged in
red across the full width of the schoolroom map. The series,
unamended as far as I know, served generations of 'scholars', and
I have often wondered if, in faraway corners of those red splodges,
future perpetrators of insurrection were having their cultures ironed
out of them by means of flat banalities in, albeit immaculate grammar.
The imagination jibs at the thought of, say, Mr Robert Mugabe being
made to stand up in front of his class and read aloud such gems of
poetry as . . .

> Dicky bird, Dicky bird whither away?
> Why do you fly when I wish you to stay?
> I never would harm you, if you would come
> And sing me a song while you perch on my thumb.

And yet, why not? Our native culture was as remote from that of the
hub of the empire as were the separate cultures of Messrs Mugabe and
Nkomo, and the grand plan was to smoothe them all out into an
acceptable uniformity.

Our teacher was a staunch upholder of the 'system' as a result of her
own indoctrination; and it was not her instinct but her training and the

policies of government at all levels, that made her labour to hone and polish us so that we could take our places in a society other than our own. 'If you don't do your sums . . . If you don't learn your spelling . . . If you don't practise your reading . . . you'll never get away from here.' These were the exhortations of school and home, and nobody ever paused to think that, particularly in those days of the hungry thirties, *here* was a damn good place to be. With hindsight it is almost incredible that, all over the Highlands, men who had fought to establish their right to the land, and to create new communities such as ours, were subscribing to a system which would ensure that their sons would seek out lives and livelihoods elsewhere.

Macdonald, Finlay J. (1982). *Crowdie and Cream*. London, Warner.

Well-known broadcaster and producer. This is the first of trilogy celebrating his interwar Hebridean upbringing.

10K                                                        Glasgow, 1940s.

Life was like a high tension wire slung out in a void and I crawled my way over it with the same fear and hesitation that marked my crossing of the backyard dyke. Every progression left me tense and exhausted. School, even more than home, was a source of continual tension, a perpetual challenge not only to your intellect, but to your survival as a free being, besetting you on all sides with bogey men that sprang up like dragon's teeth: you seized one by the throat in desperation and another grinned in its place. There was little rest. Play was never simply play, nor learning simply learning. You were always being tested. Tested in the morning for tables and whack with the pointer if you were too slow. Tested for the names of capital cities and dead kings, tested for writing, up light and down heavy so that your fingers clawed in cramp from the strain of controlling your pen, tested for spelling, tested for the dozen rule, tested for the score rule, tested every Friday so that your fingers trembled independently in anticipation when you sat down at your desk.

Liverani, Mary (1976). *The Winter Sparrows*. London, Michael Joseph.

1931– : one of ship-rigger's of family seven which emigrated to Australia just after War.

10L                                             Scottish Office, 1939.

Much of the teaching at the primary stages must be of a formal nature, i.e. it must tidy up and pigeon-hole the child's knowledge . . . Much of the knowledge acquired in the primary division must be so firmly fixed in the mind of the child that throughout life he will be able to draw on it without effort or conscious thought. Such familiarity with any subject can never be achieved except by practice and more practice, drill and more drill.

Scottish Education Department (1939).
Educational Pamphlet No. 4.

10M                                             Aberdeenshire, 1953.

ENGLISH SUBJECTS

**CLASSES P. I AND II (Infant).**

SPEECH TRAINING –
  (1) Handkerchief drill (clearing one nostril at a time and never both together).
  (2) Breathing exercises for speech, e.g., 'blowing a windmill', 'blowing a soft breeze and a strong breeze', copying an engine letting off steam to whistle.
  (3) Ear training – listening to and reproducing sounds.
  (4) Vowel sounds in singing – imitating animal calls.
  (5) Consonant sounds – during teaching of word building.
  (6) Naming of objects – in the form of games.

ARITHMETIC

**CLASS P. IV.**

Revision of work up to date.
1. Notation to 10,000.
2. Addition and subtraction up to 4 figures. In addition, column total will be limited to 40 and rows to 5.
3. Tables: 7 times to 12 times (7 and 9 last).

4. Multiplication and division by numbers up to 12. (Taught together in oral work). Written work follows.
5. Long multiplication by 2 figures.
6. Money: (1) Addition and subtraction involving pounds, shillings and pence (with not more than 2 figures in the pounds).
   (2) Multiplication and division by one figure.
7. Suitable oral examples on above work and simple problems.
8. Long division to be introduced during third term.
9. Reading ruler and inch tape: a knowledge of the names of weights and measures which will be met with later in the course. Ton, cwt., st., lb., oz., yd., ft., inch – e.g., coal is bought by the ton and cwt., cloth by the yard, etc.

HISTORY

**CLASS P. VII.**

Period from 1714 to present day:–
A. (Not more than *six* items)
   (1) The Hanoverians and the Jacobite Rebellions.
   (2) The Struggle with France.
   (3) The French Revolution.
   (4) War with Napoleon: Moore, Nelson, and Wellington.
   (5) Reforms of 19th Century; The Poor Law; Parliament; Abolition of Slavery.
   (6) Mutiny in India.
   (7) Revolt of the American Colonies.
   (8) Settlement of Australia and New Zealand.
   (9) The First World War.
  (10) The Second World War.

B. *Biography* – (not more than *two*) –
   (1) Wesley (2) Clive (3) Wolfe (4) Cecil Rhodes.

C. (not more than *three* topics) –
   (1) How people lived in the days of the Georges.
   (2) Roads, Canals, and Railways.
   (3) New ways of farming.

(4) New inventions and new ways of making things (e.g., James Watt, Kelvin, Friese-Greene, Baird, Watson-Watt).

(5) Advances in Medicine (e.g., Simpson, Lister, Hunter, Fleming).

(6) United Nations Organization.

County Council of the County of Aberdeen Education Committee (1953). *Schemes of Work for the Primary School.* [Extracts]

# 11 SENIORS AND JUNIORS: SECONDARY SCHOOL EDUCATION 1918–65

Figure 20. **Frederick Street School, Aberdeen, 1907** One of the score of establishments raised by the city's School Board to house its East-end population. Although its roof playground is innovatory, the old gender divisions still hold fast. *Aberdeen City Libraries*

Edinburgh Ladies' College.

Figure 21. **Edinburgh Ladies' College, c. 1920** Another roof playground – but a rather different ambience. The College was one of several private establishments set up in the late nineteenth-century city to serve the growing middle-class 'West-end' market for a select education. *Scottish Life Archive*

At the age of twelve, Mary Liverani came through the biggest of all her primary school tests – the Qualifying examination run by the City of Glasgow Education Authority. For its officials, this was the device by which they determined the type and location of school to which each of that year's senior Primary children should next be sent. For the young Mary it was 'the exam that decided the rest of your life'. The immediate alternatives were the Academy and its prestigiously academic regime of Latin, Chaucer, Higher French and Fifth year hockey – or Lambhill Street Junior Secondary where 'sewing, cooking and office work' would be the daily fare. To pass was to be granted her ticket of 'exit from the tenements'. So, as she stands at the back of the assembly hall (11A), the spectacle of gowns and senior prefect uniforms fills her with a sense of romantic quest. She will spurn the old alley ways; this is the dawning of the new life.

Her contemporary James Murray was not so lucky. Although the routines of the bigger school give him some initial stir, the limited nature of the timetable soon disillusions him (11B). There is the growing awareness that its syllabus amounts to nothing more than a diluted version of what his favoured counterparts at Queen's Park Academy would be receiving as the first stages of the five year course that would guide them onto Highers, university and the professions. The fact that 'the English' and 'the Algebra' are supplemented by a couple of afternoons in the Woodwork room merely confirms that he and his kind are being processed towards some lowly-rated manual job and, with it, their acceptance of a socially relegated future.

These contrasting futures, played out in the Glasgow of the 1940s, exemplify the way the SED's bipartite policies had evolved since the Act of 1918. While the priority remained the academic elite, the Department had been busy attempting to promote its 'Post-Primary' courses as the credible alternative for the non-'bookish' majority. The Supplementary years, age twelve to fourteen, had been rebranded as 'Advanced Division'; Day School Certificates were introduced; teachers were encouraged to incorporate real-life activity into their classrooms. And, increasingly, the examination which determined allocation to its curriculum was acquiring a psychometric status by the utilisation of Intelligence Tests, as developed by Professor Godfrey Thomson of Edinburgh University.

Within the larger urban areas, the Education Authorities' response was to group its final years' pupils into 'Central' schools where a proper concentration on Advanced Division work could be achieved. The concept of the old all-through Elementary education, thus, became superseded by the visible evidence of two distinct stages in operation. The term 'Junior' Secondary began to be employed; the Grammar, High and Academy counterparts became the 'Senior' version. The principle of secondary education for all had now been established – but in a way, and through a pair of titles, that confirmed the old relative rankings.

This was clear even in the much smaller centre of Inverness. Sheila Mackay's description of the means by which she, rather than 'they', was propelled towards its Royal Academy (**11C**) demonstrates how Scottish children, right into the 1950s, were being trammelled by a sociocultural mechanism, which, at the age of twelve, took upon itself the power to adjudicate friendship patterns, adolescent lifestyles, cultural expectations and, ultimately, whole destinies. The apparent indifference of this system to the personal sensibilities involved is exposed by the callously public announcement by which it delivers its verdicts.

As these three witnesses attest, the Senior Secondary was associated with the middle-classes. Its architecture and antiquity, the trappings of uniform and of regalia, its very name, proclaimed a superior standing. Many of them were, indeed, still permitted to charge fees – even as late as 1965, twenty-six public authority establishments were still doing so. One of them was James Gillespie's High School for Girls. Encountering Muriel Spark's 'Marcia Blaine' in *The Prime of Miss Jean Brodie*, it is difficult to realise that the establishment on which it is based was administered not by some independent Board of Governors but from the offices of the City of Edinburgh.

It was schools of this type that set the standard for the newer Senior Secondaries. Whitehill, in East-end Dennistoun, had been one of the 'Higher Grade' schools which Glasgow had set up in the 1890s in order to meet the demand by the city's growing ranks of middle-class and ambitious artisan parents for a more advanced curriculum. Never satisfied with remaining at any 'Elementary' level, Whitehill rapidly developed the capacity to prepare its pupils for the full academic range, including Leaving Certificate work. The pattern was repeated elsewhere: by the 1920s, the SED had come to recognise such 'Higher Grade' places as properly 'Secondary', thus adding some 200 further names to the select 55 to which it had accorded that status before the War. And by its 1936 Education Act, the label 'Elementary' finally gave way and the title 'Secondary' was adopted by officialdom as denoting the stage of education which all pupils entered on completion of their primary syllabus.

If this was evidence of the way in which local initiatives were broadening the boundaries, the later development of the country's Whitehills showed how the gap between Senior and Junior was yawning ever wider. Having secured its academic status, the school began to cultivate an extensive extra-curricular programme of team sports, prefect systems, awards and clubs, to procure a School Song and set up a Former Pupils' Association. This East-end school was to act not merely as a preparation but as a corporate experience, sufficiently all-embracing to instil the higher social graces. One of its chief expressions was the School Magazine: its Sixth form editor is here (**11D**) urging on his readership towards a loyal participation in the collective ethos.

For many twelve-year-olds, entry through the portals of tradition made for a daunting journey. A working-class kid like Alan Spence could find it quite bewildering (**11E**). His bemusement at being 'pitched' into it all is compounded by the calculated repression imposed by some of its staff.

But, once settled in, Spence adjusts. Six years later he will emerge fully armed with the Highers that will enable him to go on to university – and a notable literary career. Other young Scots, also able, also motivated, were not able to join him. The capacity to take advantage of the system's 'equality of opportunity' depended as much on economic circumstances as it did upon native wit. The frustrations of Roderick Wilkinson were suffered in the Depression years (**11F**), but even in Spence's decade some seventy-five per cent of entrants into Senior Secondary courses were quitting before the crucial Leaving Certificate stage, to opt into employment. Yet, despite such figures, the conclusion that they unmasked the system's democratic pretensions would not be a balanced one. Into Spence's account is worked a sense of wonder at the new subject worlds and enlarged society now being opened to him. For the likes of him, the Senior school is an opportunity to work out his own strengths and interests. He is beginning to ascend 'the ladder'.

And, if the company he is in is rather select, its numbers had grown considerably since the days of forty years before. In 1923, the SED had devolved the administrative burden of the Qualifying Examination to the local Authorities; they had proved more and more willing to exploit its measurements as generously as possible. By 1960, the Department's original assumption of a 10:90 split had shifted to 40:60 – and a significant ten points higher than England's.

Nor did the excluded sixty per cent always find their Junior experience a disappointment. Ethel Kilgour's Frederick Street gave her a feeling of expanding horizons and some inspirational teaching (**11G**). To a later age, her account of well-equipped kitchen-rooms and mandatory sprays will be evidence of a paternalistic determinism at work, one that is both sexist and sociological in force. But, to her, it was all proof of a provision that was sufficiently caring as to give the details of its operation an appreciatively nostalgic sheen.

Her testimonial shows that, for some, the system could work. But its functioning depended upon a static view of society in which the majority would always be leaving for manual employment and into fixed class and gender roles. Nor, despite Kilgour's accolade, were the Junior Secondaries as well furnished as their Seniors. The accommodation was inferior, their siting likely to be imprisoned within a raw new housing scheme or perched on some downtown street corner; staff were less well qualified and worked with scantier resources. The curricula they delivered were also, as Murray comments, less 'well thought out'. Despite the appearance of 'Technical', 'Commercial' and 'Domestic' strands, the bulk of the timetable still consisted of the standard subjects, offered in hopeful imitation of the prestigious local High or Grammar. The SED's attempts to persuade their staff into a more innovative approach, and the adoption of the 'doctrine of interest', became a persistent feature of the period, the lack of their penetration shown by the frequency of the repetition.

Above all, there were the social realities. Following the 1945 Education Act, the nostrum 'age, ability and aptitude' was enshrined in official explanations of the individual pupil's curriculum. The public was not convinced. For its members, the different routes pointed not to an appropriate diversity but a blatant division into something that was 'Senior' and a lesser 'Junior' thing. How could it be otherwise when selection into the latter was not by any positive appraisal but a failed examination?

The raising of the leaving age to fifteen through the same Act had originally led to hopes that the extra year would force the Junior sector into the development of substantial courses – but frequently the result was a protracted sense of futility and an added cohort of disaffected adolescents. James Inglis was voicing a general view in his bleak 1950 description of a system not parallel but broken (**11H**).

The additional year had, moreover, swollen school populations and swallowed up scarce post-war resources. To the idealistic schemings of the educational do-gooders, the Headmaster of Abercorn Junior Secondary, Paisley, was moved to oppose a blunt classroom floor perspective (**11I**).

These, however, were urban viewpoints. Many Scots would have claimed that the essential values of democracy lived on in the smaller, more rural centres. At Troon, Lesley Duncan's transition from primary to secondary was in the company of every other twelve-year-old there, regardless of ability or background (**11K**). It was true that, in such places, the population level was still too modest to disturb the old practice of sustaining the one all-purpose school. Neither Troon Senior nor Troon Junior Secondary, but simply Marr College, a daily meeting point, still, for the whole community.

The values of social unity and pastoral care which filled the typical small town school are vividly recalled by A. Stephen as he retraces his initiation into Kirkwall Grammar School (**11J**), its title as freely available to the poorest Orcadian crofter's daughter as his minister's eldest son. The communal ethos the young teacher was absorbed into was sufficiently potent to overcome any deficiencies of equipment or sense of backwater isolation.

And Troon, Ayrshire, against Kirkwall, Orkney, were simply two points within a whole network of small burghs which stretched across the country and there mapped out an enduring landscape of common schooling. This was the heartland geography which stirred the Secretary of State's 'Advisory Council' when, in 1947, it produced its vision for post-war *Secondary Education*. The spectacle of the rural burgh school, at the centre and service of the whole community, led to its advocacy of the 'omnibus' school as the universal way to heal the palpable inequalities of the pre-war system and to ensure the 'full and harmonious development' of every young Scot.

In the event, *Secondary Education* was widely praised for its eloquence – and then shelved. The SED simply bypassed proposals which demanded such a disturbingly radical upset to its own bipartite structures. But there was an even more pressing reason for Departmental inaction: the Advisory Council's vision had been rooted in a Scotland of comfortably small burghs, each planted in its own organic rural soil. Its members had averted their gaze from the land which Scotland had actually become – a complex, industrialised society in which seventy-five per cent of the people were now housed in towns of more than 5,000 in population.

The enthusiasm for the 'comprehensive' tradition of the typical country school was, moreover, based upon a fallacy – that universality of entrance assured equity of treatment. It is exposed by Norman Dixon when, writing in 1965, as the new English model of the multipurpose comprehensive was being debated north of the border – and often to the conclusion that they were unnecessary in 'democratic' Scotland – he owns up to the fact that within his own Inverurie Academy, the Qualifying examination still operated, still shut more doors than it opened (**11L**). What he was Rector over was really two schools under the one roofing, an institution where the 12-plus failures were herded on to separate tracks, complete with separate staffing. Nor were the parents fooled: each one of them was acutely aware of which side of the corridor they and their neighbours' offspring received their schooling.

Right into the 1960s, the policy-makers were attempting to convince the people that their children were being served by a system in which all were treated equally, if differently. In 1955, the new Chief Inspector, John Brunton, headed a Report which urged Junior Secondary staff to base their work on the real-life world of adult work. Some interesting experimental projects did spring up and the term 'Brunton Course' entered the currency. The generality of schools, however, continued to search for their syllabuses in the textbook cupboard rather than at the local factory workshop or office desk.

It was Brunton himself who had located the abiding centre of such thinking when he referred to his Department's Leaving Certificate as 'the Holy of Holies'. Since its introduction back in 1888, its Highers had become institutionalised as the defining goal of all Scottish education, its scholarly rubrics the shaping model for all its teachers' professional strivings, however remote their pupils might be from its prestigious heights. For some of his colleagues, it was an eminence that cast shadows, not light (**11M**).

This Director was speaking at the War's end; fifteen years on, as the sixties loomed, so did signs of change. In the open glassed frontages and confident ferro-concrete of reconstruction, which was spreading itself into the green-field edges of the old places, was the promise of new schooldays. An example was Kirkcaldy High School, now transplanted from its cramped old quarters to a hillside that overlooked the town. Opened in 1958, before the presence of Her Majesty, its arrival was graced by a brochure which speaks of individual lockerbays and a swimmingpool, of the centrally positioned library and landscaped surrounds. But KHS once housed Adam Smith and Thomas Carlyle: the commemorative words talk also of continued practice and binding tradition(**11N**). The freshness of the environment is there to rehouse the old as much as it is to manage a future.

11A                                                                 Glasgow, 1940s.

There were no more fights up the alley for me, for not long after I began at the Academy. It was now called Bellahouston Senior Secondary, but I resented the change. Why did they wait till I went to it, to stop calling it the Academy? In my area, however, it retained its old name. Most of the people in my class were posh sorts. They would have been flabbergasted to see a girl fighting up the alley. They went to dancing and elocution. So I said to Robert and Jackie:

'You'll have to fight your ain battles now'.

They were indignant. 'Just because ye're at Bella, ye think ye're something'.

In fact, at no other time in my life have I felt so concretely something. I was the luckiest person alive, the most privileged. I pitied the rest of the world. The only thing that modified my exultancy, though not much, was not having the uniform. How could anyone in the streets around be expected to realise from my gaudy tartan coat, a gift from the Canadian Red Cross to Glasgow's poor and needy, or from the square-necked, short-sleeved blouse dyed gold, and the navy tunic, that I attended Bellahouston Academy. At least a badge, I protested to my mother, would be better than nothing, but even that outward sign to strangers of my extraordinary status was impossible.

In the school itself, however, standing at the back of the hall with two hundred other first year students, I felt like a Don Cossack, a Jesuit, a Janissary, a Mameluke, a crack servitor. Serving whom or what? The headmaster, our sultan, his white sausage curls carefully straddling his head like a barrister's wig? The teachers, long and black and serious in their gowns, their expressions neatly arranged for the solemnity of the weekly occasion? Or the elderly looking senior boys with their incredible moustaches and military bearing?

Liverani, Mary (1976). *The Winter Sparrows*. London, Michael Joseph.

11B                                                                     Glasgow, 1940s.

In those days, when you reached the age of eleven, you had to sit your qualifying examination, known as the 'quali'. The exam was a serious watershed as to the direction of your education and school. Would it be the prestigious Queen's Park? – uniforms and all. Next in line was Strathbungo, a school with a formidable track record. The third school in the order of merit was Calder Street Junior Secondary, which catered for the 'also rans'. You had to shape up to the exam ordeal as best you could. It was in its way quite nerve-racking. It certainly proved too much for one of my classmates who came from Jamieson Street. Shortly after the exam got underway he had to withdraw, having shit his trousers . . . It took some time for the results to come through, and when they did my worst fears were realised: it was going to be Calder Street Junior Secondary for yours truly.

I spent a period of nearly three years at Calder Street Junior Secondary School . . . A major aspect of the school programme was the use of the timetable for the various classes. I thought this was very modern and somehow important. The ad hoc example of one that follows will, I am sure, strike a cord with many a reader.

## Calder Street Junior Secondary
## Class 2.1.A. Timetable (circa 1942)

| | | | | | |
|---|---|---|---|---|---|
| *Monday* | Maths | Geography | Music | Gym | Technical Drawing |
| *Tuesday* | History | English | Science | Woodwork | |
| *Wednesday* | Art | Geometry | English | Games | |
| *Thursday* | Algebra | English | Art | Maths | Religious Instruction |
| *Friday* | | Assembly | Maths | Physical Training | Reading |

It will be seen from the timetable that no instruction was given to the learning of a foreign language, no study of stage or drama. Social studies hadn't even been thought of. The impression was given that as you were going to be an artisan of some sort it would be better not to antagonise this unspoken trend. Leave well alone seemed to be the official attitude . . .

Looking back on the last few years of my school days, I have tried to figure out what the aim and purpose was of the 'education' that I had received. When I left school at fourteen I felt inadequate in many ways. My self-confidence was poor and never helped or developed by the so-called 'teachers' . . .

The framework of the Scottish Educational system was, to my mind, a disgrace. The major duty of any such system should be to develop the child's self-confidence and point him towards 'self-realisation'. What my contemporaries and myself received was the opposite. We were cowed and made to know our place: most of the teachers were over-bearing. It was the era of touching the forelock in obeisance to your supposed superiors. Properly organised classes in stage acting, movement and speech would have helped greatly in the building of self-confidence, allowing the boys and girls to mix. As it was, we were treated like two different forms of life that happened to be using the same building. The whole set-up was poorly thought out.

Murray, James, (1991), *Three Tears for Glasgow*. Glasgow, Murray Promotions.

1930– : became well-known Glasgow boxing manager and promoter.


11C                                                          Inverness, 1950s.


In those days, you had the choice of going to the technical school – the boys got woodwork and all that sort of thing and the girls got domestic science, which was terribly sexist in modern-day terms. Or you went to the Academy and took the academic course, probably with a view to going on to university. I did the qualy; it was the bursary you called it then . . .

One memory sticks out very clearly, the day the bursary exam results were read out. We had a super teacher, Miss Smith; she worked very hard with all her class and everybody was on pins. There were quite a few, whose parents were reasonably well-to-do and obviously had aspirations, who didn't pass and one or two of them were quite hysterical. The headmaster came and handed the papers over and the results were read out. There was nothing sent to the house, it was read out there in front of all your peer group and the humiliation for those who had hoped and had been encouraged, not to say bludgeoned, by their parents into doing well and didn't, it was very hard going, it was terribly tense. Were you going to pass or were you not? . . .

It was a tremendously traumatic experience for twelve-year-olds. I remember making myself quite ill about it, wondering if I could cope with going to this school. Coming from a very poor background – my father was a guard in the railway and my mother did some cleaning in the school along the road – and then going in with all the solicitors' and doctors' children, it was a shock. I didn't particularly let it get me down and most of them were okay but there were a few snobby teachers who definitely favoured the better-off children. But most of them were pretty good.

A lot of friendships split up as well. The schools were about two miles apart, and each of these took in a catchment area from the whole town so, for a lot of old friendships with people you'd been in primary school with who didn't make it to one school or the other, that was it. You started moving in different circles.

Mackay, Sheila (1999). In *Scotland's Century*.<br>
Colin Bell (ed.). Glasgow, HarperCollins.

1939– : family hardship forced early leaving to work in butcher's shop; later became a community activist.

## 11D                                                         Glasgow, 1929.

A school is more than a stone building where classics and mathematics are taught. It is, or at least should be, an immensely personal creation, with an *esprit de corps* and a tradition which hall-mark each pupil and make its badge a stamp with a meaning . . .

Many will have noticed a tall panel in the hall. On it will be inscribed the names of those who have distinguished themselves in the school itself by winning the Henderson Memorial Medal. The list of names is being drawn up, meanwhile, and will be completed shortly.

Nor is the sports side being neglected, for it is possible we shall have photographs of Whitehill's past and present sports teams gracing the corridors before long.

All the school organizations are in full swing. Among them has appeared a baby, the Debating and Literary Society, which has proved itself a youngster with a kick in it. The debates are of the liveliest and most cheerful nature, the teachers deriving just as much pleasure as the pupils themselves. Our compliments are due to the football team who drew with Hamilton Academy, the team which so severely defeated them a few weeks ago.

Mr McGregor is hard at work tuning up the choir who hope to give a concert in the spring. They will, as usual, give us a carolling send-off at the Christmas holidays. More members, especially boys from the IV year, are invited to swell the numbers and the noise.

We must congratulate James Hercus for graduating M.A. with 1st Class Honours in Mathematics, and S. L. MacKinlay with 1st Class Honours in English.

Unfortunately, *anni fugaces labunter*, and the staff are constantly changing. Miss Muir has retired to enjoy a well-earned rest. She has left behind the most pleasant memories, and in wishing her a long life to enjoy the fruits of a strenuous 16 years at Whitehill, we speak for all who came in contact with her, and who recognized her as a capable and respected teacher. Miss Reid and Miss Rankin, too, have left us to continue their cheerful mission in Hutcheson's Girls' Grammar School.

A more pleasant duty is to welcome new teachers to Whitehill. Mr Munro is keenly interested in Rugby and Cricket, and Mr Graham has immediately made his presence felt. He is working with a fourth year girls' choir, whom he intends to present at the Glasgow Festival. Good luck, we hope, will attend this new venture. To them and to Mr Smellie, we extend a hearty welcome to the school.

Editorial (1929). Whitehill School Magazine, Christmas.

Somehow my father managed, probably by borrowing, to kit me out with the school uniform – navy blue blazer with the school badge, grey trousers, a striped tie and cap. I felt stiff and awkward in it, but the wearing of it was compulsory.

Once more, I had to adapt to a new set of constraints, restrictions, disciplines. In the new school, the day was divided up into forty-minute periods. Bells summoned us from one to the next. We had to find our way around the school's rambling corridors, its four floors, its annexes. We were not allowed to leave the school at lunchtime, for fear we might be knocked down in the city-centre traffic. In those first days I was spun and buffeted in yet another strange new world that both attracted and repelled me. I had been pitched from a little local primary school into this institution, so conscious of its own tradition and heritage. I was made to feel I had taken a step up on the ladder. There were hundreds of boys (no girls), all presumably drawn from the best pupils in schools all over the city. For the first time I encountered boys from another social class, noticed a general confident assurance, a level of articulation I had never met before.

I felt there were new universes opening up to me. There was much to learn; there was an allure in the names of completely new subjects – Physics and Chemistry, Geometry and Algebra and Latin.

But I found the general atmosphere of rigour oppressive. As in the primary school, there were teachers who saw their first task as breaking our spirit, imposing their own will. We were there to learn, and they would make sure we did. There was the physics teacher who belted anyone who carelessly botched an experiment. There was the music teacher who belted half the class for not sight-reading well enough. There was the geography teacher who gave out lines by the hundred if you couldn't churn out the names of rivers or ports or capital cities on demand. Perhaps most telling of all, there was the Latin teacher who belted all those who couldn't conjugate the verb *amare* – to love. Young though I was, I could see the irony in that!

But of course there were others; a mild and kindly English teacher, an art teacher who was flamboyant and expansive, a chemistry teacher with a manic sense of humour, and many more, just ordinary decent men, coping with a difficult job. It was simply a matter of luck which teachers you happened to be assigned to, and how they coloured your first impressions of a subject. For my part, I worked hard at the subjects I liked, made a truce with those I hated, and muddled along in the rest.

Spence, Alan (1977). 'Boom Baby', in *Jock Tamson's Bairns*.

Trevor Royle (ed.). London, H. Hamilton.

1947– : noted poet and fiction writer.

11F                                                                   Glasgow, 1930s.

It was now 1931 and there were signs that the Slump was beginning to end. Dad got work in a ship repair yard nearby and we had regular pay coming in again. I travelled by tramcar to school every day and by this time I was beginning to take an interest in some classroom subjects – particularly English . . .

My mother was ironing one day in the kitchen when I said, 'I'll be fifteen next month'.

'Ye will that,' she said.

'I was thinking.'

'What?' She looked up.

'What I should do.'

'Oh? Have ye thought about a trade?' She put hand on her hip. 'Yer faither said he'd talk to Tom Pry, the head foreman at the yard. Maybe he could get ye started.'

'Started at what?'

'As an apprentice. He was thinkin' o' electrician. Or maybe a mechanic'.

I sat down. 'Mother, listen. What would be the chances of me thinkin' about the university?'

She stared at me. 'What university?'

I shrugged. 'Glasgow. Donald Gibson and Jim Slater are thinkin' about it.'

'What!' She pursed her lips. '*That's* no' for the likes o' us. We could *never* afford anything like that. That's for them that has fathers in constant jobs, they pay for it.'

'Donald Gibson's father's no' rich.'

'Get it oot o' yer mind, son. Yer father's just started after *years* o' idleness. No, no.' She looked at me decisively. 'In fact the quicker you're oot at a job the better. I think ye've had enough schoolin'.'

I was angry. 'And that's *that*, is it?'

'Aye – that's *that*.' She continued ironing noisily and I stumped out of the kitchen.

> Wilkinson, Roderick (1993). *Memories of Maryhill*. Edinburgh, Canongate.

1918– : left school to become shipyard office boy; *Memories* concentrates on early and war-service years.

## 11G                                                      Aberdeen, 1930s.

Such was the background against which, in 1934, and with the eleven-plus examination (that dreaded 'qually') out of the way, I graduated along with most of my class to pastures new at Frederick Street School. Opened in 1905 with some 700 pupils, this was rather a handsome and unusual building with a playground on its flat roof . . .

Our register teacher, Miss Maitland, taught us maths. She was a well-built, sturdy lady who wore the usual long-sleeved overall, heavy stockings and 'sensible' shoes. Although severe of expression at times, she was pleasant and a very good teacher. Miss Cook taught my favourite and best subject, English. She was grey-haired, slim and energetic, dressed always in neat skirt and twin-set. She took us into the intricacies of grammar and deeper into reading, but even more fascinating were her stories of trips to France and Canada, travelling the Rocky Mountains in a glass-roofed train. We sat spellbound as she described these adventures to us in graphic detail, and we learned a great deal about places on the big wall map that she unrolled in front of the blackboard. Miss Cook never had any trouble in holding her young audiences, who were very fond of her. Women teachers in those days were all unmarried (this seems to have been required under the terms of their employment contract), and it still sounds strange to me when I hear children speak of their teachers as 'Mrs'.

While the boys had woodwork and science lessons, the girls were occupied with domesticity. Sewing classes on the top floor were always fun; we had two teachers, elderly ladies who were easy to work for. Art, embroidery and various other subjects were taught by a young, tall, blonde lady named Miss Wright. Cookery lessons entailed a 'crocodile' to nearby Hanover Street School as we had no kitchen facilities of our own. Hanover Street School had a large room containing a number of gas cookers and well-scrubbed wooden tables. All the necessary equipment was available for our instruction in the making of sponge, pastry, etc. I rather shone in culinary art, not so much for pastry-making (actually my sponge was better!) but for my ability in breaking eggs into bowls without dropping them on the floor. The knack was not universally shared – I had to help several of my classmates by breaking their eggs for them. Scrubbing the tables after the lesson came naturally, as most of us scrubbed stairs at home and I had been earning my regular shilling from our neighbour in return for this service for some time. Similarly, we all showed aptitude at laundry-work and ironing!

Every fortnight came a compulsory visit to the Spray Baths at Hanover Street School, another welcome break in our classroom routine. A common room was set aside as a changing-room, and there we would disrobe to our vests and navy knickers before trooping, with our towels, through to the shower area. To preserve modesty the cubicles there were curtained and we were each given, of all things, a full length rubber apron together with a thin rubber mob-style shower cap. These caps, being of pure rubber (no nylon or polyester then), were very difficult to manoeuvre, and tended to be left perched drunkenly on our heads. The aprons might have been more effective in preserving propriety if they had not been icy cold to touch. As soon as the janitor turned on the tap we dashed across to the showers with aprons held at arm's length, squealing whenever chill rubber touched skin! Laughing and joking, we would luxuriate in the warm water, scrubbing ourselves with the brushes and tiny pieces of soap with which we had been provided. The place was kept spotlessly clean and disinfected, and we thought a shower there was wonderful.

I loved every minute of the two years I spent at Frederick Street School, with its very wide curriculum. We had advanced from primary school children to adolescents, and were treated as such.

Kilgour Ethel (1992). *A Time of our Lives.* Aberdeen City Libraries.

1922– : autobiography is of 'an ordinary Aberdeen family'.

11H                                                               Airdrie, 1953.

I have the greatest admiration for those colleagues who continually year after year fight for the soul of the junior secondary pupil. But I have now reached the conclusion that they are fighting a losing battle. The job is too big for human endurance and the better the teacher the more he puts into it and the more exhausted he becomes . . . These schools have no prestige among parents and they have generated no affection among their pupils whose one ambition is to leave and get work. Discipline is a constant, almost unbearable problem.

Inglis, James (1953). Speech to AGM of EIS Lanarkshire
Branch. As reported in the *Scottish Educational Journal*, 1 May.


11I                                                               Paisley, 1950.

Tell us what are the best methods of teaching two score youngsters of varied ages, intelligences, aptitudes and social backgrounds *as a group*, in conditions of unsatisfactory rooms, furniture, equipment and time allocation, limited professional training and nervous, physical and financial strain . . . what have been the chief influences in the last decade or two on such teachers? School milk and school meals, larger classes and fewer teachers!

Russell, Alex (1950). 'From a Dominie's Notebook',
the *Scottish Educational Journal*, 10 March.


11J                                                       Kirkwall, Orkney, 1950s.

When, in the last week of the summer holidays of 1952, I went to see the Rector of my new school, he was working with his secretary at the long table in the old Board Room, smoking at a stumpy pipe with all the robust vigour of an Orkney farmer. The table was piled with papers and books, and the wall opposite the window had packed book-shelves nearly to the ceiling. Just inside the door was a wooden settle with a padded leather seat where, after term had started, one would often find a boy, awaiting either the Rector's wrath or his nod to go to the foot of the stairs and clang the brass bell which indicated the end of the period. On the mantelpiece above the open fire-place was a disused gas-nozzle.

'We're getting a new school,' said Mr Leask as we talked. 'It'll not be just yet, but it's coming. We're crowded just now, but it'll no be for long. I'll take you along to see your room: it's Room G. I'm afraid one of your third year classes is rather big, but you'll maybe manage'.

Room G had double desks of cast iron and oak screwed to the floor, and single folding desks in every cranny. It was about twenty-four feet by eighteen, and like all rooms in the main building had an open fire and a glass partition. Into this room every day came the forty-eight pupils of Class IIIA for English, and I always made sure I was ensconced at my table when they arrived, lest I should be stranded in the corridor.

I had never seen a building like this. True, the school which I had attended during the first world war had glass partitions, but it did have central heating, and the lavatories in the playground were subterranean and heated so they did not freeze, and it only catered up to the 'Qualie', and had only three doors. K.G.S. [Kirkwall Grammar School] had open fires except the Horsa Huts [the Portakabins of the day], outside lavatories above ground, seven entrances to the main building, and all the town's pupils and many country and island pupils from Infants to Secondary Sixth . . .

What kind of education did we give under such conditions? Old-fashioned, I suppose, and austere; and some would say, repressive; and certainly moral, and I hope thorough; and intimate, in spite of huge classes. Every pupil was well-known to some member of staff – his environment, his history, even his lineage. In emergencies, like snow-storms or school parties, pupils who could not be accommodated with friends or at the School Hostel were put up by the Staff. If necessary, the Staff ran a taxi service – sometimes inadvertently, as with the member who, furious with an idle pupil, kept him in, only to find he had missed the school bus and had no means of getting home; so she took him home in her own car and did not get back to Kirkwall until after six o'clock, an experience which gave a new dimension to the cliché 'This hurts me as much as it hurts you'. The School was like a large family, with all the tension, robustness, intimacy, and warmth, of family life.

The Staff – and the pupils – worked hard, long and unconventionally. Many of Mr Leask's pupils have remarked that after he became Rector he did much of his teaching after 4.10 p.m. And sometimes the staff felt they were not appreciated. In his last year, when a new chief inspector arrived full of learning, gimmicks and criticism, but devoid of understanding, Mr Leask was angry. 'Lokkers!', he said in a fierce whisper in the presence of IIIA, 'That's a terrible wife, that!' But he was hurt. Three months after that he retired, and six months later he died. Many a Kirkwall citizen heard with a pang of the death of Sandy Leask.

Stephen, A. H. (1976). 'Ending an Era' in *From Sang School to Comprehensive*. William Thomson (ed.). Orkney Education Council.

11K                                                          Troon, 1950s.

While the *haute bourgeoisie* of Scottish's cities, even 40 years ago, sent their children to one-sex, fee-paying schools, the norm for children of smaller towns and rural communities was comprehensive co-education. Perhaps this Knoxian tradition, much debased now by sociological cant, did offer something unique to the Scottish child . . .

Whether they passed the 'qualifying' or not, the children of Troon graduated automatically to Marr College. The copper-domed school was the altruistic legacy of a coal merchant who wanted to see millionaires' daughters educated with dustmen's sons. In superb wood-panelled classrooms, and under the tutelage of a distinguished teaching staff, the democratic intellect did indeed flourish. Generations of boys and girls whose fathers worked in the local shipyard or railway works, competed, and more than held their own, with the children of the wealthy and privileged. Girls were expected to shine at mathematics and science. They did.

Svengali'd through Higher Maths by 'Chucky' Peebles, initiated into the niceties of Verlaine and Victor Hugo by Dr Philippe le Harivel, numerous children from 'working-class' backgrounds graduated from university and into the professions. It was a story paralleled, of course, in academies and high schools throughout Scotland.

Duncan, Lesley (1990). 'Jock Tamson's Bairns. A Scottish Childhood'. In *The Herald Book of Scotland*. Arnold Kemp and Harry Reid (eds). Edinburgh, Mainstream.

Graduate Glasgow University; career in journalism.

11L                                          Inverurie, Aberdeenshire, 1960s.

The Scottish claim to a more democratic system of education than that which has existed south of the border is true, however, only in part. The burgh school of modern times has indeed educated all the children in its area under one roof, but the Advanced Divisions of the 1920s left a legacy of segregation that the modern 'comprehensive' senior secondary school has found hard to 'offset'.

If Inverurie Academy with its present secondary roll of over 1,000 pupils is typical of such schools – and its history from its higher grade days of the pre-1914 era has been so typical – 'omnibus' rather than 'comprehensive' courses have been the order of the day. Strenuous but as yet insufficiently far-reaching attempts have been made over the years to break the iron curtain separating junior and senior streams. Up to the 1940s the two streams in Inveruruie were housed in separate buildings and taught largely by separate staff, heads of department being confined in general to senior secondary classes with assistant teachers 'graduating' in time from the junior secondary streams to which in their earlier years they had been appointed. An echo of this cleavage is still discernable in the Inverurie community among those of its members now in middle-age – fortunate or unfortunate, according to one's attitude – taught 'in the Academy' or 'on the other side'.

Dixon, Norman (1965). 'Comprehensive Education<br>in the Small Burgh School', *Education in the North*, 3.

Locally celebrated as devoted Rector who was reputed to know every name that ever crossed the entrance of Inverurie Academy.


11M                                                      Glasgow, 1946.

We have been trained and educated as if our sole function was to groom boys and girls for the Scottish Leaving Certificate. From secondary school to university, from university to training college, from training college to secondary school again, so the vicious circle grows . . . The whole secondary course is designed with the Leaving Certificate requirements in view, despite the fact that only a matter of four per cent gain the certificate. To my mind the provision of courses

*229*

for these children [the 'non-academic' majority] suited to their age, ability and aptitude is the single most important educational problem confronting us at the present time. If the raising of the school leaving age is to mean nothing more than the taking on of an extra year and giving young people something more of what they are getting at the moment then we are courting disaster.

Mackintosh, H. S. W. Director of Education for Glasgow (1946). 'Content of the Secondary School Curriculum'. Address to teachers reported by *Scottish Educational Journal*, 15 March.


11N                                                             Kirkcaldy, 1958.

My first impression of the new school was one of spaciousness. The smooth, uncluttered buildings seemed to stand at ease in their surrounding lawns and courtyards, like a picture in a generous frame.

The vast windows emphasised the spaciousness, and let the light flood into the classrooms, even when the venetian blinds were drawn to keep out the heat and glare of the sun. Everywhere in the building there was light and colour; from every window there was a view of fields and grass and trees; the whole school wore an aspect of light and fresh air.

How different from the architectural hotchpotch, of the old school, dull and cramped in its stony playground crowded round by houses!

Now after several weeks in the new school, I see more and more clearly its advantages.

In the morning I face almost the entire school as we worship together in Assembly. Our old hall was far too small for that.

As I go about the school I contrast its simple, geometrical layout with the rabbit warren of the old building, where even seniors could sometimes get lost. As I walk to the playing fields, I contrast that short distance with the weekly trek to the Beveridge Park.

We leave the large refectory, which will be perfect for our Burns Suppers, and go into the wide paved courtyard with its beds of flowers. High on the wall above us hangs a figure designed and executed by Mr Thorburn, of Minerva, the goddess of wisdom, her hand on the head of a child. Perhaps this wrought iron presiding genius will become the symbol of the new school, as the familiar pillared facade was the symbol of the old.

The new school, the old school, how far apart they seem! And yet the work and play go on as ever, and over the door of the new school I see the old badge, the old motto. A symbolic representation of the old building is inset in the linoleum floor of the new. The War Memorial, too, is there, with its polished names gleaming from the old wood. The men who bore these names are dead, but their spirit lives. The old Kirkcaldy High is dead, but its spirit and traditions live on – in our new school and in us.

'The Head Girl's Impression of the New School' (1958).
*Kirkcaldy High School Souvenir*. Fife County Council.

# 12 ALL CHANGE: 1965–85

Figure 22. **Kirbister School, Orkney, 1955** Traditional arrangements still, in this small island school of seventeen pupils. *Orkney Archives*

Figure 23. **St Leonard's School, Banchory, 1962** But within a few years, the 'progressive' methods evident in this infant class are beginning to take hold. The message on the blackboard indicates, however, that little had changed in the weather. *Aberdeen Journals*

When, at the end of the 1960s, the Principal of Aberdeen College of Education attempted to offer his young teacher graduates their end-of-course wisdom, it was to advise them to expect the unexpected (**12A**). Abruptly, after 'centuries' of entrenched practice, the landscape of Scottish education had apparently dissolved into a blizzard of agitated change, one that was assailing more than the surface features of syllabus and methodology. The ground structures of teacher authority and insitutional hierarchy were themselves being tugged loose from their ancient moorings.

The storm had not blown in from nowhere. In 1965, the SED had unleashed *Primary Teaching in Scotland*. The memorandum announced that, after decades of unquestioned academicism, the Department was now seeking to plant 'the child' at the centre of the school world. Joan Low's account (**12B**) explicitly confronts the age-old fixtures, of fixed desks and silenced tongues, in order to sweep them aside before an onrush of unfettered pupil activity. In many respects, she was doing no more than advocate a wider adoption of what was already being done in the more adventurous primary, both at home and abroad: what was unprecedented was the commitment with which all this newness was being propounded, not as interesting innovation, but as established orthodoxy. 'Discovery', 'freedom', 'activity learning' were now to replace 'drill', 'discipline' and 'the subject' as the watchwords.

The breathless enthusiasm of Low's classroom tour captures the driving idealism with which the 1960s educationist was seeking to revitalise – and perhaps to atone for – all that grey formalism which had marked the Scottish way. And, as her position as 'Supervisor of Primary Schools, Edinburgh' demonstrates, in the march of the new progressivism, it was the Inspectors, Advisers and Colleges that were the leaders.

Yet, within this general turbulence, one of the surest ways to reform – and certainly to ensure its spread into the secondary – remained the examination system. In 1962, the SED introduced a Fourth Year Certificate, the O (Ordinary) Grade. Its uptake outran all projection. Brought in to reverse the long-standing problem of early leaving, it not only did that but quickly spread its syllabus into the Junior Second-aries. There, both staff and parents proved eager to seize hold of a national Certificate which was not only accessible to their more able students, but the means of proving the academic credentials of a sector whose intake had been inextricably associated with '12–plus' failure.

The repercussions were far-reaching (**12C**). Within a decade, some two-thirds of the total year group were being entered for it, twice the figure for which it had been intended. The position of the remaining, and very much excluded, third had become ever more invidious. Pressure to revise the whole secondary curriculum became irresistible: by the end of the 1970s, the principle of 'Assessment for All' had been accepted; the 1980s saw the establishment of the Third and Fourth Year Standard Grade courses and, with them, the promise of an award – whether it be at Credit, General or Foundation level – to all sixteen year-olds.

The progress towards full educational opportunity for all could not stop there. Both the cause of social justice and of wealth creation demanded a further step. All political parties were turning towards investment in the skills of the nation's young as the key to economic growth; research was appearing which showed that a system which divided itself into 'Junior' and 'Senior' was one that depended upon a selection, and a pupil staying power, that was intimately linked to the determinism of social class. In 1965, the newly returned Labour Government announced its determination to convert the secondary school structure throughout Britain into a non-selective one. By 1970, all Scottish authorities had introduced plans to enter every twelve-year-old into the one common, neighbourhood comprehensive school.

As significant as the content of these changes was the manner in which they had been fashioned. Although the *Primary* memorandum had been issued in the name of the Department, its formulation had been the product of a joint working party on to which teachers had been invited. Policy was no longer by Departmental fiat but a participative venture. By the time of James Scotland's address, a series of supplementary bodies had become established: a Scottish Examinations Board to administer not only the new O Grade but the talismanic Highers; a Consultative Council on the Curriculum to advise on all aspects of school life and, in the General Teaching Council, the teachers' own professional organisation to oversee standards of entry and conduct. The whole system had been opened up.

In acting with such expansive energy, Scottish education was participating in the spirit of the age. The 1960s were when the post-war austerities could be finally thrown over and the benefits of growing affluence and technological capacity be extended to all. With the rise in material prosperity, went a sense of liberal emancipation in personal behaviour – and it was the young who were its most visible practitioners. The phenomenon of teenage culture, of Elvis and the Beatles, was born, and with it, yet another challenge to the traditionally authoritarian ethos of the school, one that was exacerbated by the intention to raise the leaving age to sixteen in 1970 (**12D**).

Then there was the Pill. Nowhere was the assertive liberty of the young more vividly on display than in the individualistic permissiveness of the new Sex. The contrast may be illustrated by the regulations which operated in James Scotland's own college. Back in the 1920s, its lady students were made to reside under careful supervision (**12E 1**); fifty years on, it was not the 10 o'clock curfew or the weekly bath which their granddaughters were being advised about (**12E 2**). Yet, as the initiation of one of its graduates, Flora Youngson, in the Aberdeenshire glens was to show, the conventional decencies had survived into their mothers' era, even if the outcomes did, on occasion, yield to a more earthy imperative(**12F**).

Reaction soon set in. The loosening of rules in sexual behaviour and mental arithmetic alike was causing disquiet long before the Aberdeen *Press and Journal* was reporting that the latest batch of trainee teachers – the first such generation brought up under the new liberalism – was now unable to perform operations which, until their day, had been the secure possession of the average Primary 7 pupil (**12G**). To many longer-serving teachers, it appeared that the first casualties of the official enthusiasm for the uninhibited play of the child's creative powers were the well-drilled features of the traditional classroom – grammar, spelling, the times table and factual knowledge (**12H**). All of them, it seemed, were now being left to the hazard of incidental discovery, to be stumbled across in the course of some grandiosely imaginative project or other.

Yet, if the primary school's emphasis upon the individual child was intended to engender a lasting identification with the processes of Scottish education, the sense of rejection that was still being experienced by those who arrived at the final years of their secondary careers without prospect of academic recognition was all the sharper. In the late 1970s, the Centre for Educational Sociology interviewed recent school leavers. Their testimony revealed that the old divisions festered on (**12I 1, 2**).

The incidence of such perceived exclusion tended to correlate highly with that of economic deprivation. These were social factors which comprehensive education had so far failed to surmount: indeed, the fact that it was based upon the district school only seemed to reproduce the starkly contrasting worlds of the 'good' middle-class academy and the struggling housing-scheme institution. Such disparity could only perpetuate a cycle of social determinism to a degree which makes the effort of Craigroyston all the more notable. Situated in a vast post-war estate on Edinburgh's periphery, it had come, by 1970, to be regarded as the 'bottom of the heap'. The tag is Hugh MacKenzie's; under his radical headship (1972–93), a vigorous attempt was launched to lift it up. Corporal punishment was phased out, rules of dress and institutional decorum were relaxed, outdoor pursuits were followed, ties with the local people were strengthened. The aim was to call off the futile attempt to ape the manners of other, more salubriously positioned, city establishments and, instead, to forge its own identity as a school, not for the system, but its own community. The results may be read in the testimonial of one of its ex-pupils (**12J**).

The Craigroyston strategy was the opposite to that of the majority of the old Junior Secondaries which were now being elevated to six-year status. Their approach had been to build up a local standing as a decent second best. This had been done by working the 'better' pupils towards whatever academic success could still be achieved, by offering vocationally useful activity to the rest and firm standards of discipline all round. Typical of these had been Aberdeen's Rosemount under the unflagging paternalism of Dr Alex Cormack (**12K**).

Up at Summerhill, on the city outskirts two miles to the north, Willie Christie had performed a similar job. In that respect, he had given his successor a solid foundation when he took over in 1968. R. F. MacKenzie, however, was neither Cormack nor Christie and had no desire to be. Having already proved to be a controversial innovator at Braehead in Fife, he was determined to use his Aberdeen posting as his opportunity to transform a typically disadvantaged urban school into an example of what a neighbourhood school, empowered not by the belt but by 'love', could achieve. Central to his vision was the notion of liberation – from coercive discipline, from academic drudgery, from institutional regimentation, from the stony confines of the city (**12L**).

More romantically idealistic, less of a hands-on tactician than his Edinburgh namesake, R. F. failed to stay his course. The felicitously expressed contempt, which he showed for exams and control alike, split his own staff as much as it agitated external opinion. The unrest gathered; by 1974 he was gone, sacked by Aberdeen City Council.

It was a fate which confirmed that, in Scotland, the revolution of the 60s was, after all, a strictly limited affair. In this regard, the country was simply re-enacting a customary intolerance of the innovator who refuses to compromise with the enduring disciplines of its educational regime. Half a century before, A. S. Neill had been forced to take his outrageously child-centred notions – and growing international reputation – to a private establishment in Suffolk. Ironically, that, too, had been called Summerhill; in his later life Neill acted as a friendly supporter to both Hugh and R. F. MacKenzie.

For the ordinary majority, the reforming energies of the 1960s and 70s settled down into a useful refreshment of the system. Its effects were never wholesale but resulted, rather, in a broadening of the curriculum to add the arts and personal activity to its still recognisable centre, while also affording the opportunity to discard some of the rigidities of the old ways. The long career of Flora Youngson demonstrated where, in retrospect, the balance came to lie (**12M**). But, as her account also shows, by the late 70s, optimism was ebbing. The move was to larger, more aloof, units of administration; it was, moreover, a time for economic cutback. The consequence was a more intrusive bureaucracy in which 'value for money' began to render the 'Golden' spirit of just ten years before a naïve aberration.

When the time came for James Scotland to deliver his final yearly reckoning (**12N**), the consciousness of gain was troubled by the conclusion it had been won against a background of moral and social diminishment, that the two great fundamentals of their Scottish tradition – respect for the work ethic, respect for the local school – had withered. Most telling of all, perhaps, is the way in which, as the country comes to consider its returns from the investment of faith and resources it has recently placed in the nation's education, it is now to be referred to not as 'community', but as a division into 'politicians' and 'voters'.

12A                                                      Aberdeen, 1969.

There never was in Scottish education – so I believe at any rate, and I can bring hosts of witnesses – there never was a more perplexing, a more continuously challenging time. After centuries in which tradition ruled and conservatism was in, change has become our daily companion. The curriculum this year is not the same as last, and a year from now it will have altered again. New methods, new materials, new textbooks, new organisations come out like monthly magazines. Nothing remains simply because it has always been; nothing, I sometimes feel, is so strange that it cannot find some prominent educationist or committee to take it seriously. You may have seen one of those little glass balls with a winter scene inside. When you shook it, the scene vanished in a blizzard. The sixties have been like that in education: someone is shaking the ball and the blizzard continues to rage.

You have all seen this, of course, happening around you. The old hierarchies have been – are being – assailed. The hierarchy of schools, which ascended from the 'modified secondary' to the fee-paying academy, is under demolition order; we are all convinced that comprehensive education is right, and we are all busy trying to find out what it means. The hierarchy of the classroom has also gone with the days recalled by the Buchan poet, J. C. Milne, who lectured for many affectionate years in this College:

> As I gaed doon by kirk and toun
> Quod I, 'a skule, guid faith!'
> And there I heard nae sang nor soun
> But bairns as quiet as death.

Few of you will teach in a school like that next winter; try to play the martinet and see what happens to you. Even the hierarchy of higher education, which seemed impregnable, is now under siege. Fiats can no longer come down ex cathedra, justice must be widely seen to be done, there are riots in the peaceful groves of Academe . . .

You may expect, as I have suggested, new ideas, new methods, new parcellings of the curriculum every year or two from now on. They will vary from inventions of Copernican moment to flashy pieces of gimmickry, and you will not be able to understand them all alone, far less to evaluate them. It is for all of us, in the schools and the colleges, the universities and the education authorities and the teachers' organisations, to work together at this process of evaluation. For you this means that today is not 'The End', merely the 'End of Part One'. A short commercial break – if you have a summer job – then back to the main feature, courses, conferences, seminars, discussions.

What I am proposing for you this afternoon is a stiff programme, a continual blizzard in the glass ball, for I do not see any signs of this settling down in the immediate future. A continuing need to attend courses and conferences, perhaps to study, part- or full-time, for an additional degree or diploma. A constant bombardment by new ideas and unrelenting pressure to evaluate them, not only for their general import but for what they mean to you, personally, in Paradise Academy or Purgatory Institution, seven hours a day, five days a week, forty weeks a year. Some of you, perhaps, are not willing to make the effort. To you I am not talking; the Scottish schools in the seventies will be no place for dilettantes, and you would do well to find something more tranquil, like deep sea diving.

Scotland, James (1969). Graduation Address. Aberdeen College of Education.

1917–83: served as Principal at Aberdeen 1961–83; urban lad o' pairts who rose from East-end Glasgow to enjoy noted career both in Scottish education, as teacher, administrator and policy-maker, and in drama for radio and stage.

12B                                              Edinburgh, 1969.

Many parents today are mystified about what goes on in school. It seems to be very different from their young day. Their children are certainly not afraid of their teachers. Indeed, 'my teacher' has a very special place in the child's life. New toys, postcards from abroad, caterpillars and pieces of coloured rock all find their way to school to be shown to 'my teacher'. Odd requests come home for empty cartoons, silver-paper, cotton-wool and other bits of 'junk'. The school day seems to consist of painting, playing and something called projects.

Anxious parents, and grandparents, quiz the children about school. 'Are you good at composition?' 'Are you in the back seat?' 'Who's top of the class?' The children in their turn are mystified. What is composition? What is the significance of the 'back seat'? Top of the class? Parents have a queer idea of school!

Schools are certainly different nowadays. They look different, sound different and even smell different! Older buildings may still have grim exteriors, but inside, the walls are painted in light colours and the long corridors are decorated with children's work. Good schools are not silent. Classroom doors may be open and a busy hum of activity heard. Children are found working outside the classrooms. Some may be reading in a quiet corner, some planning how to measure the area of the hall. Younger children may find more space for painting on the floor of the corridor. And what about the old school smell? Perhaps there is a suspicion of something cooking! But at least it is an appetising smell!

Have a look at an infant class. The children are so absorbed in their work that they hardly notice a visitor. Every available inch of floor space seems to have been used. In one corner a curtain has been strung across to make a house. Two children are setting a table. They count the cups. 'One for Daddy, one for me, one for you, and one for Baby. That's four.' They do the same with saucers and spoons. Another corner has a painted sign to say, 'This is the Post Office.' 'Four threepenny stamps please', asks a diminutive housewife in a smart hat, handbag and long skirt. The efficient assistant holds out his hand: 'That's a shilling'. A plastic baby-bath is the scene of a delicate operation of filling a bucket with jugfulls of water. The little group helps by counting to see what the bucket will hold. Another group works at easels and on the floor making great bold pictures in vivid reds, blues and greens. Four children stand at a table earnestly discussing what size of carton will be needed to complete their spaceship. This large object is made of cornflake cartons, toilet-roll cylinders and other unidentified articles. A boy sits beside them writing about how it was made. 'We made a spaceship and we're going to paint it.'

Where is the teacher? She is sitting at a table with a group of children who are sorting small objects into sets. John collects the blue things, Billy the red, and Mary looks for the yellow. The teacher talks to them as they work. 'How many have you got, Billy?' 'Have you got more than John?' 'Who has the most?' 'Who has the least?' She leaves this group with further suggestions for the next step and joins a group which sits in the book corner. She listens to some reading, discusses the story, and talks about some new words the children will be meeting. Leaving the readers she stops beside the sand tray. 'That must be very heavy, Susan, when it's full. When you empty it it will be very light.' 'Just playing' they tell their mothers. But they are learning new words, new ideas; how to read, to count, to compare, to measure, to be considerate, confident and independent.

> Low, Joan (1969). 'Primary Schools', *Scottish Education*
> *Looks Ahead.* Edinburgh, W. and R. Chambers.

Taken from collection of campaigning articles on the 'new' outlook by College lecturers, Inspectors, Advisers, Directors – but no classroom teacher.

12C                                                           Scotland, 1965.

When seen in retrospect, in future years that change may come to be regarded as one of the most significant in the history of Scottish education . . . the introduction of that certificate has set off changes in Scottish education which deserve, in the language of today, to be called 'an educational explosion', so far reaching have they already been in their consequence. Indeed it might in truth be said that only now are the promises of the 1945 Education Act being fully honoured in regard to Secondary education.

> 'An educational explosion', Editorial (1965).
> *Times Educational Supplement,* 30 July.

12D                                                           Scotland, 1966.

Adolescence is a period of tremendous change which the boy or girl nearly always feels acutely. Rousseau once said that we are all born twice; once into existence as a member of a race and once into life as a member of the sex. Probably the only feeling common to all adolescents is a feeling of insecurity.

The change is most marked in the early years of the secondary school. In the first year pupils are still inclined to lean on adults but a year later their contemporaries have taken precedence. They tend to become scruffy and untidy as a gesture of defiance and parents are written off with the rest of the adult world as 'squares'. In the third year they undergo yet another change. They become interested in the other sex and with this growing sexual awareness they become tidier and smarter in appearance. It is also about now that the boys begin to affect outlandish hairstyles and the girls badly-applied cosmetics. This is probably the most formative phase in the new development of the adolescent and at this stage social training is all-important. The teacher must learn to understand the growing self-awareness of the adolescent and sympathise with the deep-seated, emotional and intellectual urges that motivate him. He must in short encourage the process of maturing, e.g., by giving his pupils more responsibility.

The most significant thing is that although all children pass through this awkward stage of development, the difficulties associated with it become most acute as a general rule in the case of the less academically successful children, of whom most, although by no means all, find their way into non-certificate courses of secondary education. It is these children who appear most unruly and rebellious and least inclined to conform. The successful senior secondary school child seems to take the vicissitudes of adolescence in his stride and comes back to school in the fourth year not much different from what he was in the third, except that he is a little older, a little more mature and possibly more settled in his outlook. It is some of the others that cause difficulty. Until they approach the age of 15 they require no different treatment from the rest; then it seems in their case the problems of maturation become fundamentally different. They are seen to kick over the traces in their third year, impatient to get out of school into the adult world. And the thought of their being detained in school for a fourth year has caused some foreboding among teachers and others.

What makes these children difficult? It is not enough to say they do not see themselves getting anywhere in school and are bored and frustrated, though this may well be so. School is only a part, and the smaller part, of their environment and it has to fight a constant battle against external influences. When the pupils see little meaning or purpose in what they do in school it is a hopeless, losing battle. They are lost in advance to the mass culture of the new teenage society with its easy spending habits and its artificially created tastes and fashions in pop music, clothes and hair-styles into which many of their older friends have already escaped.

This culture, or sub-culture of the modern teenagers, presents a formidable challenge to education. It is part of the new social pattern of our time in which old values and customs are shifting and changing. Whether they change for better or for worse will be determined largely by how well education and teachers succeed in exerting a formative influence upon the new society. To do so they must first come to terms with it.

Educational Institute of Scotland (1966). *Towards 1970*. Edinburgh.


12E                                         Aberdeen, 1921; 1965.


1) The rules for residence [in 1921] were also strict. All students had to be in by ten p.m.; in fact this rule applied to female students only, and if they told their landlady where they were and she approved, the time might be extended to midnight. No young man might be invited into lodgings without the sanction of the Director or Lady Superintendent. No landlady was permitted to accommodate a male lodger in the same house as female students. The minimum space for each lodger was 500 cubic feet. Where there was no fixed bath, a portable one had to be provided.

Scotland, James (1983). *History of Aberdeen College of Education*. Unpublished.

2)

## ATTENTION – LADY STUDENTS
### NEVER

1. trust any male as regards contraception.
2. have intercourse without contraception (the Pill or the condom or spermicide).
3. have intercourse with anyone whose name and address you do not know.
4. have more than the equivalent of three single whiskies with any male unless you are protected from the consequences of intercourse.

Notice issued to female students (1965). Aberdeen College of Education.


Issued by Dr Horace Thomson, College's new Medical Officer; his frank commitment to the cause of sex education aroused some stir throughout the North, especially in Church circles.

12F                                                      Aberdeenshire, 1938.

The mile-long walk – or rather plough – to the small school-building
with its adjacent schoolhouse was accomplished on foot of course and
I met my boss Mrs M. and was quite kindly received, although I
detected some reserve in her welcome. She told me that I would be
responsible for Prs. 1, 2, 3 and 4 (ages 5–8) while she taught the 9–
11+ stages. Also I would be expected to supervise the needlework of
*all* the girls! Horrors! Then, with a slightly embarrassed air, Mrs M.
produced a small dark red-covered book and muttered 'You'd better
read that when you have time', and left me to make the acquaintance of
some 15–20 solemn round-eyed country bairns who were obviously
just as uneasy as I . . .

The book which Mrs M had given me was 'Married Love' by Marie
Stopes! This writer may be unknown now but was widely held to be
*the* authority on sex relationships in my young day. As I read it in the
decent privacy of the farmhouse and found in it answers to many
questions which my reticent and rather prudish mother had wholly
failed to explain, I realised why this had been the rather unusual gift
from a Head teacher who obviously didn't wish her new assistant to
leave the job as abruptly as had her two predecessors who, in the
phraseology of the day, had been 'got into trouble' by young farmers of
the neighbourhood. And I still think that she, faced with a rather shy
twenty-year-old from a sheltered background, was quite sensible to
warn me in this practical way. But my mother was furious when I told
her and could only with difficulty be restrained from complaining
about Mrs M. to the local Education authority.

Youngson, Flora (1991). *Dominie's Daughter.*
Centre for Scottish Studies, University of Aberdeen.

1918– : daughter of village headmaster on Aberdeenshire coast; trained as teacher
at Aberdeen and taught in range of local posts before became Head at inner-city
Causewayend; noted as enthusiast for Language Arts.

12G                                                          Aberdeen, 1981.

Student teachers at Aberdeen's College of Education failed a maths
test that could have been set for 11–year-olds. Four even worked out

that it would take a bus travelling at 40 m.p.h. five hours to travel eight miles. Wild guesses and stupid mistakes were made by some of the 83 first-year students who sat the test. About ten of them did not pass . . .

The recent case of Aberdeen students failing a maths test for 11-year-olds has prompted parents to ask if maths in Scottish primary schools is suffering. Many parents are confused by the 'new maths'. The methods used are totally different to when they were at school. And parents are beginning to wonder if the change is for the worse.

Even some teachers are finding it difficult to understand the new methods. And several teachers think the pendulum has swung too far towards 'understanding' at the expense of 'knowledge of basic maths'.

Against this background, a Grampian Region working party have just produced a new report, secret at this stage, which will introduce yet more changes into the primary maths curriculum this August.

But a return to more traditional methods of teaching maths is favoured by Aberdeen maths teacher Malcolm Savidge from Kincorth Academy, who is also regional secretary of the Educational Institute of Scotland. 'Some advisers are pushing trendy, novel ideas and in some cases, I think have gone too far', he told me. 'I was horrified at seeing one Primary 4 exam paper in which pupils were expected to understand and use phrases like 'commutativity' but simple multiplication was not included because it was thought to be too difficult for them. There is a strong feeling among many secondary teachers that not enough simple, basic arithmetic is being done in some primary schools'.

Nickson, John (1981). 'Countdown to Maths Muddle',
*Press and Journal*, 9 February.

Malcolm Savidge later switched careers to become a Labour Member of Parliament

12H                                  Kirkintilloch, Dunbartonshire, 1960s.

I got sick of watching all the things that were happening in the schools. This was in the 1960s when they were throwing spelling out of the window, grammar out of the window, the tables out of the window. I enjoyed parts of the new maths like teaching algebra and geometry, but most of the changes made me uncomfortable. They weren't detailed enough for me. Too much laissez-faire. I felt children weren't being given enough general knowledge – that had always been my Friday afternoon bit of fun, along with meanings of different words and so on. But an embargo was put on such things. 'Old hat', I was told by an inspector when he was examining my books. 'Well, maybe, but every child leaves my class able to read, to write and to count'. He had no answer to that.

The majority of Headteachers that I knew were in favour of a middle-of-the-road approach. I remember speaking to one of them about the inspector I'd had – he'd been watching me for three nerve-wracking days – and he told me that exactly the same thing had happened to him: 'Old hat!'

The new aim was freedom of speech, of self-expression, a belief that grammar should be curtailed in case it inhibited the child's expression. But, my goodness, you should have seen the rubbish I got! They said we had to get the children to keep a diary every day, into which they should be allowed to put anything they liked. For my own peace of mind I used to go through them. When I came to entries like, 'My daddy hit my mummy last night', I used to think, 'What good is all this doing?' And then there was the red face of a colleague who attended parents' night at her son's school and saw written into his diary, 'We are going to get twin beds put into our house when my mother gets her salary at the end of the month'.

Brocklehurst, Mabel (2002). Interview with author.

1918– : brought up in Grantown-on-Spey on 'traditional' values at both home and school; long career as teacher and primary head, both in North-east and at Kirkintilloch.

<br>

12I                                       Somewhere in Scotland, 1980s.

**1)** Okay Education is a good thing but you want to know what they taught me Yes I think I should tell you it starts early when kids not up to academic standard a particulr *Academic* standard are placed in whats commonly known as the *Daft* group where they learn Humileation a very cold lonly Humileation I know because I was in a group yes the Daft group I was the one to survive whats called Primary

Education mabe because I realised in time what the Daft group was Designed for I only realized because as I wached the kids around me clam up and by allowing themselves to become so inferior they became just to afraid to open up the rest of there school lives would be spent in the Daft group Yes that's right there all in factories now just doing what there told to bloody scared to Do anything else they were sensetive feeling children once now there nothing more than zombies or slaves take your pick.

Hughes, Joan (ed.) (1984). *The Best Years? Reflections
of School Leavers in the 1980s*. Aberdeen University Press.

**2)** I want to see in later education, pupils and Teachers being a sort of family. When I was at school my teachers made me feel thick really stupid so I did not bother to study, they made me feel as if it was not worth my while thinking of what I wanted to be. I had set my heart on being a child nurse but I have no confidence in myself anymore so I shall never forget my teachers and how they made me feel. I hope when I have my children they will be encouraged as I don't want them to be hurt like me. I don't think my teachers meant to be like this but if they had encouraged me I would have went to college or something but I started to skip school and not study. But they encouraged the more brighter girls to go on and be what they wanted to be.

Gow, Lesley and McPherson, Andrew (eds) (1980).
*Tell Them from Me*. Aberdeen University Press.

12J                                                    Edinburgh, 1970s.

For most children, a teacher is a kind of two-dimensional blackboard accessory who may as well be put away for the night like a rollerblind and brought out again, raring to go, in the morning. Yet Craigie teachers volunteered in alarming numbers to become real people in the lives of their students – real people with homes of their own, husbands and wives, habits good and bad, hang-ups large and small, idiosyncrasies weird and wonderful and an assortment of talents which made them colourful, three-dimensional characters whose company I actively pursued . . .

Back in the classroom things were probably a bit different from the normal Scottish secondary school. Craigie was pretty informal. No uniforms, very few rules and, as my schooldays passed, gradually there was no belt. Until the belt was finally banned, it was used fairly frequently in my early years at Craigie. I've watched a teacher haul one of my classmates out for some long-forgotten misdemeanour then play a double-or-quits game of cards with the child, teasing him along with a friendly fun-filled game before reducing him to tears with one brutal blow of the belt.

Though the belt would eventually have no place in Craigie, it took some time to phase out completely so, like anyone who ever went to school, I can tell a few horror stories. Yet I like to think my collection of negative school memories is abnormally small. Of course, stacked against the warm rosy glow which will live with me forever, there are a few bitter moments. But when they came, they probably hurt more because Craigie's spirit of mutual trust and co-operation was so ingrained it was easy to take it for granted . . .

Last August marked the 20th anniversary of the day I started at Craigie. Standing in the big hall in my Oxford bags and my yellow shirt with the sticky out collar, I'm waiting for my name to be called out in the class list for IW1, waiting to embark on a six-year adventure which would provide lessons to last a lifetime.

The world has changed since then but the guiding principles which drove the Craigie culture should be at the foundation of any school. Education is not about exams or league tables. It isn't about the three Rs, school boards or the Parents' Charter. Education is about people. It's about giving young people the opportunity to fulfil their potential with the gentle support of committed professionals whose work is more than just a way to earn a living.

Craigie cared. The certificates gather dust, the logarithms are forgotten but the values carry on. Craigie cared, and that's what counts.

Munro, Alan (1995). In MacKenzie, Hugh. *Craigroyston Days*. Edinburgh, Mainstream.

Student – the school refused to employ the term 'pupil' – 1974–80.

12K                                                              Aberdeen, 1950/60s.

Rosemount Junior Secondary School provided an all-round education that would lead to apprenticeships for the boys and nursing, office, hairdressing and shop careers for the girls. The staff was a mixed group of teachers, some of us returning from the war and others who had kept the school during the emergency.

The head was Dr. Alex A. Cormack, a tall, imposing figure who had gained his doctorate for translating the Scottish Poor Law into French. He was among the last of the dominies, those figures respected in the community along with GP, the minister and the local Bobby, for their distinction and dependability.

True to type, he was a disciplinarian, yet loved by the pupils, each of whom he knew by name. When he entered a class, the children sat to attention and there was a hush of expectation. The Doctor always had an anecdote delivered in a rich, booming voice and spiced with the Doric. He had his finger on the pulse of the intimate activities and needs of the families in the area; who had a 'bidie-in' [unmarried live-in partner], and what child was in need of a new pair of shoes . . .

He ran a happy school where teachers and pupils established a rapport based on a mutual understanding of the need for good discipline. The children came from varying backgrounds but the parents, many of whom had seen war service, were almost without exception in favour of the school's ethos. Staff stayed on and on, bringing continuity to the teaching.

There was a full programme of social events – Sports Day, Concerts, Trips to London, Summer Camp etc., for which teachers gave unstintingly of their free time. The good Doctor himself, twice a year, at Easter and Xmas, dutifully held up the traffic in Rosemount Place, while the whole school, class after class, passed in relay across to Rutherford Church for the traditional Services. On one occasion he was having difficulty with a boy who refused to keep in line. When the recalcitrant reached the church door, prodded on by the angry Head, he was given a dressing-down. At last he managed to blurt out: 'But I'm not at school  – I work for Clark the butcher!'

Baird, Archie (1999). 'The Happiest Days of our Lives . . .' *Leopard*, October.

1919– : professional footballer (Aberdeen and Scotland), journalist, PE and Italian teacher in Aberdeen.

His Dr Cormack is the author of *William Cramond* – see Chapter 8.

Most human associations have been uneasy efforts to get a variety of people to settle down together, the lion and the lamb. Any establishment underplays its stresses; the slaves are generally well-treated and happy, it assures itself; the natives wouldn't know what to do with the money if you paid them European rates. But each civilisation contains within itself the seeds of its own decay.

These seeds were already growing in the Summerhill soil before I arrived there. The staff pushed out of their consciousness the kind of lives that the factory-fodder, non 'O' grade pupils would live; they minimised the mutterings of revolt that came from a few independent, resolute spirits who refused to bow to Baal . . .

Craig had an independent streak and an immunity to establishment carrots that made him unacceptable in the school. Any authoritarian society has an allergy to these characters. In the army they are called 'bolshy', 'barrack-room lawyers', and cajoled and threatened. For centuries they persisted against all the odds, however small the minority in which they found themselves. Porcupine characters, uncomfortable and inconvenient. When I was at school we did what we were told; we feared criticism and denigration, we fought one another for promotion and preferment. Craig had different values; he was independent at whatever cost to himself, he insisted on human dignity . . .

In 1970, Craig Peterson's pioneers were merely a headache in the body of the educational system. They could be isolated and prevented from spreading the infection. They received the admiration of a large number of the pupils but they could be removed from the classrooms by the provision of practical jobs round the school. I asked some of the senior staff to recommend half a dozen boys to go and tidy up the Highland lodge the school had been presented with. The Education Committee were going to visit the lodge to see if they would support us in this venture and there was three days' work sweeping and dusting and scrubbing to make the place presentable. The pupils whose names were given in for this work were Craig Peterson's and five of his lieutenants; they were expendable; and teachers were relieved at their absence. They helped to sweep a chimney, dug a pit to bury rubbish, cleaned and scrubbed and hammered. It was an impressive eruption of energy and goodwill. They enjoyed, I think, both the sheer hard physical activity and the awareness of doing something of value. Years later, leaving a first division football match at Pittodrie, I met Craig. He said: 'Did you ever get that Highland lodge going?' I replied, 'No, the education committee wouldn't support us'. He said, 'Do you know, that was the best three days of my life'.

> MacKenzie, R. F. (1976). *The Unbowed Head.*
> Edinburgh University Student Publications.

1910–87: brought up in rural Aberdeenshire; famously liberalising headteacher and eloquent campaigner – *Escape from the Classroom, A Question of Living* etc.

12M                                                          Aberdeen, 1940–75.

When, during the war years, I had taught at Middlefield, the conditions for pupils and staff were far from ideal. Teaching materials were barely adequate and the curriculum very narrow. Social conditions were poor and East-end children with whom I dealt all through my 'career' were the products of poor housing, poor feeding and of poor cultural background. But by the 60s the climate for education had changed. More money was available and Aberdeen City was fortunate to have a Council who, although Socialist in politics, were most Liberal in their outlook, and soon we were to enter what I regard as the 'Golden Age' of primary education. The effects of the easing of finance in the country in general were also felt in the further re-housing of the people in the slum areas of the city. Bathrooms became commonplace and no longer did we have the nits and other side-effects of poverty and lack of hygiene . . .

At this time, education in the City was at an all-time high. Money was reasonably plentiful and we had a liberally-minded Town Council and a caring and interested Administration. If a teacher or H.T. had a new idea, the money for the materials to try it out was forthcoming. Audio-visual aids, Reading Laboratories became available even in Primary schools, staffing ratio was generous, and in this climate the child-based revolution throve and prospered. I'm not implying that everything was perfect, but on the whole, this was a co-operative, interesting and innovative period in the field . . .

Causewayend was the next school to fall vacant, and again I remember my first impression when the H.T. Mr F, invited me to tea in the staffroom prior to his transfer to a larger school. It was a huge, grey, cheerless building in the centre of the city, a cross between a castle and a prison. I received a polite but hardly warm welcome from a staff who had never suffered petticoat government before and didn't like the prospect. Whether by coincidence or design, eight of them transferred or resigned before I took over! At that time Causewayend had about 300 pupils, twelve permanent staff, a deputy head and an infants' mistress. Twelve years later when I retired it had seven teachers, no promoted staff and only 150 children, and the old granite tenements had been razed to allow passage of a new ring road.

Well, I moved in. On the first morning early I was seated in my small office on the first floor, overlooking the playground. The children were milling about below my window and I heard a chant begin, 'Granny Headie, granny headie'. As if that wasn't sufficiently depressing, there came a loud bang at my door and in burst a large and scruffy 11-year-old. 'Hey Miss,' he said 'Hiv you got a strap?' Fixing him with a steely glare, I replied 'You'll soon find out!' That lad, by the way, now a handsome smartly dressed young man in a good post, came to see me every few months right until I retired, just to ask how I was doing and to give me his news.

But how lucky I was at Causewayend. With only a few exceptions, the children were friendly and receptive, the parents pleasant and co-operative and the staff, once they got over the initial shock, enthusiastic and capable.

Due to the liberal outlook of the current Council and to the encouraging atmosphere generated by our Directors we were able to give the children a wide cultural experience as well as to teach the basic subjects thoroughly. We took them on exciting visits, they had gardening and cooking classes, they were able to engage in many activities outwith the set curriculum – badminton, volley-ball, chess, football, gym, to name but a few. We were able to augment what was a rather poor cultural background with an attractive library and with visual aids and musical instruments, in short, to do what all keen teachers would wish to do, namely, to educate the whole child in a happy yet disciplined environment.

Then alas, in 1974, came the twin evils of recession and regionalisation. With either of these, separately, we might have coped, but it was, and still is, I hear, a hard struggle to cope with both. We in Aberdeen City had a particularly difficult situation to face. With few exceptions, our respected and admired Directorate retired and newcomers, mainly from the former county, moved in, determined to upgrade the other parts of the new Grampian Region to the high standards of the City. This inevitably led to a corresponding downgrading of the city schools' amenities and, in consequence, to a feeling of dis-satisfaction and disappointment among the staffs of these schools.

On reflection, I can now understand the enormous task which this new Directorate in conjunction with the new Regional Council had to undertake – that of merging all the widely differing district authorities into one regional whole. I believe, now, that most of our new Administration worked mightily to achieve this end. But oh! the agonies of those first years – the endless paper edicts from Woodhill House [administrative HQ, Grampian Region], the endless returns of such meaningless statistics as the square measurement of every room, store and cupboard in every school, the constant flow of 'Do nots' and the equal plethora of 'Dos'. One funny story illustrates the futility of these paper mountains – I received a circular addressed to all H.T.s which read, 'It has been brought to our notice that, in some schools, flammable materials are being stored in the boiler rooms. This dangerous practice must cease immediately, so please notify your Janitor to remove all such material from the boiler rooms forthwith'. I gave this missive to my Aberdeen Janny and he read it carefully, then looked up and said, 'Aye, and fit am a tae dee wi' ma coal?'

> Youngson, Flora (1991). *Dominie's Daughter*.
> Centre for Scottish Studies, University of Aberdeen.

12N                                        Aberdeen, 1983.

The society we live in is deeply perplexed. In the last couple of decades there has been a colossal redistribution of the world's goods, both nationally and internationally, with all the social evils that brings. The greatest of these, I believe, is the possible breakdown of the work ethic on which our educational system depends. You will be faced with a paradox when you start teaching. You and I know there never was a time when our society needed education more, but hordes of your pupils, and their parents, utterly disenchanted, will believe there never was a time when they needed it less.

You will also come up against young people as they are, not as they ought to be. Unfortunately, some of the decisions in education are taken by people who think they already are what they ought to be. You, not the decision makers, will have to cope with them, and some of you will have a hard row to hoe.

Is it worth the struggle then? Year by year in these addresses I have said goodbye to thousands of your predecessors and many of my own old friends. Now the time has arrived for me to bid you all farewell. I have spent over thirty-six years in the business of Scottish education, as a teacher, lecturer, as Principal of this college. If I have anything helpful to say to you, this must surely be the time. The temptation is extraordinary to echo the centenarian once interviewed on Radio Scotland: 'Ay man, I've seen a wheen o' changes and I've ben against every dampt one o' them!' It is tempting, but it wouldn't be true. I've seen changes in which I delight – a place in the sun, for example, for the aesthetic subjects: when you think of all the joy people have in music and art and drama, it is no more than they deserve. A beginning at least to the breaking down of the religious barriers which have troubled us for centuries. A chance for teachers to play a real part in running their schools and profession. Here in Scotland we set up the first General Teaching Council in the world, and it is a matter of enduring pride for me that for three years I was its Chairman.

Alas, there have also been changes in which I take no pleasure. The long struggle to smooth the path of the less gifted has combined with the huge increase in labour-saving devices to reduce, I am afraid, the value of effort. As teachers in Scotland, moreover, we seem always to preoccupy ourselves with means rather than end, and I have seen no change in that phenomenon. Let me plead with you – don't let the waves of day-to-day detail close over your head. Don't just concentrate on doing things better in the class-room: try to think about why you are doing them. But the saddest thing I see is that education has shrunk into a smaller, less respected place in our community. The politicians still spend a lot of money on it, but there are increasing signs that they grudge it, and so do the voters.

Scotland, James (1983). Farewell graduation address.

Aberdeen College of Education.

# 13 THEN AND NOW:
## 1985–2000

5–14: A Practical Guide: The Scottish Office, 1994
Too many targets, so little joy: Herald, 1999
Back to the basics in schools: Press and Journal, 1999
St Margaret Mary's; James Gillespie's: Scotsman, 1992
Why comprehensive schools work for Scotland's youngsters:
Linda Croxford, 2002
The Scottish Identity: Christopher Smout, 1977
'In every country, except Scotland . . .': Scotsman, 1979
School History and the Shaping of Scottish Identity:
Sydney Wood, 2002
The Senga Syndrome: Leslie Hills, 1990
Scotland spirals down to blissful ignorance: Norman Harper, 1999
On the Evils of a Neglected Education: Scots Magazine, 1802
Villagers fight to save their primary: Scotsman, 2001
A School in the Hills: Katherine Stewart, 1996
What children think of school life a century ago:
Dunnottar Primary School, 1989
Going to School in the 80s and the 90s:
Some Recent First-hand Accounts

Figure 24. **Garnetbank School, Glasgow, 1914** 'Teacher and Class at Drill' – a familiar image of the period which gave the city School Boards the opportunity to demonstrate the order that was now being introduced into the lives of its younger citizens, not only through formalised exercise, but the solidly imposing building which looms behind. *Glasgow City Archive*

Figure 25. **Abbotswell Primary School, Aberdeen, 2000** Pupils carrying out some individual investigation work in the school's computer bay. *Abbotswell Primary School*

By 1985, it could be claimed that Scottish education was making its own vigorous response to the comprehensive system which had swept through Britain, twenty years before. Selection had been abolished; the new Standard Grades were providing a certificate to match all ranges of interest and ability; the large majority were staying on past a leaving age that had now been raised to 16; as many as fifty per cent were taking the Highers that had once been the preserve of a tenth of that number; for the less academic, the modular units imported from the further education sector were feeding in practical, work-orientated materials. And, everywhere, the tempering of the old subject-centred approach was leading to a more relaxed and flexible learning environment.

The argument was, however, moving on. The developments of the previous twenty years had opened up the full benefits of a system, which had formerly confined its higher reaches to the able minority, to all of Scotland's young people. But these were advances which were to bring the nation's education hard up against the meaning of a tradition which had always attempted to hold both 'democracy' and 'excellence' within the one web of inherited values.

Any chance that, after the agitation of the 60s and 70s, the system would be able to settle down to a decade or two of steady development was removed by the arrival of a committedly right-wing Tory government and, within it, as Secretary of State, the combative Michael Forsyth. For him, the issue of quality was to be resolved by turning it into a matter of customer satisfaction. Parents were to become consumers of educational services. Devices such as School Boards, entitlement to opt out of Local Authority administration, the right by 'Parents' Charter' to choose their child's school and devolved school management were introduced as the required leverage against 'failing' schools; league tables of examination performances, teacher appraisal and the publication of Inspectors' reports were to arm them with the necessary information.

The SED – now translated into the 'Scottish Office Education and Industry Department' – was charged with drawing up the curricular specifications by which to drive the schools into acting as publicly accountable bodies. The employment of such terms as 'delivery', 'development plans' and 'targets' was to impress upon them the managerial nature of the new systems approach.

In these respects, the reforms paralleled what was happening in England – where it could at least be said that the UK Conservative governments of Margaret Thatcher and John Major had received a majority vote. The lesser enthusiasm evident at the ballot box for their New Right policies in the north helps to explain the softening of their implementation in Scotland. Inspection remained under the steward-ship of St Andrew's House: the full harshness of the national testing scheme was resisted; almost all schools remained within the Local Authority domain; Chris Woodhead and his OFSTED stayed south of Hadrian's Wall. For many observers, this more canny response was also evidence of continued public trust in the national system.

The impact on the character of school life was, however, un-deniable. Throughout the 90s, the SOEID, from Unst to Galloway, was dispatching van-loads of documentation to teachers everywhere, and with them the detailed syllabus directives required to implement its '5–14 Curriculum and Assessment Programme'. Every conceiva-ble aspect of the child's first ten years of schooling was to be accounted for. **13A** is characteristic, both in its tone and its bullet-point content, of the planning disciplines which all were now required to obey.

Such a burden of regulation had not been experienced in Scottish schools since the days of Sir Henry Craik. It was as if the age of the Codes had returned and, with it, the same sense of teacher oppression that had been voiced a century previously [see Chapter 9]. (**13B**).

The 'performance' of the school was now exposed to a wider audience than ever before. When the Inspectors' Report, *Standards and Quality in Scotland's Schools 1995–98*, was issued, and, with it, the intelligence that one school in five was failing to attain a 'good' rating overall and that forty per cent of pupils in Secondary 1 and 2 were below par in Maths and Language, the media were empowered to pronounce a national failure. The *Scotsman* ran its editorial comment of 19 November 1999 under the heading 'The Scandal of Scotland's Schools'; the *Press and Journal* saw in it the much anticipated revelation of a twenty-year-long betrayal (**13C**).

If Scotland's schools appeared to be failing, it could also be said that they were now attempting much more. In many ways, the rankings that were being lined up in the league tables of examination results, which were now receiving annual publication in the eager press, told the reader more about the distribution of socio-economic deprivation than it did about specific academic efficiencies (**13D 1, 2**). The verdict depended on which particular bit of the national scene was under scrutiny. James Gillespie's had always been a high-achieving – and West-end – Edinburgh establishment; St Margaret Mary's, in Glasgow's raw housing schemes, could never have been. Yet, nationally, more and more, and from an ever wider spread of background, were staying on in their local school, there to gain the qualifications which had once been confined to a relatively favoured minority. To that extent, it could be concluded that by 2000 Scottish education had become more truly democratic than ever it had been in its celebrated past (**13E**).

At that date it had, however, become, more than ever, a matter of publicised agonising. Its controversies continued to be quarrelled over by the media through the customary mixture of statistics, opinionating and selective reference, both social and individualised. Indeed, the significance of the national tradition had, itself, become a matter of debate. While there continued to be general agreement that, historically, the school has offered a potent expression of such cherished Scottish qualities as 'democracy', the 'work ethic' and 'getting on', doubts grew as to the positive effect of such symbolism.

Over the last twenty years, reaction has gathered against any easy acceptance of the old wisdoms. Critics have now come to insist that tales of lads o' pairts and sturdy village schools be set in a wider, more questioning sociological context. Some historians have pointed out that the fitfully heroic success story has been used to distract from a more general record of repressive indoctrination, one in which teachers have been reliant upon harsh discipline and narrow-minded academicism. The most biting attack in this vein has been made by Christopher Smout (**13F**). While the rasping directness of language suggests that he is substituting one caricature for another – an anti-myth for a myth – there is no doubt that, for many Scots, 'schooldays' provoke memories of bleak sessions at dull repetitive exercises, beneath the unsmiling tyranny of tawse and test.

There have been further revisionists, concerned to question the right of Scottish education to be carrier of the nation's best identity. Although he has concentrated on the universities, George Elder

Davie's account of the extent to which, in the nineteenth century, the country's higher education fell prey to an Anglicising influence, produced, in 1961, a book whose title offered the contemporary critic a famously compelling slogan – *The Democratic Intellect.* It appeared to crystalise all the undermined virtues of a system that once gave the student a broadly-based grounding in mental rigour and, with it, independence in thought and debate. And in its desire to imbue its products with a competitively standard education, especially within the context of British citizenship and Imperial service, the native system has been notorious for its neglect of Scottish literature and Scottish history (**13G**). Although efforts are now being made to repair the omission, concerns still remain (**13H**).

The most incisive criticism, however, has come from those commentators who have brought a sociological awareness to their re-examination of the old stories. The account by Leslie Hills (**13I**) of her tortuous career in the education ranks of the 70s and 80s demonstrates how the cherished exemplars of a 'democratic' system may underwrite a culture of acceptance which perpetuates inherited, and institutionalised, power structures at work in Scottish society. It comes from a volume whose contributors have drawn upon the insights of Edinburgh University's Centre for Educational Sociology. There, its researchers have reconstructed the individual biographies of politicians and SED officers who have been at the centre of policy-making in twentieth century Scotland. Through a combination of interview and documentary analysis, they have argued that the dominant thinking has, classically, been that of men – no women – who are the products not of the more populous and, therefore, representative urban centres, but of a rurally parochial small-town Scotland, where the local school and a supportive community were, indeed, vitally formative influences. In so doing, they have given the national tradition another icon – 'Kirriemuir Man', so named after the douce little Angus town which was the breeding ground not only of James Barrie but his brother, Alexander Ogilvy, who rose to become an influential Inspector of Schools in the late nineteenth century.

The maintenance of a sense of national identity must always be dependant upon a certain measure of myth-making and selective construction. These are, after all, the means by which shared ideals are not only established in the people's imagination but become lodged in the individual memory. Set against such symbolism, the current actuality must always fall short. Norman Harper's lament (**13J**) is simply the most recent in a sequence of decline which may be tracked back two hundred years and more (**13K**). What joins the present-day writer to his 1802 predecessor is the degree to which the perceived shortcomings of the school are implicated in a more general sense of moral and social fall. And, as Harper's regret for his schooling in his own Howe of Alford indicates, when seen at its most quintessential, it is the rural that continues to compel. The traditional colouring remains pastoral, not urban grey. The image of the warm little local school, sitting at the heart of a stable, organic community, is one that can still beguile the national imagination and, where the rationalisations of progress menace, offer a cause (**13L**).

In the 1990s, the memoir of a personal life carved out among the glens or along the howes became sufficiently prolific to constitute a minor genre. Writers like Jean Cantlie Stewart, with *Pine Trees and Sky* (1998), and Katherine Stewart, with *A School in the Hills* (1996), are not simply being nostalgic: their experiences are intended to conserve. When the latter recounts the chronicle of her attempt to take over an old croft in the Highlands of the 1950s, the plain one-teacher school of Abriachan, to which she sends her daughter, is depicted as a place for a deeper, more purely ethnic education (**13M 1**). Even when the economic policies of Inverness-shire County Council force its closure, she can still urge the reclamation of the school as an educational centre, one where the young may re-enter a past whose spirit will live on within their reawoken understanding.

The hope is that the old place will continue to give out its lessons. The effectiveness of such a venture is called in doubt by what can happen when the nation's young do revisit their past. When, in 1989, the children of Dunnottar Primary were led into the celebration of their school's centenary, through television reconstructions and excursion to the preserved old classroom in the Aberdeen Urban Studies Centre, the imprint that the education of their great-grandparents made upon their own memories was inescapably, dismissively contemporary (**13M 2**).

In attempting to estimate the progress of Scottish education, and to decide how best its traditions may be reworked, it is important to get inside the experiences of its most recent inheritors. These are voices not yet widely broadcast. Their schooling has been too immediate, too raw, to have generated the considered long-view. For them, the personal encounter has not had time to settle into the reshaped memory and to be refined by knowledge of the life-development to come – nor to be imbued by prejudicial nostalgia or consolidated into the definitive judgement. The biographical statements of the latest school generation must await a further twenty years of gathering retrospect.

A sampling of the experiences of a range of young Scots has, however, begun to be compiled by the author's interviews of those who have left school within the last decade. (**13N**). At this early stage, any comment on what they reveal can only be tentative. What may be noted, even so soon into their adulthood, is that the speakers have already become aware of 'change' as a remorseless complication to both the school and the social fabric that binds it. Nevertheless, according to their testimony, the abrupt upheaval in teaching methods and institutional disciplines since the 1960s has been fabled rather than actual; rather there was a series of pragmatic adjustments which – now – have been caught up in something of a swing back to basics and to structure. Theirs is, it would appear, the evidence of a body of people, pupils and teachers both, who must do what they can to pick their way through a school world caught up in a turbulent social setting, one which has been disturbed by injury to many of the old shared forces such as the church, the priority to be accorded to communal welfare, job continuity and to the very concept of the family.

Their contemporary school has, as ever, had to act as much as a social organism as it has been host to a series of procedures which are merely curricular. To the concerned and ageing onlookers, what they have to report may appear to be of a world that has become disordered, degraded even. But, to those who have newly emerged, its processes continue to make sense, and do so as an honourably modern way of attempting to mediate between the immediate want and the longer-term future. If the local primary can still retain something of its familiar, comforting immediacy, the neighbourhood comprehensive appears to be accepted as the latest agency which Scottish society, and its history, has evolved to meet the nation's democratic aspirations. In their reports, it emerges as the great melting-pot, to which, as never before, all of the nation's young are welcomed, there to bubble their way through a flux of experience, which is both educational and educative.

13A                                                    Edinburgh, 1994.

### School Policies

Whether you work in a primary or secondary school you and your colleagues need to have a shared understanding of what you are trying to achieve for your pupils. This can be done by including a succinct statement of agreed aims and policies in the school development plan and school handbook. The 5–14 Guidelines can relieve schools of the need to provide extensive **curriculum and assessment** policy statements . . .

The **national guidelines** provide all the policy needed on
- **the structure and balance of the curriculum** – see The Structure and Balance of the Curriculum 5–14 and the sections in each guideline on time allocations and weightings;
- **the aims of each area of the curriculum** – see the statement of aims within each curriculum guideline;
- **the main components of learning within each curriculum area** – see attainment outcomes and strands;
- **the key indications of progress** – see attainment targets within attainment outcomes in each curricular area;
- **a framework against which progress can be assessed, recorded and reported; and**
- **a description of appropriate learning and teaching methods** – see programmes of study in each guideline.

**Education authorities and schools which endorse the national guidelines have gone a long way towards having a set of policies on the curriculum.**

> HM Inspectors of Schools (1994). *5–14: A Practical Guide*. Edinburgh, Scottish Office.

13B                                                    Greenock, 1999.

### Too many targets, so little joy

A former headteacher at one of the country's highest-achieving state schools warned yesterday that officials were becoming obsessed with assessments and targets at the expense of giving children a well-rounded education. Mr Allan MacDougall, who retired from Greenock Academy last month at the age of 50, said teachers are under so much pressure to ensure pupils reach certain grades in national testing that they are reluctant to release them for activities such as the Duke of Edinburgh awards, or school musical rehearsals, in case they let the side down.

He said, 'We have become terribly accountable. I wonder if some people have become so obsessed with examination results and league tables that understandably we have had to pay less heed to those non-measurable but equally valuable aspects of education.' Mr MacDougall said he was suffering from high blood pressure and the beginnings of an ulcer – problems probably connected with the stress of the job. 'I wasn't going to drop dead, but the way I do my job and the way my colleagues do their job is to give it 100 per cent at least. I couldn't continue to do that for Greenock Academy,' he said.

In a farewell letter circulated to parents, Mr MacDougall said that one of his greatest regrets was that 'the pendulum has swung too far towards the ethos of assessment, evaluation, examination, account-ability and targets'. He added: 'some of the spontaneity in teaching has been lost and the steadily increasing curricular demands on teacher and pupil alike have tended to "squeeze out" some of the activities which, although hugely beneficial and educational, are less able to be measured and assessed in any formal way and thus are seen by some of those whose task it is to formulate educational policy and planning for our country as less "essential".'

Buie, Elizabeth (1999). *Herald*, 3 November.

13C                                                  Scotland, 1999.

**Back to the basics in schools**
The surprise is that it has taken so long. Most employers and many university lecturers have long deplored the decline in literacy, numer-acy and basic general knowledge of Scottish school-leavers. They have despaired of an education system which, for 20 years from the mid-1970s, followed fashion and trend, not the fundamentals. They stood aghast as senior figures at the Scottish Education Department, regional councils and colleges of education airily dismissed the basics as relics of the unfashionable old days; an obsession of those who

could not or would not understand that new methods, rooted in the psychology of education, would allow pupils to flourish far more effectively and efficiently than before.

It was nonsense 20 years ago and remains nonsense now. The gurus of education are taking a little longer to see that than are the rest of us, but they seem to be getting there. HM Schools Inspectors have issued a report declaring that writing skills in nearly half of Scotland's schools are not up to standard. This is certainly true . . .

Until the late-1960s, Scotland had an education system which believed that sound foundations allowed the building of strong and able pupils. It encouraged those who were academically inclined and drew out the other talents of those who were not. Now the country has a system which tells pupils and parents that failure is not really failure; that reading, writing and counting are over-rated, and certainly not as vital as employers believe. In short, we have a system in which the system knows best, despite all evidence to the contrary.

Editorial (1999). *Press and Journal*, 13 January.

13D                                           Glasgow; Edinburgh, 1992.

**1)** St Margaret Mary's School in Glasgow's sprawling Castlemilk district is an unremarkable looking school, a series of uninspired 60s style buildings on a main drag into the estate which once had the dubious distinction – if it no longer does – of being Europe's biggest housing scheme. This week St Margaret Mary's enjoys a similarly unwelcome pre-eminence with the publication of the controversial school examination league table which reveals that it has an among-the-bottom 'performance' rate in Scotland. With only 4.2 per cent of its 90 school-leavers emerging with 3 or more Higher certificates, the school with about 550 pupils has the country's lowest recorded pass rate in the category.

Nevertheless it could have been worse: 16 other schools in the region, mostly in the deprived Glasgow periphery housing schemes, had fewer than 5 pupils leaving with 3 or more Highers. Such is the education authorities' sensitivity to the tables – Strathclyde Regional Council is bitterly opposed to the idea on the grounds that it does not reflect the differing social and economic circumstances prevailing in the school locales – that a request to interview the Headteacher yesterday was refused. But local people were quick to defend St Margaret Mary's' record of success in an area inextricably linked to the evils of high long-term unemployment and widespread poverty. Immediately opposite the school, an alcohol advice centre shares a ground floor site with Dougrie Nursery School and in St Margaret Mary's Roman Catholic Church 300 yards down the road, the notice-board features helpful reminders on drug abuse helplines and where to get help on welfare rights and debt-counselling alongside a bright poster for a pancake evening.

The school chaplain, Father John Quinn, feels the relative lack of academic success can be attributed partly to a lack of parental aspiration, which instills and perpetuates a lack of motivation in the youngsters. But the table, he feels, does not reflect the valuable work going on in the school on the social and personal development of the pupils for whom such measures as special tutorials and homework classes have been instituted. 'The teachers are very encouraging to the children but the self-esteem of the parents is very low,' he said.

**2)** Throughout its 189-year history, James Gillespie's High has earned a reputation as one of Edinburgh's top schools. Many fee-paying institutions cast envious glances at the school's consistently unim-peachable standards and up to 70 parents a year living outwith Gillespie's catchment area appeal to have their children sent there.

Set in Marchmont on the city's south side, Gillespie's hovered on the brink of becoming an independent school when it was a grant-aided school but eventually threw in its lot with the state sector. The school draws pupils from a largely middle-class background, the same area from which George Heriot's and George Watson's private schools take their children. But the Headteacher, Colin Finlayson, has said in the past that he is not competing with the independent sector, rather aspiring to high standards in the state sector.

The 1,100 pupils benefit from impressive facilities, the result of £3,000,000 spent a few years ago. The Business Studies department is well-stocked with computers and every department has its own desk-top computer. Pupils have the use of cycling and running machines in the PE department. It also has a fitness room, a gym and a swimming pool. Young musicians have a host of keyboards on which to practise in the Music department. Out of school hours there is no shortage of activities on offer to the pupils: orchestra, choirs, field-trips, public speaking events and visits to Europe all feature on the extra-curricular agenda.

John Hart, the Chairman of the School Board, said he believes Gillespie's place near the top of the examination league results in Scotland reflects its catchment area. 'The difficulty with league tables is that they suggest we are making comparisons,' he said.

Dean, Susan and Gillian Harris (1992). Scotsman, 2 March.

13E                                    University of Edinburgh, 2002.

The introduction of comprehensive schooling in Scotland has been a major success story. By 1984, just 20 years after the end of selection, researchers were able to report, 'comprehensive schooling is better and fairer'. (McPherson and Willms 1989). After analysing differences in attainment in schools in fully-comprehensive catchments between 1976 and 1984, they concluded that standards of attainment had risen overall, the increase was greatest among females and pupils of lower social class, and social inequalities in attainment had declined.

If we look at average levels of attainment in the Scottish Certificate of Education (SCE) from 1956 to the present we find a dramatic improvement in levels of attainment. Figures show the decline in the proportion of young people who left school without achieving at least one SCE O-grade/Standard grade award (at A–C/ 1–3) from 70% in 1965 to less than 20% in 1998. The decline is most rapid in the years following comprehensive reorganisation. In the period of selective schooling there had been an expectation that only the top 30% of the ability range were suitable to take SCE examinations, but once the barrier of selective schooling was removed, many more pupils were successful in the examinations than could previously have been thought possible. Similarly there was a tripling of the proportion of school leavers achieving three or more Higher grade passes.

A further measure of success is the high level of entry to higher education in Scotland. In 1998–99 the age participation index was 47% in Scotland compared to 29% in England . . .

The research suggests that the more uniform system of comprehensive schooling in Scotland has reduced social segregation and led to a high quality of education for the vast majority of pupils.

271

In contrast, the introduction of comprehensive schooling in England was piecemeal and perpetuated a system of socially-segregated schools.

Croxford, Linda (2002). 'Why comprehensive schools work for Scotland's youngsters'. *Scottish Educational Journal*. April.

13F                                            University of St Andrews, 1977.

And lastly, the Scottish working class and middle class have been exposed for a century to a miserable education system (Scottish run too) which believes that teaching consists of trying to smash facts into children. How can constructive consensus, adventure and innovation be produced in a society where phalanges of silent children arrive at the universities with their pens poised to catch truth as it drips from their teachers' lips?

Smout, Christopher (1977). 'The Scottish Identity', *The Future of Scotland*. Robert Underwood (ed.). Edinburgh.

'Much has changed in the last 25 years and I would not make that comment now.' Professor Smout to author, June, 2002.

13G                                                              Scotland, 1979.

In every country, except Scotland, it is taken for granted that national history and literature should be well taught in the schools.

'In every country, except Scotland . . .' (1979). *Scotsman*, 8 February.

13H                                                              Scotland, 2002.

Pupils were asked to explain the importance in Scottish history of twenty individuals ranging in time from St Columba to Winnie Ewing. Here too the open-ended strategy produced a very high number of nil responses. Boys proved more ready than girls to hazard a guess, however wild; girls who did not know the correct answer were inclined not to respond but to leave a blank. Pupils provided a very varied range of replies and a generous interpretation was given to give credit to any answer that showed some relevance. William Wallace and Robert Bruce were recognised by 40 per cent, John Logie Baird (a little surprisingly) by 33 per cent and Flora MacDonald by 24 per cent. For the rest, nil responses loomed large, reaching a level of 90 per cent for Sir Archibald Grant, Adam Smith and Tom Johnston. One per cent recognised the first two of this trio, none were able to identify Tom Johnston. Pupils' knowledge of religious history again seemed sketchy with 6 per cent managing a relevant answer for St Columba (whilst 10 per cent thought he had discovered America), 7 per cent identifying John Knox and just 1 per cent recognising St Margaret. Social and economic history fared little better, as the fate of Archibald Grant (1 per cent) and Adam Smith (1 per cent) indicates. 13 per cent knew something about Thomas Telford, 3 per cent made relevant points about Sir John Sinclair and, to my surprise, only 8 per cent linked James Watt to steam power, 26 per cent of pupils connecting this great man to the development of electricity, most commonly the invention of the light bulb.

Political figures other than Wallace and Bruce remained a mystery to most pupils. Eighty-nine per cent were unable to say anything about Kenneth McAlpin (2 per cent identified him), Ramsay MacDonald stirred 3 per cent of pupils to provide a relevant response, nobody knew who Tom Johnston was and 73 per cent could find nothing whatever to say about Winnie Ewing.

Wood, Sydney (2002). 'School History and the Shaping of Scottish Identity'. *History Scotland*, March/April.

131                                          Lothian, 1966–88

I am a child of the land of the Democratic Intellect; the land of the lad o' pairts. A land famed for its excellent egalitarian education system. This is a strong male myth which has served the women of Scotland ill. Since women have been largely invisible there is a habit of silence. When women seek to break the silence there is no precedent and they are isolated and vulnerable. Gender codes and behaviours are so instutionalised as to go unnoticed. My professional education and working life spans the years of equal opportunities legislation in Westminster and, at local level, the introduction of codes of practice designed to eliminate discrimination. My experience leads me to believe that legislation and codes of practice have made little difference to the ability of women to influence and shape policy and thus the future. Neither have been applied to significant effect on the system of patronage and appointment which systematically excludes women. There was a smaller proportion of women in positions of power and influence in Scotland in 1988 than there was in 1966 when, armed with a belief in the eventual triumph of natural justice, I took up my first teaching post . . .

The vast majority of advisers were men. A small but significant number resented women in their midst. It was necessary to tolerate repeated derogatory references to competent women and 'jokes' about the inability of women (and more disturbingly, of female pupils) to understand the technical and scientific. I heard myself described as forceful and articulate in tones which made it clear that it was not a compliment. I heard one senior official describe me to another as very intelligent and then beam at me, waiting for me to wag my tail. Worst of all, was unthinking and demeaning and insulting behaviour of senior officials who regarded treating a middle-aged professional colleague as though she were a naïve, flighty and essentially frivolous slip of as girl as gallant. One offered at the top of his voice in a corridor, not to spank me this time, when I reported some trivial slip of memory. At the time I was forty-one.

> Hills, Leslie (1990). 'The Senga Syndrome: reflections on 21 years in education'. *Girls in their Prime*. Fiona Paterson and Judith Fewell (eds). Edinburgh, Scottish Academic Press.

1945– : from Glasgow University in 1960s to Lothian's Advisory Service in 1980s, with range of teaching and national working party posts in between, Hills reports on the perpetuation of institutionalised sexism.

13J                                          Aberdeenshire, 1999.

In the Sixties, ours was an average primary-school class in an average village in an average part of Scotland, but every one of the 40 of us knew the capitals of Europe, the key dates of British history, potted biographies of 20th century figures, the basics of musical notation and a thousand other things. We could identify different species of trees and knew rudimentary botany. Most of us could parse, and all of us could tackle mental arithmetic. These days, you're lucky to find 15-year-olds as well informed as we nine-year-olds were in the Sixties. They're filled with opinions, and able to identify the latest Playstation game from a still picture, or any Top 40 band just by listening to the opening bars of the latest hit.

Otherwise, they're mostly lost.

Harper, Norman (1999). 'Scotland spirals down
to blissful ignorance'. *Press and Journal*, 28 July.

13K                                                        Scotland, 1802.

As the spirit of the times has been complained of as favouring too much laxity of morals, and growing depravity; and there is too much reason to apprehend an increase of vice and ignorance rather than of virtue and knowledge . . . The systems that have been introduced, by particular schools, are little calculated to produce any effects on a plain and simple education.

'On the Evils of a Neglected Education' (1802). *The Scots Magazine*, August.

13L                                                          Angus, 2001.

### Villagers fight to save their primary

Like many rural communities in Scotland, the tiny village of Kilry in Angus has seen its fair share of difficult times. The combination of depopulation since the Seventies and an inability to attract new families to the area has led to the steady closure of many important facilities, from the Post Office to the local shop. Now the community, 12 miles from Blairgowrie, is facing its toughest challenge as Angus Council is considering the closure of its 13-pupil primary school.

Officials from the education department insist that talk of closing the 121-year-old school is premature. They say a review has been launched to ascertain how viable the school is – an exercise made necessary by falling pupil rolls. However, parents and other residents from the Kilry area believe the review exercise is a smokescreen for plans to close the school – saving just £40,000 – and have launched a campaign to save it for future generations.

Jeremy Martindale, spokesman for the group, said a recent meeting attended by 90 local people showed how important the school was. He said, 'If you close the school then you rip the heart out of this area. Since 1880 this school has been a centre of excellence in the community. Standards are extremely high, children do extremely well and the teaching is of the highest quality. We have lost so many of our facilities in the past few years and the school is the only thing left which provides the strong focus that a community of this kind needs to bind it together' One farmer added: 'Institutions like the church and school create a sense of cohesion which is of the utmost importance to a small isolated rural community like ours.' . . .

However, Brian Milne, the council's education convener, said it was the council's duty to seek best value in all its services.

Denholme, Andrew (2001). Scotsman, 19 December.

13M    Inverness-shire, 1990s; Stonehaven, Kincardineshire, 1989.

1) Children of today, coming to visit, might come to understand and appreciate the difficulties their forbears, perhaps their own grand-parents, had in acquiring knowledge. No flickering computer screens brought them fascinating glimpses of things in far-off parts, but they did learn how to deal with the things that immediately concerned them – getting to school on a day of drifting snow, in leaking boots, for a start. Then, on the way home, in summer, they learned which plants were sweet to chew on and how to guddle small trout from under stones in the burn to take home for tea. There would have been jobs to cope with before and after school – bringing in the cow for milking or washing tatties in the ice-cold water of the burn. Holidays were not long and punishments could be harsh. Taking the strap on fingers reddened with chilblains in winter must have been an agony of pain. But lessons had to be learnt. The well-being of the school and of the master depended on scholarly achievement in the days of 'payment by results'. Truancy was penalised, parents being fined or even impri-soned when a grant for good attendance was at stake.

The children, looking round the old classroom and comparing it with their own brightly-lit, well-furnished premises, would shudder at the thought of being educated there, though when the 'new' school was completed and Mr Maclean [its first dominie] arrived, it was regarded as a palace.

Today's children could have a lesson in the old style, sit at desks, copy some magnificent writing from the blackboard, do 'spellings', recite the multiplication table, add, subtract, divide 'mentally' (no fingers to be used!). Books being in short supply, they would listen to stories and poems the master read to them. Stories, tales of 'olden times', when their forbears lived and died, would make their history lesson. The poems they would have to write down and learn 'by heart'. Singing, with the master and his magic tuning fork, would be a relaxation, but a disciplined one, with no excuse for wrong notes or giggles. A dunce's cap or a flick of the tawse were always to be dreaded, but a glint of approval in the master's eye was something to be prized.

After a while the children might well be surprised at the extent to which they'd been 'stretched', pleased with their achievement or eager to do better. It could be more than 'play-acting'. It could be an eye-opener to those watching and those taking part.

Stewart, Katherine (1996). *A School in the Hills*. Edinburgh, Mercat Press.

With husband Jim, became crofters in hills near Loch Ness in 1950s; daughter went to Abriachan school, which had once housed 100 local pupils but was forced to close when roll dwindled to two in 1958. Later, the Stewarts were to live in the old school-house, converting it into a conservation Field Centre.

**2)** 'You got a ruler over your knuckles.' (Primary class 6)

'Your legs could go bent if you didn't drink a pint of milk.' (P4)

'The classrooms were not bright and colourful – they were grey.' (P5)

'They used to stop you getting off your chair.' (P2)

'I don't think the teachers and pupils were very kind.' (P5)

'The school would not have electricity, central heating or any new-fangled things.' (P7)

'They checked your hands to see if they were clean.' (P3)

'They did gym in long skirts – they couldn't move.' (P4)

'Primary Ones had a very hard time.' (P3)

'They got the cane if they wrote with their left hand.' (P3).

'The big ones were dreadfully horrible and the little ones were frightened.' (P3)

'You had to go to the toilets outside.' (P6)

'It must have been hard for the children before – but now it's brilliant.' (P5)

Nicol, Alisoun (1989). 'What the children think of school life a century ago'. *Tak Tent O'Lear. A History of Dunnottar School, Stonehaven*. Aberdeen, School Resources Centre.

13N
                    Aberdeenshire, Angus, Caithness,
                         Edinburgh, Fife, Glasgow,
                    Kincardineshire, Perth, 1980/90s.

**Primary School**
1) The school, though relaxed, was quite solid in what it did. The expectation was that you would co-operate and generally behave. One or two pupils stood out as having difficulties with that, but that's the point – they stood out. We just accepted that there were lines you didn't overstep . . . Certainly some teachers did go in for 'new' methods. Really, it came down to the individual teacher. If the ideals of child-centred education were being championed I don't think they were being applied right across the school. I think there were a few forward-looking teachers but most tried to draw on the modern methods as they saw fit. Sequence was a bit of a problem though. We seemed to be moving from scheme to scheme and following some commercially produced package like Oxford Junior English or Top Ten Mental. The school had invested in all these new materials. It seemed almost as if the thinking was, 'We've got these shiny new materials, we're supposed to be modern and do away with whole class lessons so let's give them these schemes where they can do things at their own pace and in groups – that's us being child-centred, isn't it!'

**2)** I was at [Edinburgh] till P4. Then I went up north, to Caithness. Looking back, I realise this was the rough school for the town. It certainly came as a great culture shock. I hated it and cried and cried. I couldn't understand what the children were saying; there was no uniform. Mum was affronted so she made me wear a kilt and jumper and tights and – oh dear – I was just ripped to shreds for wearing such a get-up to go to the school! I wanted to wear jeans just like the rest but mum wouldn't have this so I had to go in and get ridiculed every day. And there seemed to be no structure to anything. All the children seemed to be all over you; they were very touchy, always wanting to sit up against you and touch and bosie in . . . But they were lovely people; there was lots of love too – but it was all so different from what I had been used to. At [Edinburgh] everything had seemed so coherent, to be within my capabilities and with no sense of struggle – but in [Caithness] some things were very easy and some just didn't seem to make sense at all. I remember the long division and the huge struggle that seemed to involve. At my Edinburgh school we'd been grouped and our curriculum was structured. The days were ordered, you got your work to do and everything went along in a neat and ordered fashion. You had your own little tray with everything in it that you needed. But in [Caithness], it was bedlam. If there was a radio programme, then the radio would just be turned on without warning. I remember constantly thinking, 'What's going on now?'

**Secondary School**

**3)** At Secondary, we started off with a broad introduction to all the subjects. Only in S3 did we start to choose and to specialise. We all had to take English, Maths and French, and then you could pick from a basket of subjects. I did English, Maths, French, German, History, Economics and Physics to make up my seven. There was a range of teaching styles. It depended very much upon the teacher. Some would talk at you for an hour and then give you work based on that; some would try and involve you from the start. I would say that they were all generally competent. You don't really question what you are being taught at school or why exactly you are having to do things in that precise way, but they all appeared to me to know what they were doing. Some belonged to the old school of chalk and talk. The younger ones were less like that, as a rule. But you just accepted it all.

4) To be honest, I could have passed the Standard Grades without any study at all. Perhaps Maths was a bit of an exception for me. But the other subjects, if you listened in class, you were going to be all right. Whereas with the Highers, I became aware that if I didn't study, I would fail. One thing you did notice: in the general school, in your register class, there was still this great mix. I remember realising my friends there were no longer the same as me, necessarily, that while I was doing my five Highers, they might only be taking one or two. Up till then, we'd all seemed much of a muchness. We'd all done pretty much the same at Standard [grade]. Suddenly, at Higher, things shifted: those who were academic and prepared to work now stood out. I suddenly had to work hard, to write essays, do homework. It felt like a real school then! Up till then it had been a bit more of a social centre, a place you made friends in, attended classes and did a bit of work on the side.

## Community

5) I am quite unusual in that I grew up with a strong church link. But there were friends of like mind and we ran the Scripture Union at Secondary – we got called the God Squad. Certainly, I can look back and say that the church played a significant part in school life. The school stood opposite the church, both were in the centre of things. They got involved in Lifeboat Gala day; Brownies and Cubs were held there. But it's evident that that role has diminished. A recent survey has shown that if numbers continue to fall at the current rate, there won't be a Church of Scotland in 2050! What the Church aims to do is for the social good but society is changing in such a way and at such a speed . . . I went to Sunday school and all my friends did too but then it got to the stage when it was just a few of us. Its fortunes have changed so very fast.

6) The teacher, bank manager, minister – they used to be pillars of society. They had a house, a big house provided; automatic member-ship of the Golf Club and so on. These things gave them a definite position. Times have changed now and people don't get that kind of perk any more. My Headmaster belonged to the age when certain people, because of the roles they filled, were valued by the community. The local paper-shop man wouldn't be regarded as anything special now – but he was then. Once, if you had a shop in the village you would be thought of as someone with a definite position, as a man of

substance. The butcher, the baker, the newsagent – these were men who still wore ties, went to work in suits, were always well presented. It's not like that now – but it was still there in the 80s. I remember Mr W had the newsagent and he was smart, very proper. It was always, 'Good morning Mr C; good afternoon Miss W.' He would drive people home; he would deliver to their house. These were the old-fashioned little services that were accepted as part of our community life. The main difference now is the people. They're very nice – but when I walked to school I would know everyone along the route. [Angus] is still a safe place, touch wood – little disturbance, hardly any vandalism. But then I could walk to school and I remember a typical instance when I once got caught short on my way and just ran up to the nearest house and knocked. It was old Mrs T – 'Can I use your toilet, please Mrs T?' 'Of course, Gordon. Come away in!' Neither of us thought anything of it. I just knew that behind that door would be old Mrs T and that she would let me in for a pee on the way to my school . . . It was a very stable community then. The main thing that's changed is that I no longer know all the people. You meet fewer and fewer people in the old way, out and about. Now they just jump into their cars and drive by you, off to work elsewhere or to do their shopping at the supermarket in Montrose.

**The School Today**
7) I know the impression can be that the modern Comprehensive is a big untidy incoherent monster and something of a decline from the ordered place of yesteryear but – and maybe I'm an optimist – I think it's less inclined to be like that now. You still hear horror stories but they are more to do with the society we have created and I don't think schools can take responsibility for that. I think there's this consumerist fix-it mentality around now, that if there's drugs and vandalism and bad spelling then it's the government who should fix it . . . but ebb and flow: the quality of teaching is probably higher now in terms of being accountable and professional. I think we're discovering now what is really meant by 'child-centred', that it's recognising the individual child and being sensitive towards them – not letting them go their own way in an undirected fashion. From the inside, the school makes more sense than an outsider can ever imagine. It's part of a different society in any case – kids stay on at school longer and when they leave it's not to go straight into some life-long career job. Yet

society has got this fix-it notion that it's for the school to give the pupil a place to go and fix them up with a job for life. But society itself no longer supports such an outcome. In the past you knew from your parents' example where you were going; nor did you have all these distractions around. The breakdown in the traditional family, the models given by the media and the soaps . . . To criticise the curriculum for being different nowadays misses the point – is it trying to be relevant for the kind of society that young people are now having to enter? You could argue that people are less dutiful, less reliable nowadays, but is that the school's fault? When, actually, the school as an institution is more reliable and coherent than the society around it!

8) As a pupil you aren't aware of any 'decline' in education. You are there and you accept what happens to you and that's that. But I couldn't say there's been any falling off. A lot of the people who go on about the 'scandal' of Scotland's schools haven't experienced it at first-hand since their own day. I know that when I tell people I'm training to be a teacher, there's often a recoil – 'You can't be going into that!' It can be difficult to explain; it's such a different world now. There's a lot more to it than just standing up and explaining things. You try to go through your day in a school and it all seems so untidy but it makes sense enough to those inside it. It can't be seen through some distant memory. People look back and they rationalise their memories. I could certainly follow this experience of going from a little eager 5-year-old to the Sixth Year adult, but it all flies past – the changes in what you are and what you're becoming are just phenomenal. It's the total experience that counts, the experience of growing up and the school is the place more than any other where it happens. At the time, it's a great flow of experience, a steep learning curve that the school helps you over . . . The school can't just stand there and enforce the past. Kids are a lot more savvy now and have a whole lot more in their lives. The school has to mediate between the past and today and ought to be allowed to get on with it.

## The Scottish Tradition

9) I think I've had a good education. School did enable me to get on, to go to university. I was brought up on the work ethic. My mother would do anything to keep us moving in that direction. There was no noise in the living-room while we were studying. She was anxious we

would do something she'd never done – take Highers and get to university. There was this belief that if you worked, you'd get on.

**10)** Scottish education  – I've always thought of it as high quality. Maybe that's just automatic patriotism but I've always been taught that Education, along with our football team, is one of the few things different about us compared to England. I've always assumed that it's held in good esteem generally, in the world. I'm not sure whether that's still the case, but it's what I grew up with. If you look at powerful people in British public life, then you'll find a lot of them were educated here – Tony Blair, Gordon Brown, Robin Cook and the new Transport man, Alistair Darling.

# CONCLUSION

# 14 THE TRADITION OF THE SCOTTISH EDUCATION TRADITION

*Targeting Excellence: Modernising Scotland's Schools*:
Donald Dewar, 1999
*'Scottish education means excellence!'*: Archibald Watt, 1999
*School Education open for debate*: Scottish Executive, 2002
*Hopeless but not Serious*: Jack McLean, 1996
*Good Vibrations*: Evelyn Glennie, 1990

Figure 26. **Balerno School, Edinburgh,** *c.* **1900** The distance that Scottish education – and Scottish society – has travelled in the last century may be observed by comparing this group presentation with the images on the school website shown below.
*Scottish Life Archive*

Figure 27. **Balerno High School, Edinburgh, 2002** By the beginning of the new millennium, many of Scotland's schools were running their own website. This vivid example offers a ready collage of the range of activity that now makes up the daily life of the present-day Scottish school. *http://www.balernochs.edin.sch.uk/*

Whenever, during the 1997 British election campaign, the leader of the Labour Party was called upon to identify his three national priorities, he would reply: 'Education! Education! Education!' In this way, Tony Blair – himself the product of a sort of Scottish education – was claiming for the United Kingdom what, in its northern portion, has always been a common preoccupation. If, elsewhere, the repeated emphasis had the thud of the political slogan, in Scotland the words could be heard as a compelling historical echo.

In January 1999, his new Labour government duly produced its White Paper on the future direction of the Scottish education system. They called it *Targeting Excellence*. It also carried a subtitle – 'Modernising Scotland's Schools'. In its Foreword, Donald Dewar, then Secretary of State, offers us the title's keyword five times in two brief paragraphs (**14A**).

In the document itself, however, the word receives no explicit definition. Instead, it is left to emerge as a system, by which to bullet the page with an urgent punctuation. The difficulty is that while 'Excellence' is, indeed, a term to elicit universal assent – how could it not? – the checklists, the tabular imperatives and technocratic abstractions which here track it up and down, are detached from the way in which people actually talk about the matter. Ask, for example, Archie Watt, an octogenarian living and chronicling life in Stonehaven, to sum up 'Scottish education' and he will certainly reach for the word, but will then immediately, instinctively, go on to embody it in a celebrated local figure (**14B**).

Such definition is, of course, scarcely scientific. Archie's words freely mix in the fabled with the particular and relate local anecdote to an idealised history. They also ride over such complicating actualities as the young Leslie Mitchell's unhappy subsequent spell at his own Mackie Academy or, indeed, the hostile caricature of Scottish schooling in *Speak of the Mearns*. Rather, this recasting of material into rhetorical form is the natural outcome of a desire to invest the particulars of an individual experience with the wider meanings of its national setting which Watt, as a Scot, speaking to fellow Scots and to the world at large, feels it to possess. And what reads here as a conclusion was a paragraph heading in what turned out to be a lengthy interview account of his many years of teaching in the nation's schools, first as an idealistic young member of Elgin Academy's English department pre-war and, then, after five war-time years in the RAF, three decades at Mackie Academy. His was a service in schools and at a time, when examples of democratic classrooms, of rewards to be gained only through the ethic of work, of dedicated dominies and lads who got on, were still to be talked of as living tradition.

Any response to a present-day government's claims for a 'restoration of excellence' will itself merge into an ancient landscape of debate and anecdotage that is already peopled not by political spin or sophisticated data but by countrywide tellers of everyday stories. For the real targets of the government's Paper – the electorate – 'excellence' is more a matter of shared recollection and inherited precedent than it is of politicised logistics. The failure to engage with history's personal power empties the White Paper of sustained human meaning for the very people it claims to be consulting. In the interests of businesslike purpose – being 'focused', they call it – the language it employs is void of colour, variety or tangible reference. Instead of an invitation to visit the store of native experience in order to sift out its possibilities for growth, the reader/voter is treated to a civil-servant's whiteboard demonstration.

*Targeting Excellence* does not seem to be interested in history at all. A bare mention of 'Scotland's educational tradition' is proffered, but only to support the warning that 'one of the greatest threats to continuing improvement is complacency as a result of our strong educational heritage'. So briskly are we hurried on, that the impression is conveyed of the past as so much debris to be cleared away in order to set up the greenfield site on which something called 'a world class system' may be erected. Globalisation has been at work; *Targeting Excellence* is a document without a memory.

And now, following devolution and the installation of a Scottish parliament, we are to have a 'Great Debate' (**14C**). Concerned to take the management of education as its most distinctive responsibility, the Scottish Executive is currently inviting the people to attend meetings, to send in letters and to post advice upon the Holyrood website as to the future direction of the nation's schooling. It remains to be seen whether the electorate and the Departmental officials, after two decades of modernising technicalities, really will be able to rise to the 'big answers' and do so in a way that would recognise the relationship between the Scottish inheritance and today's 'knowledge economy', between the individual experience and a nation's belief in itself.

But, then, the developing narrative of Scottish education has always been such as to offer its policy-makers and its spokespersons a ready set of big words. Yet, if the terms have pointed to the constants in its history, experience has shown their meaning to be more a matter of the accumulated understandings of individual people and the local communities they inhabit than of official utterance. Scotland's system has aspired to values, which themselves have been subject to the relativities of material advance, of cultural change and social development. As such, 'excellence' and 'democracy' are qualities that have been realised – and in ways various and varying – in the experiences, both actual and remembered, of Scots at school.

Archie Watt's 'excellence' is undoubtedly an individually constructed account but, as the instances in this work have shown, it is so in ways that are representative, not merely idiosyncratic. Frequently, when individual Scots come to set down their own life-stories, now as always, the section which deals with schooldays will be recreated in terms of vivid enactment rather than straight recall. It is the common, and shared, process: as childhood events are recollected under the dispensations of maturity, the familiar and protracted drama of going to school can be made to tell of the fate of the nation.

Take the two autobiographies extracted here (**14D** and **E**). Each is of a well-known contemporary Scot who grew up in postwar Scotland. Each presents an entirely different version of the Scottish tradition at work. One is of an inner city experience of a bleak schooling endured in the grimy slumland of Townhead, Glasgow; the other of a reassuringly protective early education in rural Aberdeenshire. Yet, it is not the details that separate them – ordeal by mental arithmetic, assembly rites, the 10:45 bottle of milk – this is the daily round which shows that Evelyn Glennie and Jack McLean inhabit the same system, were at school in the one Scotland.

It is the shape that the memory takes which makes them different. Both writers are conscious of the school as a place of initiation and moulding; but whereas the country girl is concerned to affirm the solid continuity which she entered in her little, family-familiar Cairnorrie, the East-end boy wants only to expose the inhumane repression which he has come to see as the underside of what is meant by a 'good Scots education'. Neither is straight recall, both are dramatic in tone; their particulars are invested with a strongly held attitude towards the formative value of their schooling, for themselves as children and as maturing members of the wider Scottish community. Evelyn grows up to build upon her early musical encounters to become an internationally famous musician; Jack will turn himself into the 'Urban Voltaire', the irreverent wit-about-town, ready to spear all native pretension at the end of a well-turned phrase.

The schooldays of twenty, thirty years before are reconstructed in the image of what their pupils were, what they went on to become – and of the connections between the two. Yet their depictions remain recognisable – the walls, the prints, the physical presence of the teachers, the childlike bemusement at the intricacies of mental arithmetic – all are basic to the classroom world, each catches 'Scottish education' at a particular and human moment of time. It is this combination of the universally familiar with the personal response, held together within the framework of an insistent tradition, which has the human power to tell us something of what it felt like to go to school in Scotland – and of how Scottish schools have made Scottish people.


14A                                            Scottish Office, 1999.


Education is at the heart of the Government's policies in Scotland. Our vision is of a world class school system founded on excellence, in which all young people, regardless of their background, have the opportunity to learn the skills required to take their place as citizens in the learning society which is modern Scotland. Our young people are our greatest asset; by targeting excellence, we will ensure that they are all given the opportunities to reach their full potential.

We have committed ourselves to restoring Scotland's educational system to the position of world leader. Such a system will have many characteristics, but above all it will identify and celebrate excellence. The commitment to excellence is shared by all teachers, pupils and parents. Each has a role to play. Working together, we must single-mindedly target excellence in everything that we do.

'Foreword' by the Right Hon. Donald Dewar, Secretary of State for Scotland (1999). *Targeting Excellence: Modernising Scotland's Schools.* Edinburgh, HMSO.

14B                         Stonehaven, Kincardineshire, 1999.

Scottish Education? It means excellence! It comes from the time when the ploughman's loon could sit down with the minister's son at the same hard bench of their parochial school. It's a system that could throw up talent like young Leslie Mitchell down at Arbuthnott and a village dominie like Andrew Gray to lead it on – and so turn him into Lewis Grassic Gibbon. Scottish Education? It's the expression of the indomitable character of the Scot who wrestled with the rigours of the land and who strove for what is truly worthwhile in life.

Watt, Archibald (1999). Interview with author.

Archie Watt died, aged 87, in 2001. Was for 28 years first Head of English, then Deputy Rector Mackie Academy, Stonehaven – the school Leslie Mitchell (1901–35) attended unhappily after his productive time with Gray at Inverbervie Public School. Under the name Lewis Grassic Gibbon, Mitchell became the North-east's great novelist, author of *Sunset Song*.

14C                               Scottish Office, 2002.

### School Education open for debate

In an unprecedented move, the future shape of school education is to be opened for discussion in a countrywide National Debate on Education.

Organisations and individuals inside and outside the education system will be asked for their views as the first step towards producing a long term vision for Scottish education. Launching the Debate in the Scottish Parliament, Minister for Education and Young People, Cathy Jamieson, said:

'This is the start of a genuine and inclusive dialogue on the way ahead for learning and teaching in our schools. Instead of the traditional method of a consultation paper from Ministers, we are seeking the public's views on the "big questions" in order to inform and shape a vision for the future. Briefing packs are being sent to every local authority and school in Scotland, and to every organisation who has already expressed interest in hosting a National Debate event. A national phoneline is up and running and details are available on our

*293*

website. There will also be press and radio advertising to raise awareness of the Debate, and to let people know how they can participate.

I've said many times that there is much to be proud of in Scottish schools. But society is constantly changing and we must look at what will be best for children and young people in 10 or 15 years time. Now is the time to seize this opportunity and make their voices heard.'

Scottish Executive, (2002). www.scotland.gov.uk

14D                                                    Glasgow, 1950s.

Lessons kicked off with the Lord's Prayer which Mr Kidd performed perfunctorily. Next door Miss Kirk, an angular lady who sported steel-framed spectacles to go with her steel-framed theology, intoned the morning religious ablutions with gusto, as though it were a revivalist meeting in some dark glen. She had clean hands inspections and rewarded those too exiguous in their toilet with a dose of the tawse on each unwashed extremity. How this cleansed the mitts I know not but I suspect Miss Kirk had the cleansing of the soul in mind. Then, as in every school in the Scotland of those days, we plunged into the first lesson which was mental arithmetic . . . It was public and so was your humiliation. Monkey-Lugs Bruce and Tam Elvin could answer any question involving numbers in seconds and Ronald Millar, taking after his bookie dad, could compute with even more lightning speed, but the teacher knew that and ignored their upraised hands when they tried to answer his open question which involved adding and dividing and all the other curious antics of this almost religious rite. Kidd asked the ones who couldn't do it . . . A whole bloody morning it was, I seem to remember, taken up by this nonsensical liturgy. It ruined mornings for years . . . We did have reading, too, but it followed on from the numbers, and was somehow contaminated by the calcula-tions of the a.m. ordeal, which lasted, always, from prayers till the milk break.

Milk came in small bottles, a third of a pint. It smelled, as milk still does for me, of slept-in pyjamas and was another trial to be got through. Other children seemed to like it though and vied with each other for extra bottles. They slurped it and drank it up greedily and I despised them for wetting themselves for the bloody milk and for liking it in the first place.

> McLean, Jack (1996). *Hopeless but not Serious, the Autobiography of the Urban Voltaire.* Edinburgh, Mainstream.

1945– : before he became a full-time writer, was a secondary school Art teacher.

14E                                              Aberdeenshire, 1970s.

Shakespeare's famous schoolboy may have crept 'like snail unwillingly to school'; I showed no such reluctance on my first day at Cairnorrie Primary School, a small country school a mile and a half from our farm. My father had been a pupil there . . .

Stretching across one wall of the junior class were the letters of the alphabet with colourful drawings: *a* for apple, *b* for bat, *c* for cat, *d* for door, and so on. There was a rack of Ladybird books in 'the reading corner' which I loved to browse through; another corner had bricks and wooden blocks and puzzles of every description, and there was a corner for plasticine, crayons and paints. All around the room were cupboards, and trays of equipment, labelled in big letters, with instructions, 'KEEP TIDY – OR ELSE!' Next to the big green door was a crate of twenty-five bottles of milk. At the morning break, or 'playtime' as we called it, we were each given a bottle with a straw poking through the silver top. If there were any bottles left over, then 'Hands up' for another; my hand always went up . . .

Our mornings always started with a song at the electric organ with our teacher Miss Flett. Everyone loved Miss Flett; she was warm and happy, but authoritative and very nice to be near. She always wore delicious perfume and we adored having a lift home in her little red Mini, because it smelt so good . . .

After singsong would come the horrid part of the morning – sums! Maybe if they had happened later in the day I would have understood them better; as it was, the figures would stare up at me out of the ugly pages with no feelings of warmth or imagination. My two best friends, Isabel (Issie) Gordon, and Edna (Eddie) Cadger did their best to drum what were probably the simplest of equations into my head, but I hated the whole mechanical business. Playtime followed at 10:45 and we were sent outside for games of Stuck-in-the-Mud, Hide-and-Seek, rounders or Stringyingins (String-the-Onions), or simply a good natter under a tree.

Glennie, Evelyn, (1990). *Good Vibrations*. London, Hutchinson.

1965– : farmer's daughter; despite onset of profound deafness became internationally renowned percussionist.

# GLOSSARY AND
# ABBREVIATIONS

*Bursary Competition*: competitive examination for university scholarships, organised by the individual universities. Celebrated mark of individual and local school achievement.

*Chapels of Ease*: created for parishioners living at distance from parish church.

*Code*: from 1860 onwards various regulations laid down by government to regulate award of annual grants to schools were consolidated into 'the Code'.

*Dame School*: privately run by a woman, generally elderly, and usually concentrating on early basics.

*Dick*: endowment scheme from estate of John Dick, Morayshire son who made his fortune in Jamaica. Supplemented salaries of appropriately qualified schoolmasters in the North-east counties and, thus, did much to raise academic standards there, from 1830s onwards.

*Dominie*: from Latin 'dominus' (master). Common adoption for 'master' of burgh and parochial schools; demonstrates his assumed standing.

*Dover House*: London office of SED; till 1930s and full development of St Andrew's House, Edinburgh, its effective headquarters.

*EIS*: Educational Institute of Scotland. Founded 1847 as world's earliest such organisation; developed into country's leading body for qualified teachers, promoting their professional and material interests.

*Heritors*: as owners of significant areas of land, charged under pre-1872 parochial system with provision of local schoolhouse and its master's salary.

*Highers*: In 1888 SED introduced its Leaving Certificate to establish accepted national academic qualifications and regularise entry to universities and professions. Quickly developed required authority to become goal of all secondary school-leavers; since 1960s, its administration has passed to Scottish Examination Board and, now, Scottish Qualifications Agency.

*James Coats*: Paisley cotton millionaire who funded provision of schoolbags for pupils throughout Scotland in early 20th century.

*Lad o' pairts*: local lad of sufficient ability and diligence to conquer humble circumstances and, with help of a devoted dominie, go on to high academic honours. Although one of Scottish education's traditional icons, term only introduced – according to Robert Anderson's researches – through Ian Maclaren's 1898 story 'Domsie' (in *Beside the Bonnie Briar Bush*). However, its wide adoption establishes its ability to sum up age-old virtue of 'getting on'.

*Lancastrian*: utilitarian system introduced by Joseph Lancaster in early 19th century to deliver economical schooling to the masses; use of pupil monitors and concentration on basics enabled one master to deal with multiple classes.

*Normal School/College/Seminary*: teacher training institution.

*OFSTED*: 'Office for Standards in Education'. System of commercially contracted school inspection introduced by Conservative government of 1980s for England and Wales – but not Scotland. Seen as attempt to move from collaborative to managerial model of school governance. Chris Woodhead was its first – and controversially zealous – head.

*P1, P2 etc*: gradually established in 20th century as denoting school year of pupil; entry at age 5 is into P(Primary)1 and so on up to P7 at 12, when pupil moves on to secondary school and 'S1'.

*Pupil-teacher*: system of apprenticeship teacher training introduced on UK-wide basis in 1846. Enabled able boys and girls at 13–plus to receive extra academic and pedagogic training alongside own studies. On completion of (usually) 5 years, became eligible for admission to Training Centre. System continued till First World War.

*Qualifying Examination/Quallie, etc*: test to determine pupil's fitness to proceed beyond Primary education, whether to Secondary school, or post-primary stages of elementary school, and its 'Supplementary' or 'Advanced Division' classes. Persisted till phasing in of Comprehensive schooling in 1960/70s.

*Quoad sacra/spiritualia*: parish created and functioning for ecclesiastical purposes only.

*Rector*: headmaster of secondary school.

*Revised Code*: ('Payment by Results') under original Code, grants were awarded against standards achieved on whole school basis; in 1862, 'Revised' version was introduced to examine schools on a pupil-by-pupil basis. The move proved contentious, being seen as leading to concentration on mechanical coaching in basics. Resistance was especially strong in Scotland where its full implementation was delayed till 1872; the SED made its abolition one of its first acts, in 1885.

*Seceders and Burghers*: two examples of sects who began split from Established Church from 1730s onwards. Such groups stood for more purist interpretation of Church's founding Presbyterian principles, against growing 'worldly' practices such as appointment of ministers by laird's patronage.

*SED*: Scotch/Scottish Education Department.

*Session(al) schools*: founded by a parish congregation, usually urban and instituted as response to problems posed by rapid growth populations in towns.

*Side schools*: additional schools founded by heritors in very large parishes.

*SSPCK*: 'Society in Scotland for Propagating Christian Knowledge' ; subscription body established in early 18th century to bring benefits of regular education to more remote areas, especially in Highlands. At peak – 1758 – responsible for 'planting' 176 new schools there. Especially in early years associated with anti-Gaelic and anti-Catholic policies.

*Standard*: Six successive, yearly levels of academic performance specified under the Code (see above) to trigger award of grants.

*Subscription schools*: schools provided by parental subscriptions.

*Taws(e)/ taurds*: stiff leather strap used as standard weapon of punishment till its abolition by law in 1980s.

*(Ad)Venture school*: school set up by individual outwith standard parochial and burgh system and, therefore, entirely dependent on fees – run at teacher's own 'adventure'.

# INDEX OF PEOPLE AND PLACES